151 Secrets of Insurance Direct Marketing Practices Revealed

151 Secrets
of Insurance Direct
Marketing Practices
Revealed

By

Donald R. Jackson

Nopoly Press, Inc.

Wilmington, Delaware
U.S.A.

ISBN 0-930950-38-0   Hardcover

Library of Congress Cataloging-in-Publication Data

Jackson, Donald R., 1938 -
    151 secrets of insurance direct marketing
practices revealed / by Donald R. Jackson ;
foreword by Sy Okner.
        p.   cm.
    Includes index.
    ISBN 0-930950-38-0 : $49.75
    1. Insurance--Agents.   2. Direct
marketing. I. Title.   II. Title: One hundred
fifty-one secrets of insurance direct
marketing practices revealed.   III. Title: One
hundred and fifty-one secrets of insurance
direct marketing practices revealed.
HG8091. J33   1989
368′ .0068′ 8--dc19   88-32365
                                        CIP

For David Reichberg

Few of us pass through a career without being touched by special people. For me, David Reichberg was one of those special people.

He was one of those fortunate few who enjoyed not one but two successful careers—the first as one of the pioneers in the direct marketing advertising agency business.

The second was as an insurance direct marketing entrepreneur...who discovered the key to third-party marketing profit.

He was a remarkable character—intellectually acute and exceedingly sensitive to the demands of the consumer marketplace. A lateral thinker, he called on a continuous stream of creature energy that lesser lights found debilitating.

David possessed inner resources that compelled him to reach out to success. He combined knowledge and experience with a business intensity almost unmatched in direct marketing.

Like all successful men, he was driven. This quality came from a standard of excellence that caused him to demand more than most people were capable of giving, or willing to do so.

For good or ill, he touched almost everyone with whom he came into contact. For most of us, the experience turned out to be positive. And, working with David Reichberg was nothing if not an "experience."

I am proud to have been his student, his associate, and his partner. But, most of all, I am thankful that, through more than a decade's relationship—seldom calm and frequently stormy—he called me *friend*.

I am lucky. He not only shared with me his business acumen, he shared himself. What greater benefit could he have given?

We are all poorer for his passing. But, we are all richer for his legacy.

David Reichberg made a difference to the direct marketing profession. In the early days—and for generations to come.

He would have liked that.

Acknowledgments

Any book is completed with an enormous amount of help from a variety of people. This work is no different. First, a big "thank you" to the more than thirty insurance direct marketing clients, with whom I have worked over the years, for the opportunity to learn.

In addition to David Reichberg, to whom this book is dedicated, I owe an enormous debt of gratitude to George Abouseid, currently Executive Vice President of the American International Group, Inc., and formerly a *mentor*, who motivated me to learn more about this business than I thought—at the time—I wanted to know. In the same category was Al Block. We are poorer for his passing.

In the very beginning of my career, Warren Levy, Creative Director of the book club division of Doubleday & Company and his associate, Ed Stern, introduced me to the mystique of writing copy—and pounded me until I learned to think beyond the "nine-dot square."

In the writing of this book, Jon Hamilton, a Partner in Brady & Hamilton, rendered valuable assistance in developing the telemarketing chapter.

My thanks to Dick Nevins, Vice President Marketing, of Commercial Travelers Mutual Insurance Company; Jack Wolf, Senior Vice President Life and Health Marketing of The Signature Group; Dick Miller, President, Market Response International, Inc.; Jay Jaffe, Consulting Actuary; Henry R. "Pete" Hoke, Jr., Publisher of Hoke Communications, Inc.; and Irwin Lowen, President, Intersure Marketing, Inc. Each generously provided cogent advice, trenchant comments, emotional support, direction, and shared experiences, without which the final draft of this book simply could not have been written.

As well, Anne Bulger, formerly Creative Director of Continental American Life Insurance Company, provided assistance in writing the creative chapters. Don Millsaps and Mike Stricker, talented partners of MBS+K in Philadelphia helped with design. Christine Hall Thornhill and Kelly Green assisted in the preparation of the manuscript for publication.

Finally, I am indebted to my proofreader, partner, friend, critic, and biggest booster—Betts. Through it all, she displayed "the patience of a saint."

Foreword

by Sy Okner

Some years ago my associates and I coined the acronym "DFWAC." Don't fool with a control. In direct marketing jargon a "control" is your current winner—the creative solicitation package that outpulls all others. It's the one you test against and attempt to improve upon.

Don Jackson has written a book that I believe will immediately become the "control" for insurance direct marketing. That Don is an excellent writer will, of course, come as no surprise to those of us who have known him professionally. However, the scope and detail of his book fill a void that has long existed in our industry. There are other direct marketing books available, but none are dedicated exclusively to insurance. And, none are as thorough in their "step-by-step, how-to approach" to our industry.

Now many marketing skills are interchangeable. If you know your product, your costs, your price points and your customers, you can find a way to do business. Direct marketing, however, demands its own expertise.

We all know direct marketers who seem to be able to sell anything from gadgets to widgets...to anyone—from giants to midgets. But, insurance is different. Insurance is unlike electronics, appliances or clothing, which satisfy—or not—on receipt. Related services and claims have to keep satisfying during a life span that can, actually, outlive the consumer.

Combining the two, *direct marketing* and *insurance*, into *insurance direct marketing* requires unique knowledge of a special nature. Obviously product specific knowledge is essential, but that is true of any product sold through the direct marketing system. Insurance direct marketing demands more. Because it is a marketing system...interactive...intricate and organized.

And, it is complicated by an *institution* normally not faced by either "general marketers" or "non-insurance direct marketers." There are fifty regulatory bodies...fifty-one counting the FTC...which closely supervise insurance direct marketing. Policy language, advertising, benefits—all have the potential to differ from jurisdiction to jurisdiction. Insurance policies are complex contracts, difficult to understand. Time and time again the courts have upheld that "what you say is what you pay"...advertising materials will prevail, even over actual policy wording.

As you can see, employing the direct marketing system successfully requires the balancing of all the complex individual elements so that each works effectively with the others.

To make the point, not long ago the vice president of one of the large Eastern old line insurance companies asked me what I considered a good response rate to a direct response solicitation. I replied that I had no idea, and I launched into a discussion about profitability, trying to explain that initial response rates are only one number in a somewhat more involved equation. An equation that considers average annual premium, persistency, mortality, morbidity, lifetime value and more. How much simpler our discussion would have been, if I had been able to offer him a copy of Don's book and direct him to the appropriate chapter.

I believe that any discipline within the insurance direct marketing community will find *Secrets* one of the better investments in self-development, and/or management of any particular responsibility. Actuaries, marketers, administrators, lawyers, even bean counters can benefit from this broad overview of insurance direct marketing, as well as the specific details dealing with their own areas.

Now, the quintessential question: Are we insurance people using direct marketing techniques as another channel of distribution (which according to its definition it is not)...or are we direct marketers, who have chosen insurance as our product...and does it make any difference? Since Don has covered the field from Applications to Zip Codes, the reader will have ample opportunity, and a wealth of information, with which to reach his or her own conclusion.

One final thought. A number of colleagues have become consultants to insurance companies and have realized the need to broaden their marketing efforts. With the publication of *151 Secrets of Insurance Direct Marketing Practices Revealed*, the consultants may well find that they will be working harder for clients who know more than ever before.

[Ed. note: Sy Okner is President of MarketUSA Direct Response, Inc., 2454 E. Dempster, Des Plaines, IL 60016, 312/803-1900. He was formerly President, The Signature Insurance Group; a past recipient of the *Direct Marketing Insurance Executive of the Year* award. He is also a Founder and past Chairman of the Direct Marketing Insurance Council.]

Contents

Chapter XIV The Secrets of Administration　　**256**

Policy issue and policy maintenance, developing the system, DP-system architecture, cost/benefits of effective administration, billing and collection, claims, customer service, underwriting

Chapter XV The Secrets of Insurance　　**272**
　　　　　　Direct Marketing Mathematics

Nature of insurance direct marketing mathematics, product marketer vs. customer marketer, iteration method/acquisition allowance model, apps/M, concept of breakeven, lead generation breakeven, concept of net present value, concept of payback method, reporting and projecting results

Chapter XVI Vexing Issues and Tomorrow's Trends　　**292**

Compliance, people, product and service quality, graying of America, new American family, new reality in consumer marketing, geographic relocation, video/visual revolution, new American lifestyle, individualism

Nopoly Press, Inc.

P.O. Box 7245
Wilmington, Delaware 19803-0245
U.S.A.
Telephone (302) 764-8918

Introduction

Some years ago, I was attending a meeting conducted by the chief marketing officer of a moderate-sized insurance direct marketing company. In the space of ten minutes I heard this senior, experienced marketer make three vital errors.

See if you can spot them. Here's what he said—more or less:

"We're going to set up an AD&D (accidental death and dismemberment) program designed to generate applications from people who have recently moved. We'll use a snap-pak to keep creative costs down. Our offer will be $1,000 of all-risk AD&D *free*, with an opportunity to purchase additional benefits amounts on an invitation-to-contract basis—up to $100,000." This was to be a new product, not one in the company's product portfolio. "I've made a special first-use-for-insurance deal with XYZ Company to mail all the compiled names with which they can provide us on a monthly basis. And, I want to start as soon as possible."

Can you guess what happened when we executed the program? If you spotted the three vital errors, I bet you can.

> We mailed an UNTESTED product, using an UNTESTED creative package, to an UNTESTED *compiled* list!

In fact, we mailed 800,000 pieces of direct mail! When the results were totaled, we had spent $345,000 in marketing costs on the program, sold 281 AD&D policies, which produced $34,000 in total annualized renewal premium.

1

Now, in all fairness, a good number of "free takers" were added to our "prospect list." And when mailed additional offers, later on, it is *possible* that the six-figure acquisition cost was recovered.

Frankly, I wasn't around long enough to find out. And, not surprisingly, the chief marketing officer didn't stay around all that long either.

My point in sharing this vignette with you is to show that the most experienced marketers take risks. But, when they forget, momentarily, the basic tenets of insurance direct marketing practices, failure usually follows.

Now, for those of us who populate the insurance direct marketing industry, learning the business is a *hands-on* experience. While there is a surprising number of resources to call on in checking things out, there isn't a single source available that compiles various experiences of a number of marketers from a number of marketing environments. *That's what this book is all about!*

Fortunately, as a consultant, my window on this business is unique. I have worked with more than thirty insurance direct marketing companies in the United States and ten in foreign countries—from writing direct-mail solicitation packages to planning new business ventures. These ranged from product development to production, from DP system definition to administration, from managing profit centers to developing support services, and from strategic planning to consumer market research and database creation.

This cumulative experience offers a vantage point not frequently available to most insurance direct marketers. I've had to learn a lot about how the "other guy" markets. Every time I worked on a new assignment for a company I was learning how their people applied their own unique methods to the marketing opportunities they were pursuing—within their peculiar corporate culture.

The results have been a series of observations.

For example, in a general way, most companies involved in insurance direct marketing have a *tendency to sacrifice long-term financial health for short-term profit.*

Relational marketing, using the tools provided by *lifetime value* and databasing, is not a strategy generally available to marketers.

Surprisingly, a remarkable number of marketers don't know a whole lot about insurance products—their development, their architecture, elements of expense and profitability, risk assessment procedures, and more.

Further, senior management infrequently shares overall corporate objectives with their marketers. And, when they do, the objectives are impossibly vague, or—even worse—simply unachievable.

Insurance direct marketing is considered "nontraditional" marketing among the greater number of insurance companies. Of course, that bothers me. But, I understand the label is assigned in deference to the agents and brokers who have succeeded in becoming the "traditional" means of marketing insurance. The good news is that an increasing number (4 out of 10, in fact) of insurance company chief executive officers (CEOs) expect to use nontraditional marketing within five years.

They will learn a lot, just as I've learned a lot. I've learned, vicariously, through a group of marvelous clients and, "hands-on," by actually working in a number of insurance direct marketing environments. I have never been bored. I have failed. *And,* I have succeeded.

Perhaps the biggest lesson I've learned is that insurance direct marketing is a complex, detail-ridden business of numbers. Also, it is a business driven by passion.

Through it all, my passion has grown. By sharing the principles of the practice of insurance direct marketing which I have learned and evaluated over these years, perhaps a lamp will light. And, it seems to me, to light a lamp is to illuminate the extraordinary possibilities that exist within this extraordinary discipline.

George Bernard Shaw wrote: "Progress is impossible without change; and those who cannot change their minds cannot change anything."

If minds change—if understanding grows—then progress wins. What follows is a geometric progression in opportunities and possibilities.

In preparing to share this journey with you, I have tried to examine possibilities and have attempted to introduce ideas—some proven, some prospective, but all rational. Let it be known that *the coin of insurance direct marketing is concept!*

Some concepts, I suspect, will generate argument. Good! Debate is healthy. Others will generate a "nod." Good, too! All 151 secrets, I hope, will be useful.

Useful, that is, to companies in the business and those—both large and small—thinking about entering the business. Useful, also, to agency and brokerage operations interested in using these techniques to increase business. Useful, as well, to the dozens of businesses living in tangency to the insurance direct marketing environment.

Now, a short note about sources. In preparing this book, I have consulted a significant body of printed material. As well, I have consulted with my associates, current clients, and former clients. Much of the information contained in the various "secrets" is proprietary. Therefore, acknowledgment needs to be masked to maintain absolute confidentiality. A lot of the information is empirical, based on my own experience. In every case, I have tried to verify, from at least two other sources, the validity of the material presented, all of which is based on actual testing.

The focus of the book highlights both accident and health and life business. Many of the principles, however, are as applicable to property and casualty direct marketing as they are to A&H and life direct marketing. They are, it seems to me, equally *applicable to both large companies and small ones.*

Finally, I want the record to show that the insurance industry is one I admire. I hope that I have given back to it some small portion of what it has given to me.

II

The Window of Opportunity

Why write a book about insurance direct marketing? Because it's big business—bigger than you might think! And, it's growing faster than anyone thought possible just a decade ago. Sales are just the tip of the iceberg!

Below the waterline, insurance direct marketing is intriguing, challenging, demanding, complex, and sheer fun. It offers all its practitioners remarkable chances to succeed—because: a) it is accountability marketing and b) it is expanding.

First, what is accountability marketing? It is marketing that is measured instantly. This is unlike the broad functions of marketing, where measurements often are made in terms of market share and take considerable time to assess. It functions less on share of market and more on the financial success, or failure, of its efforts. So, it contributes greater flexibility to its practitioners, allowing them to take advantage of opportunities more quickly than their general marketing brethren.

Second, it *is* expanding—expanding into companies that a few years ago laughed at the thought of using its techniques.

Take a look at the growth of just the mail-order segment of insurance direct marketing. In 1974, the system wrote $850 million in premium, while being pursued by only a handful of companies. Five years later, the system wrote $4 billion— and became the fastest growing segment of the direct marketing industry. In 1981, it booked $5 billion in sales, written by fewer than 100 companies in the business—dominated by four major, publicly-held corporations. In 1985, the system wrote $6.9 billion, by just the 100 companies engaged in its practices. In 1986, it increased its sales by $450 million, and twenty more companies joined the ranks. This is a 20% increase in just one year in the number of companies using the system. The latest figures show that sales now top $8 billion annually, rapidly heading toward the $10-billion mark.

And, that's just for the mail-order portion of the insurance industry. If you factor in direct marketing practices employed by companies in support of agent sales, as well as the business-to-business portion of the industry, the dollar volume increases dramatically.

Yes, insurance direct marketing is big business.

Now, where did it all begin?

It may well be true that there is nothing new under the sun. Advertisements for annuities, for example, appeared in leading 18th-century British newspapers. Ben Franklin, during the same period, organized early fire insurance plans, and advertised for participants in the colonial press.

Today, when you walk into the quiet, marble lobby of Commercial Travelers Mutual Insurance Company in Utica, New York, you discover a glass display case filled with direct-mail offers aimed at "traveling men."

Think of it: *Published in the 1880s.* A century ago!

The Equitable Life Assurance Society of the U.S. wrote, in 1912, the first employer-employee group plan covering 2,912 Montgomery Ward employees with $5,946,564 of life insurance.

The late Charles Binger, in the pages of *Direct Marketing Magazine* (January 1985), spins a wonderful yarn about a pioneering journey of insurance mail-order discovery. As a young advertising salesman in the 1930s, Binger introduced the same company to the wonders of direct-mail-inquiry generation.

Binger was approached by the Equitable, asking him to come up with an idea to use his self-mailer, "Reply-O-Folder," to promote life insurance. In those days, salesmen had to be creative to sell. So he put on his copywriter's hat and wrote a headline: "$250 A Month For Life. Make It Yours By Adopting This Simple Plan!"

During the depression, $250 a month for life was "big bucks," and—according to Binger—required about $40,000 of life insurance to be in force for thirty years. An unreachable dream for most folks.

The Equitable placed a total order for 1,000,000 Reply-O-Folders for a national mailing. A total of 52,000 inquiries was received for Equitable agents to follow up. The kicker? Only one-half the order was mailed! That

10% response started Charles Binger on a career in insurance direct mail! And made direct-mail "believers" out of The Equitable, Connecticut Mutual, and a host of other companies.

The 1930s saw Allstate begin to sell accident and auto policies. A decade later, Old American started up. During the 40s and 50s, Banker's Life and Casualty Company built its business by exclusively generating agent leads through direct-response methods. In fact, in the late 60s this company sold more than 1 million Medicare supplement policies through the mail. On the life insurance side, Guarantee Reserve Life Insurance Company of Hammond, Indiana, became one of the largest direct-mail marketers during the 1950s.

In the late fifties, Executive Fund entered the insurance direct marketing arena. Then followed DMCA in California. Next came the Delaware Valley Trio—National Liberty, Colonial Penn, and Union Fidelity—all of which entered the business. These were followed by USAA, Physicians Mutual, GEICO, and even Wilmington-based Continental American Life.

The legends began to develop. Legends pioneered by men like Mike Fields (Executive Fund), Leonard Davis (Colonial Penn), Art Demoss (National Liberty), Harry Dozer (Union Fidelity), Al Golden (DMCA), Joe McGee, and Martin Baier (Old American), and a host of others.

During the sixties, there was electricity charging through the insurance industry. Invitation-to-contract mailings, sent to millions of American consumers (by a handful of underwriters), was seen as an attack on the agency distribution system. The introduction of newspaper free-falls—single sheets and booklets—virtually revolutionized the ability of this handful of underwriters to reach audiences long neglected by the agency system. American Republic Life Insurance Company achieved amazing success, selling a combined term-life/decreasing-term product (Americare 39), using Jack Benny as their spokesperson.

The introduction of Art Linkletter and Roy Rogers and Dale Evans, as spokespeople for hospital indemnity coverages, caused applications to flow. Then came the skyrocketing expansion of the most successful endorsed-marketing program in the history of the industry—American Association of Retired Persons (AARP) and National Association of Retired Teachers (NRTA). This combination generated unbelievable sales of insurance—as well as creating one of the most powerful lobbying groups in American history.

Inevitably, the decade of the seventies saw insurance mail-order marketing leap from the pages of newspapers into the national consciousness, through television advertising. Another revolution! As well, this decade saw the techniques and practices bred in the United States catapulted to Europe, South America, and the Far East.

From infancy to adolescence in twenty-five years. Companies engaged in the insurance direct marketing system, once spawned by the insurance "establishment," were leading a revolution—discovering and refining new distribution channels.

Using imaginative product design, in addition to specialized and streamlined selling and administrative techniques, these companies spoke directly to insurance consumers. They sold supplementary insurance coverages, identified new market segments not being serviced by insurance agents, and provided the neglected service. They stumbled. Some fell, while others experienced the astonishing growth and profitability that successful risk taking so frequently produces.

Today, regardless of the growth over the past two and one-half decades, the contribution of the direct marketing system-generated insurance premiums to the overall industry is relatively small—amounting to just about 4% of the more than $200 billion in premiums written annually. As a share of market, it was up only a percentage point in the last five years. Nonetheless, as you've seen, companies are "jumping in" all over the place.

In fact, in a recent study by Ernst & Whinney among CEOs from the top 200 life-health and top 200 property & casualty companies, it was estimated that by 1993 more than 40% of the companies will be engaged in some form of nontraditional marketing, i.e., utilizing the direct marketing system.

Now, when these companies "jump in," they face two problems. First, there is a lack of trained, talented people. Today, the insurance mail-order marketing "talent pool" is at a low level. There is a serious shortage of qualified insurance mail-order marketing personnel—people who know how to conduct database marketing.

The second problem is misunderstanding. The insurance direct marketing system—the mail-order distribution channel in particular—is acutely sensitive to capital investment. It is "capital intensive," requiring relatively large investments to ensure a reasonable chance of success. And, as with most entrepreneurial ventures, the effort comes with no guarantee of success. As well, it takes a significant amount of time, effort, and attention to detail to make it work. One thing is certain, it is not a panacea for the real or imagined ills of a company.

Insurance mail-order marketing is more than a momentary solution to an occasional distribution problem. To produce a sales impact that is highly visible on an annual statement, it's necessary to adopt a very active role, and to be alert—constantly—to a host of opportunities that:

○ Already exist within the company, such as each company's own policyholder files (internal marketing).

○ Already exist under the control of the company's inter-mediaries—such as the files of brokers and agents (endorsed marketing).

○ Can be pursued through existing contacts with organizations that have large-membership customer lists, such as banks, department stores, and associations (third-party marketing).

○ Can be developed by locating, identifying, and isolating access to markets not currently under the company's control (broad marketing).

Too frequently today's insurance mail-order marketing practitioners tend to see their business in a single dimension—depending on what part of it they are managing at any given moment.

The inherent complexities of insurance, unquestionably, demand a broader view of the distribution channel, as well as the direct marketing system itself.

The techniques that have developed over the last two and one-half decades were driven by inventive applications of generally accepted (and tested) principles of mail-order marketing.

A good place to start the search for the 151 secrets of insurance direct marketing practices is to begin with a search for a definition.

What is Insurance Direct Marketing?

Martin Baier, Henry R. Hoke, Jr., and Robert Stone created what stands today as the generic definition of direct marketing.

"*Direct Marketing* is an interactive system of marketing that uses one or more advertising media to effect a measurable response and/or transaction *at any location.*"

Remember, according to this trio, it is *an aspect of total marketing. Not a fancy term for mail order.*

Basically, if you accept the textbook definition that marketing "is the total of activities of moving goods and services from seller to buyer," then you must accept the conclusion that direct marketing has the same broad function.

But, *marketing* is really a concept, an array of ideas that integrate one with another.

Clarence E. Eldridge, author of *The Management of the Marketing Function*, clearly defined the marketing concept. He did it in sixteen words:

"*Marketing is ascertaining, creating, and satisfying the wants of*

DIRECT MARKETING - What Is It?

An Aspect of Total Marketing -
not a fancy term for mail order.

Marketing is the total of activities of moving goods and services from seller to buyer. (See chart). Direct Marketing has the same broad function except that Direct Marketing requires the existence and maintenance of database.

a) to record names of customers, expires and prospects.

b) to provide a vehicle for storing, then measuring, results of advertising, usually direct response advertising.

c) to provide a vehicle for storing, then measuring, purchasing performance.

d) to provide a vehicle for continuing direct communication by mail and/or phone.

THUS

DIRECT MARKETING is interactive, requiring database for controlled activity: By mail, by phone, through other media selected on the basis of previous results.

DIRECT MARKETING makes direct response advertising generally desirable since response (inquiries or purchasing transactions) can be recorded on database for building the list, providing marketing information.

DIRECT MARKETING plays no favorites in terms of Methods of Selling...and there are only three:
a) Where buyer seeks out seller - retailing, exhibits
b) Where seller seeks out buyer - personal selling
c) Where buyer seeks seller by mail or phone - mail order

DIRECT MARKETING requires that a response or transaction at any location be recorded on cards, mechanical equipment or, preferably, on computer.

DIRECT MARKETING can be embraced by any kind of business as defined by the U.S. Census Standard Industrial Classification system:

DIRECT MARKETING is an interactive system of marketing that uses one or more advertising media to effect a measurable response and/or transaction at any location.

Figure 2-1: Courtesy *Direct Marketing Magazine,*
224 Seventh St., Garden City, NY 11530-5771

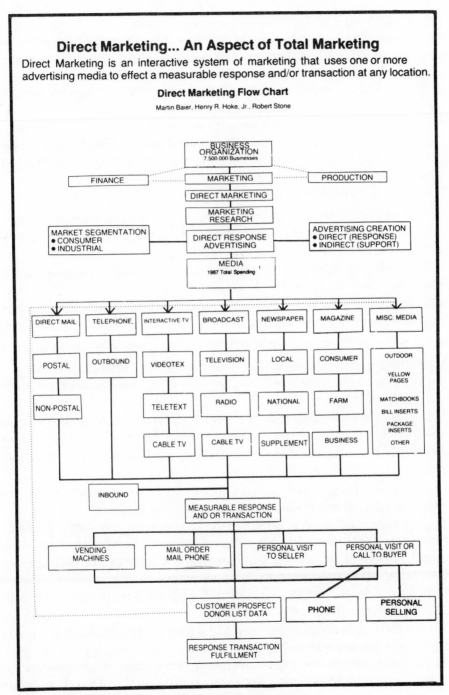

Direct Marketing... An Aspect of Total Marketing

Direct Marketing is an interactive system of marketing that uses one or more advertising media to effect a measurable response and/or transaction at any location.

Direct Marketing Flow Chart

Martin Baier, Henry R. Hoke, Jr., Robert Stone

Figure 2-2: Courtesy *Direct Marketing Magazine,*
224 Seventh St., Garden City, NY 11530-5771

11

people—and doing it at a profit."

Continuing, the insurance industry has four distribution channels: a) the agency system, b) the brokerage system, c) the direct-selling system, and d) the mail-order system. It comes as no surprise that direct marketing has been part of the insurance industry for a century, perhaps longer. *And, it is applicable to each of the four distribution channels.*

Now, you need to add the essential element of *direct marketing* to Eldridge's definition of *marketing. Direct marketing* has the same broad function as marketing, except this: Direct marketing requires the existence and maintenance of a database.

The database is required to:

1. Record the names of customers, lapses, and prospects.

2. Provide a vehicle for storing, and then measuring, results of advertising—usually direct-response advertising.

3. Provide a vehicle for storing, and then measuring, purchase performance.

4. Provide a vehicle for continuing direct communication by mail, and/or phone, and/or personal visit.

Now, insurance direct marketing begins to take on substance, because:

a. It is interactive, requiring a database for controlled activity: by mail, by phone, by personal visit, or through other media selected on the basis of previous results.

b. Direct marketing makes direct-response advertising generally desirable, since responses—inquiries or purchasing transactions—can be recorded on the database for list building and to provide marketing information.

Returning to the general definition of *direct marketing* above, and applying it to insurance, it embraces three selling methods:

First, where the buyer seeks out the seller—on-floor banking environments, or retail outlets like Sears Financial Service Centers.

Second, where seller seeks out buyer—the agency, brokerage, and direct-selling distribution system.

Third, where buyer seeks seller directly by mail or phone—the mail-order distribution system.

Now, borrowing from all these elements, let's complete the definition of insurance direct marketing.

Insurance Direct Marketing is an interactive system of marketing that ascertains, creates, and satisfies the insurance wants and needs of people by performing organized tasks affecting the transfer of services between seller and buyer; using one or more media for the purpose of soliciting a response, by phone, mail, or personal visit, from a prospect or customer; maintaining complete information on each transaction in a database; and doing so at a profit.

It is literally the "reinvention of the egg"—the perfect package. It is the *hottest* continuity program yet devised. For good reason: Insurance direct marketing is unique in that an original sale of a policy generates income over a long period of time.

As a group, insurance customers pay premiums for years as the result of an initial solicitation or offer. That means there is likely to be a steady cash flow from an original sale. It is unlike a catalog sale where a customer needs to purchase and repurchase—item by item—to maintain the seller's cash flow.

It is equally unlike, for example, a Franklin Mint sale, where the amount of insurance premium collected is usually considerably more than what is collected for a chess set.

However, in the modern age of insurance direct marketing, even though you know you are going to be collecting cash from your customers over a long period of time, the success of your system depends on organized, effective, and efficient re-solicitation!

This is known as *relational marketing.* It is conducted through internal marketing and is absolutely essential to your profitability and marketing strategy, as you will see in the chapters ahead!

Now, if you are entertaining the notion of using the insurance direct marketing system and its distribution channels to help your company, or—if you are already doing so—there are other things for you to consider.

Bob Pearcy, writing in the Danville, Indiana *Gazette,* once observed: "Starting a new year is like driving a brand-new car for the first time. You worry about the first dent you know you're going to get." Why is it, then, that companies using the insurance direct marketing system seldom think about the "dents"?

Getting into the business requires the tough mindedness of the traditional direct marketing entrepreneur—to be prepared to take the lumps, but totally committed to making the system work.

Starting out using the system is a lot like setting out on that first-time New Year's drive. Sure, there are going to be dents...but, if you are committed to making the system work for you and your company—if you have looked ahead and planned for the dents—the rewards are worth the risk.

The trouble with most companies in and out of the business is a lack of commitment. And that is the first real secret to success in insurance direct marketing.

SECRET No. 1

You cannot dabble. "Dabblers" die!

Companies who choose to dabble simply don't succeed. Make no mistake about it, there are many ways to "dabble." Each one is as bad as the other. There is:

○ The company which stops using the system after a single-test failure.

○ The actuary who adds "a little" to a product to give an extra margin of financial safety.

○ The financial officer who actually *demands* that marketing cost be recovered in the first year of product life.

○ The administrator who, when asked to alter an existing system or procedure to accommodate necessary elements of a marketing plan, declares that it either cannot be done, or it can be done, but not until next year.

At one time or another, these attitudes have been confronted by most insurance direct marketers. The way to overcome them is to make your company a "marketing company."

How is a *marketing* company different from a *product-oriented insurance* company? For the most part, an insurance company manufactures insurance products. Their markets are the agents and brokers who sell their products to the public. The attitude of the insurance company is: "Here's the product—go out and sell it."

By contrast, a *marketing company* seeks to obtain the benefits of the extraordinary possibilities in everything it does. It is market driven, seeking to fill the real and perceived needs of consumers, agents, and brokers. It adheres to, supports, and executes policies that are on the cutting edge of technological advancement.

Its dynamic is excellence. It takes risks—and reaps the huge rewards that successful risk taking produces. It is not afraid of failure. But, *when it fails*, it learns as much from the failures as from the successes.

Marketing companies are alert to change: change in composition and character of the consumer marketplace; change in consumer product needs, both real and perceived; change in communication techniques; changes in society, in government, and the world in general. To the marketing company, change is its foster parent, while *profit* and *return on*

14

investment are its parents.

What better environment for direct marketing to flourish in than to blossom in the fertile fields of *challenge* and *opportunity.* Frequently, these are exactly the same thing. The vast difference is in how one perceives them. One must look to the future possibilities, which are based on the measurable, accountable experiences and performances of the past.

Does it work? A small glimpse at performance: National Liberty Corporation is now part of Capitol Holding Corporation. In 1979, the company's return on stockholder equity was 14.35% on an increase of 27% in net income. Colonial Penn Group reported a 21.0% return on stockholder equity, along with an increase in income of just 3.3%. This has to mean that the net increase in investment was much less than proportional in relation to the earlier experience. Going much further, Geico, the P&C marketer, enjoyed a 38.4% return on stockholder equity on a 15.8% *reduction* in net income of the previous year.

The performance of major direct marketing insurance organizations demonstrates the difference between a *marketing company* and a *product-oriented insurance company.* In simple terms, marketing companies outperform the traditional insurance organizations, especially in terms of stockholder (or policyowner) equity and return on investment.

And, that is not too difficult to understand, because—during this same period of phenomenal direct marketing growth—the traditional agency distribution system abdicated an entire market.

It has been estimated that 40% of consumers are not covered by the insurance agency system. In the late seventies, the number of agencies peaked at 80,000. In 1983 that number had fallen to 65,000. Independent agents shifted their emphasis, primarily to upper-income consumer markets. The decline is not over. As many as 20,000 of the 1983 agency base will merge, sell, or go out of business during the next ten years.

However, to conclude from these facts that the agency distribution system is dead might be premature. To conclude that it is changing is appropriate. As long as the insurance agent's financial well-being is tied to commissions, it is logical that the agent will seek ways to maximize his or her commissions. Moreover, it is estimated, for example, that 10% of life insurance agents account for 90% of the new business generated each year. The "handwriting" clearly appears to be "on the wall."

This *graffiti* is not delivering a cryptic message! New insurance-distribution channels are replacing the agency losses. Banking deregulation has given rise to in-bank, on-platform insurance sales. The retail financial service centers, led by Sears, are cutting peninsulas of influence in the agency system.

And, the techniques employed to "bring in" the customer, according to the definition above, are direct marketing oriented.

Agents, themselves, are using direct marketing techniques more efficiently in prospecting for customers. And, the complexity of the agent's task has increased with: the introduction of new, sophisticated equity-based products; more complex P&C coverages; and demand for group and individual health plans. In addition, there is an array of financial-planning options. It's no wonder that direct marketing techniques are proving abundantly successful.

Twenty-five years ago the technique of mail-order distribution was, at best, obscure. In fact, it was considered only as an "extra" to the real business of marketing.

Giant life and casualty companies viewed the concept of "invitation-to-*contract*" direct-mail offers with amused tolerance. For the most part, as we have seen, many of these same companies are using "invitation-to-*inquire*" direct-mail support for their agency forces. But the concept of selling an auto policy, a life policy, or a health policy through the mail—directly—just wasn't ever going to happen.

Oddly enough, the insurance industry wasn't the only industry to look on mail order as a stepchild. Almost every industry viewed direct marketing, at best, as a second cousin.

Its use was confined to publishers—book clubs; magazines—circulation promotion; record companies—record clubs, and some legendary retailers. Sears, Montgomery Ward, and J.C. Penney had been using catalog sales to enhance their basic retail business.

Then came the growth of the suburbs, the installation of the interstate highway system, and the rise of shopping centers. All of these led to a general decline in mail-order purchasing patterns. These purchasing patterns had become relatively well developed over the century of manifest expansion and rural orientation of American society that had preceded World War II.

Since that war, two events occurred that stimulated mail-order marketing growth. The first was a shift in philosophy; the second, a new technology.

American business prior to the war, reports *The Wilson Quarterly*, was enchanted with the process of *manufacturing*.

The technological challenges and innovations of production captured the imagination of the entrepreneurial spirit. Manufacturing costs determined the price of goods. Product planning began with considerations of production and technological capacity. Inventory levels were set with production requirements in mind. Top management positions were occupied by financial or production personnel.

After the war, the American consumer, reacting to years of sacrifice, released a steady stream of pent-up *demand*. The fierce competition among companies to fill this consumer demand led to a change of attitude. The consumer became king.

For the first time, companies became less concerned about the magic of manufacturing the product. They became overpoweringly concerned with how they could sell their products to consumers and what products consumers wanted to buy!

This shift in industry focus from manufacturing to marketing became the preoccupation of American business. It was no longer enough to know what your plant was capable of producing. It became essential to find out how well your product was satisfying consumer needs and wants.

The birth of the marketing concept engineered a virtual revolution. Now, functions that had been the responsibility of technicians were becoming the responsibility of salesmen.

In fact, the marketing concept is an array of attitudes. These attitudes apply to insurance direct marketing, as well as to the variety of industries that have adopted the system. Bob Stone displays this shift in attitude by identifying the differences between a marketing company and a manufacturing company. Borrowing his model and applying it to the insurance industry, the differences become equally recognizable to novices and old hands:

Objectives The Marketing Company: Consumer forces dominate; long-range planning is emphasized. The Insurance Company: Internal forces dominate. Emphasis is on clerical administration and financial technology in the short run.

Place of the consumer The Marketing Company: Decision making begins and ends with consumer consideration. The Insurance Company: Decisions are imposed on the consumer.

Product Mix The Marketing Company: After consulting consumer wants, needs, and preferences, it creates what it feels confident can be sold. The Insurance Company: Sells products it manufactures without adequate and timely regard to consumer wants, needs, or preferences.

Marketing Strategy The Marketing Company: Focuses on *creating* new markets, as well as serving present ones. The Insurance Company: Tries to satisfy existing markets, usually their agents and brokers.

Innovation The Marketing Company: Emphasizes market opportunities and possibilities. The Insurance Company: Focuses on complicated product configurations and on administration.

Competition The Marketing Company: Sometimes leads, sometimes follows, always takes an offensive posture. The Insurance Company: Always follows, always reacts, always takes a defensive posture.

Profit To the Marketing Company: It is always an objective. To the Insurance Company: It is always what's left over, as a residual, after all costs are paid.

Other Corporate Functions The Marketing Company: Always focuses on marketing problems. The Insurance Company: Focuses on the "manufacturing," financial, and administrative problems.

Now, chances are good that most companies using direct marketing and its related distribution channels, are—at this point in time—somewhere between the extremes outlined above. In a sense, they are neither "fish" nor "fowl."

But, a constant movement toward the "best of all possible worlds"—the marketing company—ultimately will pay handsome dividends to those who have the courage to achieve that label!

In direct marketing terms, the development of the marketing concept was the first step after World War II that led to the growth we enjoy today. The second was truly technological.

The computer!

In the late 1980s, it may be difficult to remember that the post-World War II era was a time of explosions. Consumer demand exploded! The population exploded! There were new migrations from city to suburbs—and retail businesses exploded!

Those decades saw technological explosions. From refinements in productivity, to the age of television and to men landing on the moon! Information explosions—war was brought into your living room from the freezing hills of Korea to the steaming hell of Vietnam.

In the United States we became a society of "more." More women in the workforce, more awareness of our place in the world, more tension, more free time, and more discretionary income to feed societal demands for increasingly sophisticated goods and services.

The United States ceased being a market of more than two hundred million souls and became, instead, a variety of markets—each labeled a "segment." New data exploded into the marketing awareness. Demographics and psychographics, geodemography, modeling, and databasing are facts of the modern era in insurance mail-order marketing.

These facts make one concept in insurance direct marketing totally obsolete. That obsolete idea is mass marketing. Today, there is no *mass market.* Rather, there are specific and unique market segments in which it is appropriate for insurance direct marketers to sell products, ranging from hospital indemnity to universal life—in each case using a total-marketing approach.

The interactive nature of modern direct marketing requires the assembling and analysis of huge amounts of data, which is virtually an impossible task if attempted manually.

But, the computer makes it possible!

Computer technology allows the marketer to organize and make use of large quantities of information. Such technology allows the manipulation of information to form the basis for postulation. It tracks the results of decisions, making the ambiguous become obvious.

Computers perform routine tasks faster and more accurately than human manipulation. They produce useful data to guide the marketer in the decision-making process. Computer applications are universal. Computers were and are particularly critical to the direct marketer.

Insurance direct marketing has borrowed from a variety of disciplines: psychology, sociology, economics, and statistics. Mathematics and mathematical modeling are its method, information is its mother's milk, and analysis is its daily bread.

It is unlikely that the insurance industry will change overnight—with new definitions, or recognition, of this maturing marketing system.

It is a new world for this business of insurance direct marketing. If you are new to the system, you can anticipate some dents. They are going to happen. But, if you are committed to the system, you can fix the dents.

To take advantage of the window of opportunity open today in insurance direct marketing, and the many windows that will open in the future, it's best to approach the subject with a completely open mind.

For example: Yes, it is possible to market single-premium deferred annuities through the direct marketing system. Companies are doing it. As well, companies using the direct marketing system are generating millions of leads for agent follow-up sales. Companies are generating hundreds of millions of dollars of new premium every year marketing products as different as interest-sensitive whole life is from hospital indemnity, term life from long-term nursing care, and Medicare supplement from universal life. In each case, these are accomplished by using the techniques of the direct marketing system.

The opportunities appear to be endless, governed only by the imagination of marketers...and the perceived needs and wants of the consumer markets.

Insurance direct marketing has spawned its own unique techniques, its own unique vocabulary, and its own unique experiences. And, yes, a number of secrets.

The secrets that make the system work are concerned with such things as product development and strategic planning, broad marketing, endorsed marketing, internal marketing, telemarketing, the creative process and its applications, administrative systems, research, and the mathematics.

So, the first step in understanding insurance direct marketing is to take a look at the way those tasks interact. In a sense, these tasks are what make it a system.

The Secrets of the System

The insurance direct marketing system is, in its purest form, a complete ladder of logic. It is, as nearly as any marketing method can be, a precise and "artfully-scientific" system of building premium income, profit, and return on investment, on the basis of *predetermined costs and returns*.

In its most successful application, the system involves the following prerequisites:

○ A large potential target market—in the generic sense of a *market*. For instance, people over 50 years of age constitute a market. Or, perhaps, veterans. A potential target market might be savings & loan association customers, or bank credit-card holders.

○ A product of broad, general appeal within the target market.

○ A medium for *reaching* and *testing* limited segments of the market.

○ A means of accurately recording and evaluating response from the market.

○ A method of rolling-out from the test segment to the larger target market, and of eliminating market segments that testing indicates would be nonprofitable.

It is enormously *efficient* marketing—regardless of the distribution channel you use. Part of its efficiency is *the ability to control.*

Companies that have long depended, for example, on the agency distribution channel are discovering that centralizing and managing an agent lead-generation program, using direct marketing methods, produces remarkable results.

In one case, a group of companies marketing a catastrophic group health product with an average annual premium in the $1,750-to-$3,500 range is producing more than 20 inquiries per thousand from their lead-generating program.

The leads are high quality (highly qualified). On follow-up by the companies' agents, the closing rate is between 15% and 30%. At an average annualized premium sale of, say, $2,500, that roughly translates into $7,500 to $15,000 of annual premium per thousand pieces of direct mail dropped. Of course, the business volume generated is limited by the number of agents following up on the leads.

But, the database used by this group of companies has almost 10 million records available for their lead-generation program—a very significant marketing universe.

By the time all expenses, including commissions, are totaled, the marketing efficiency—the ratio of marketing cost to total annualized renewal premium (MC/TARP) is as follows: Every $1 spent in marketing cost produces slightly more than $1 in annualized premium, which will be coming in for a substantial number of years.

On the other side of the coin, a mail-order marketing insurance company, selling a graded-benefit term-life product through a television inquiry program, produces leads at a cost of about $5 each. By the time their marketing cycle is finished, total lead cost is in the $16 per-lead area.

The closing rate against their leads is about 80 sales per thousand. At an average annualized premium of $210, they are generating about $16,800 per thousand leads in sales. The MC/TARP ratio is roughly the same as the company using direct marketing techniques combined with the agency distribution channel. And, the market of the mail-order company is much larger than 10 million. Thus, because of the difference in market size, the result of the graded-benefit term-life product indicates a much greater profit volume than we saw for the catastrophic group health product, just above.

In a different scenario, a leading third-party marketer provides hospital indemnity protection (HIP) to the commercial bank credit-card-holder population. Using direct mail, it experiences response rates in the range of 3.6 to 6.1 apps (applications) per thousand pieces mailed, averaging 4.5 paid applications per thousand.

The average annualized premium for the product is $265, and each mailing is producing somewhat more than $1,192 in annualized premium

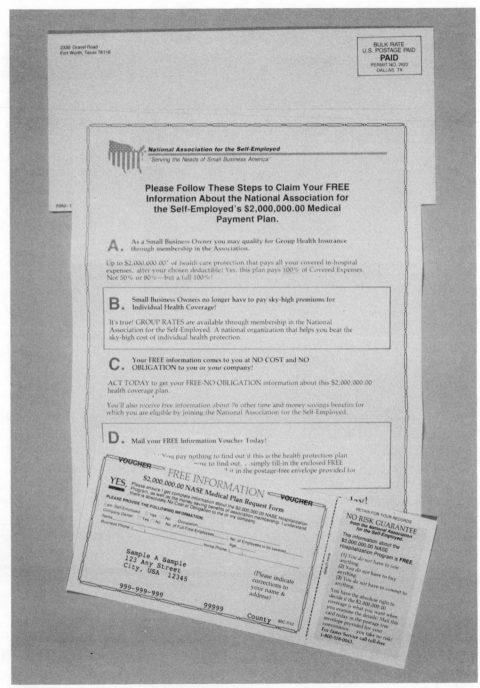

Figure 3-1: High-ticket inquiry generation in support of an agent sales program uses simplicity as a key.

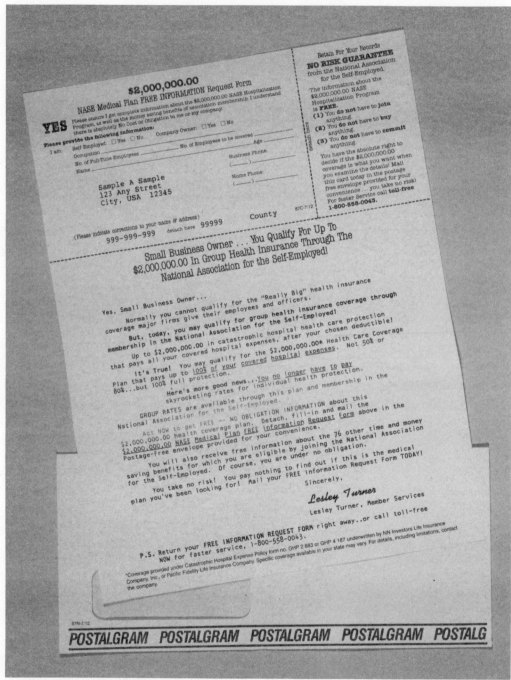

Figure 3-2: Both samples "beat the control."

for each thousand pieces mailed. When all the expenses are totaled, including commissions and list fees to the endorsing organization, the MC/TARP ratio is about $1.00 : $1.35.

The point here is that by employing direct marketing methods, these companies have considerably more accountable control over their marketing than do companies that do not employ the system.

However, and this *however* is a big one, direct marketing is not designed to replace the insurance agent. A whole array of co-operative techniques is available to show that it need not. And, best of all, this is true on a national, regional, or local basis.

The way direct marketing is helpful, actually, is to amplify the effectiveness of each distribution channel. Through market segmentation, certain markets become targeted by each distribution channel.

For example, agents use direct marketing techniques to generate interest and business in higher-priced products—basic coverages needed by just about everyone. Brokers use the techniques to help capture the interest of business markets. Direct writers generate leads for their consumer products—especially in property and casualty coverages. Mail-order companies specialize in supplementary products, and some basic P&C coverages.

In fact, a majority of insurance companies operating in the United States today—wittingly or unwittingly—employ some of the more common direct marketing techniques in their day-to-day operations. For, whenever a company sends out a small brochure describing a new product with its premium notice, it—to a small extent—is making use of insurance direct marketing!

Now, the thing that is important to remember about insurance direct marketing is its systems aspect. *An insurance direct marketing system is a complex of interactive ideas, events, principles, techniques, and philosophies that form a coherent whole.*

The system owes its efficiencies to the development of the computer and its vast array of applications that are particularly suited to the unique needs of direct marketing.

Three concepts govern the successful and profitable use of the insurance direct marketing system.

SECRET No. 2

Elements used in the system must be designed to function within the system—as well as designed to sell!

SECRET No. 3

You can afford to spend considerably more money to acquire a policyowner than a single product's marketing allowance would lead you to believe.

SECRET No. 4

Your customers and qualified inquirers are the best prospects for future sales.

These three secrets are fundamental to establishing, or revising, your direct marketing efforts. This is so, because they form the basis for *relational marketing*—a concept absolutely essential to the system.

Relational marketing is the process by which you build sales on the interest of inquirers, and the purchases of your customers, your policyowners. You see, this process is based on the fact that, to these people, you are a known quantity. You have established a relationship with them. You are either providing them with a service—a policy or certificate of insurance— or you are answering questions about a service you have offered. In the case of customers, you have established a clear *affinity*. In the case of inquirers, the affinity is not nearly as strong as it is with customers, but it exists nonetheless. In both cases, you have less to prove than another company, about which they know nothing.

Now, how does all of this relate? Take a look at an overview of the elements and events of the insurance direct marketing system:

- o *Research and development*
- o *Product development*
- o *Market development*
- o *Computer system development*
- o *Strategic market planning*
- o *Program tactical planning*
- o *Market promotion*
- o *Fulfillment, premium billing/collection*
- o *Customer service*
- o *Response analysis*
- o *Customer/inquiry sales programs*
- o *Claims handling*
- o *Database development and use*

Some elements or events happen simultaneously, some are prerequisites for the next event. But this "baker's dozen" identifies the most critical parts of the insurance direct marketing system.

How does it work?

Let's follow a simple example through the events which transform an idea into a potentially profitable book of business.

As a marketer, you've decided to mount a marketing effort using the direct marketing insurance system. The initial questions you ask yourself are: What product will I sell? To whom will I sell it? Where will I sell it? Why will I sell it? When will I sell it?

Pretty good questions...and rather common questions. These usually start every project—regardless of the field you're in.

You need the answers, so you turn to the first event in the direct marketing system—research and development. Your R&D folks develop a working hypothesis, identify a market segment, and begin to conduct some phone and mail surveys.

The result of their initial efforts seems to indicate that there's a good market out there among families in midlife...about 40 to 65 years of age. Most have children, some are homeowners, some apartment dwellers. Nearly all are auto owners, have relatively modest savings accounts, and are job holders earning between $15,000 and $25,000 annually. These folks have many concerns...but among them is the high cost of hospital care.

Next, the research folks begin conducting focus-group interviews among this market segment. A focus group simply assembles a number of consumers in a controlled environment and, through a leader, asks questions to determine attitudes and preferences of the assembled group. This technique confirms the initial findings of your R&D people, and also discovers that the real fear is of catastrophic illness and long-term hospitalization.

Now, the research people also discover that the average hospital stay in the United States is four and a half days. So...they recommend that some kind of indemnification product be developed, linked to hospital stays of longer than, say, four days and delivering a minimum benefit of, say, $150 for each day beyond the fourth for a period of at least two or three years. The product will sell best, if it is guaranteed issue, priced in the range of $15 to $25 per month.

Three things happen next.

The results are delivered to three groups: a product development group, a market development group, and a systems development group.

The product development group is going to construct your product for you. This group will develop *rates and benefits*, exclusions, limitations, and reductions. Thus, the group creates the insurance contract. Moreover, based on a series of assumptions, the product development group will assign a

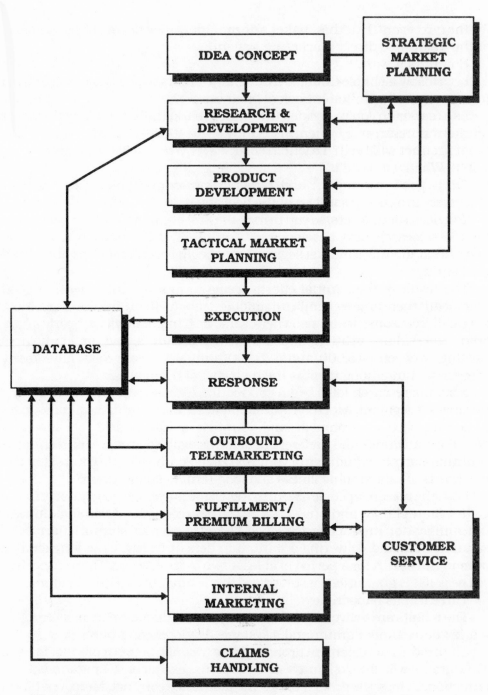

Figure 3-3: A basic model that considers the generic elements of the insurance direct marketing system

target for the *required return on investment*, as well as the degree of *profitability* "built into" your new product.

The market development group investigates the market and determines for you whether the market is *reachable*, and what *your* possibilities are for reaching the market. More details concerning the market population—not only their numbers, but their motivations, fears, hopes and desires—are developed.

The systems development group concentrates its efforts on determining the *computer requirements* for issuing policies, billing and collecting premium, providing proper levels of customer service support, as well as the myriad administrative details connected with *recording and analyzing the results* of your marketing effort.

Depending on the size of your company, these groups are either separate entities—like departments—or teams made up of representatives from each of the functional areas.

The next step in the process is strategic market planning. Either by concept or document, your marketing strategy is a broad statement of the who, what, where, when and why with which you began your research. Now you have information and can begin to develop your strategies. At this point, you can coordinate those strategies with the larger corporate strategies within which you must work.

These steps, so far, have given form to your developing an insurance direct marketing system. The skeleton is in place. What remains, now, is to add the flesh.

The tactical marketing plan delivers the detail of the program you are about to execute. It is the specific "how" and "when" you are going to market. It is the start of your time-line-to-target date, when you are going to expose your new product to the marketing universe you've chosen.

The tactical marketing plan also indicates a critically important *number*—it is the breakeven! The *breakeven* on any program is the number of paid policies you must issue to meet the financial requirements of your product and your program. Financial requirements might be expressed as *profit, return on investment,* or *internal rate of return.*

Breakeven is directly related to *acquisition allowance,* which is the amount of money you can afford to spend to acquire the new policyowner. The acquisition allowance of any direct marketing insurance product is a complex of numbers developed as part of the marketing strategy and product development phases of the system.

Now...we are ready to go to market. Let's assume we have decided to solicit our market through direct mail. The direct-mail material has been created and produced. The computer and support system are alerted and ready to process. The target date arrives and tens of thousands of direct-mail packages, or "kits," are scattered throughout your chosen market segment.

Market promotion is under way. The waiting starts; the risk has been taken; time passes.

Then, one day...there it is...your first response. Five, ten, or twenty business-reply envelopes containing applications from your target market for your new, guaranteed-issue, hospital-indemnity product. More the second day, more the third, and so on. Slowly, the response soon builds to hundreds. Perhaps, even thousands of applications are pouring into your facility every day.

The steps called fulfillment and premium billing and collection now swing into action. Let's assume the offer you made was a *send-no-money offer*, which simply means that folks in your target market do not have to send along the first premium with the application.

Application data is entered into the computer system. The computer system does all of these things: prints out a form containing all the details of the insurance contract, creates a tape that is used to emboss a plastic credit-type identification card, generates an initial premium bill, and a welcome letter thanking the prospective customer for responding and pointing out how important the protection is. The computer system also stores all the personal data contained on the application, and it generates a whole series of reports to inform you and your management team about what is going on. All of the output material—the fulfillment material—is then assembled and mailed back to the applicant.

When the consumer receives his conversion package, he is faced with a decision: to purchase or not to purchase. It may be that, at this point, our prospect has a question. If so, all he needs to do is call an "800" telephone number and he's in touch with the customer service department.

Customer service answers questions...*before, during, and after a sale.* Since our contact, in this case, is primarily by mail, the customer-service function is critical. It is the consumer's window of opportunity to verify that the company exists and to help raise his comfort level in his decision-making process.

Now, the consumer has your material in his hand. One of three things can happen. Your applicant can study the policy, decide he wants it, pay the premium bill—putting his policy in force—and then store his policy in a safe place. Or your applicant can simply trash the material. Perhaps your applicant will look at the material and set it aside to make a final decision later.

If the applicant pays his bill, it arrives at your company and is entered into your computer system. In the masterfile it is marked paid. From now on, the customer's bill will be prepared automatically and mailed out when it is time to do so.

In the other two cases, the system generates another bill, then another, if the second is not paid. Perhaps, it continues even after that. This is the *billing series*...and at some point it ends. Those applicants who have not paid are placed in a special segment of the masterfile. Those who have paid are your *policyholders*.

While all of this has been going on, you have been receiving reports telling you what is happening relative to the mailing program as a whole. You may have used as many as twenty different direct-mail lists. The response is being reported to you on the basis of how each list is performing. You are, as well, receiving reports on the average annual renewal premium being generated, how many policies have been issued, how many have been paid, how many individuals—with breakdown as to gender—and how many families, how old the main insured is. And more.

The response-analysis part of your program is telling you what happened, and you are comparing it with what you thought was going to happen. The results are also being stored in your computer *because you are going to revisit those results in a variety of ways later on.*

In the systems-development part of your planning, you arranged to have your computer automatically check on how long a policyholder has paid his premium. When your policyholder makes his third payment, a trigger is toggled in your system.

An offer is automatically generated to your policyholder soliciting an increased-benefit, surgical-care rider to add on to his basic coverage. Sometime later, another offer is made to increase his daily indemnity, and—sometime after that—another offer to improve some other aspect of this medical coverage...and so on and on.

These add-on rider offers are essential to the profitability and persistency of your book of business! First, because your response rates in policyowner marketing may be as much as 60 times higher than front-end solicitation. Second, because the marketing efficiency—the relationship of sales to marketing cost—is on a parity with response. Third, because persistency will increase. Policyowner retention gets better in direct proportion to the strength of your policyowner marketing effort.

There's more.

The same principle applies to crossloading. *Crossloading* is the process of selling a different type of coverage to your *own* policyowners, for example, life insurance to hospital-cash policyowners. While the response rates are somewhat lower—perhaps only 10 times front-end-solicitation response rates—the marketing efficiency remains significantly higher than that associated with new-customer solicitation.

Crossloading and rider-add-on offers can greatly enhance the profitability of a policyowner. The process gives to a policyowner a far greater value than is generally acknowledged. This concept, known as *lifetime value*, will—if properly understood and calculated—give you more marketing dollars for the purpose of attracting the policyowner in the first place. Obviously, the more policyowners you acquire, the more policyowner marketing you will be able to do. The more of this you are able to do, the higher your profitability will be. It is simple arithmetic. *And it is relational marketing in action.*

Mining your policyowner file is not restricted to direct mail alone. Although chances are good, if you are just starting out, that's the direction in which you will go. Outbound telemarketing programs to policyowners greatly enhance response rates to add-on and crossloading offers.

Within the system, outbound telemarketing provides a person-to-person contact with your consumer. As important as your inbound operation is for customer service, so—too—is your outbound operation.

Combining outbound telemarketing with direct-mail solicitations provides you with the strongest "clout" in generating high TARP to MC ratios. Together, these techniques greatly enhance your profit—and, your credibility.

The next step in the process really reinforces your credibility. Since the product you are selling is essentially a "promise," it is important that, when the time comes to pay a claim, it be done sensitively, efficiently, carefully, and effectively. Claims handling is an integral part of the insurance direct marketing system. It is the ultimate service you provide.

To be effective, whenever possible, your claims system should be automated to the highest degree. It must have access to the masterfile— obviously, a random-access capability. This process allows you to instantly verify a claim, and—in some cases—claim checks can be on their way to your policyowner within twenty-four hours. In fact, you can program your system to do it for you by setting up a claims payment subroutine.

All the while, many events have been happening in this hypothetical display. Information has been accumulating on: gross response rates, issue rates, policyowner marketing data, demographic data, external file enhancements, payment patterns, monthly lapse rates, and claims. And, it is all being stored, day after day, in your database.

Database marketing has become one of the fundamental concepts of direct marketing. A *database* is a comprehensive collection of interrelated information providing the marketer with an enormous amount of knowledge about his customer.

Because of its inherent capabilities, it allows marketers to perform more sophisticated analyses than ever before. It can examine relationships between data, and it is a tool that is used for planning, executing, and measuring direct marketing programs. It runs from sophisticated, multivariate, statistically-predictive modeling to the discovery of market segments previously considered unproductive...but, in fact, highly profitable.

This is the insurance direct marketing system at work—a complex of ideas, concepts, philosophies, events, techniques, and principles—all interactive, all interconnected. The glue that holds the system together is the computer.

Perhaps what is most important, however, is the attitude. The direct marketing system is as much a state of mind, a complex of attitudes, as it is a commitment to making it work. At its heart is the research function.

That's a good place to start.

IV

The Secrets of Research
and Development

SECRET No. 5

Research unlocks reality!

At best, *reality* is an elusive concept, in a philosophical sense. But in a marketing environment, the research function delivers *information* to the insurance direct marketer. This information mirrors the attitudes and the facts concerning the people populating a market segment. To the marketer, this reality sets the confines in which he or she has to live.

Now, there are many kinds of research: market and product research; attitude research; database manipulation for statistical analysis; and broader forms, like generic market research.

Here's an example of the last kind. In Chapter II, while looking at the overall background and opportunities in insurance direct marketing, information was reported about the downsizing of the agency distribution channel. As well, it was noted that there is a variety of applications for agent insurance direct marketing.

James Fouss reported on research conducted by Response Analysis Corporation, of Princeton, NJ, to attendees of the Twentieth International Direct Marketing Symposium in Montreux, Switzerland. The research discovered that two-thirds of the insurance agents, themselves, believe that there will be a significant reduction in their numbers during the next five to ten years.

Therefore, insurance companies will be seeking other ways of reaching wider consumer segments in order to sell—in this case—life, as well as property and casualty products. They will be doing so for several other reasons, according to this study. It costs over $200,000 to train a successful insurance agent. Such extraordinary expense, in tandem with high turnover and the declining number of people entering the field, is forcing companies to re-examine their distribution techniques. These are the alternative distribution channels cited by the CEOs surveyed in the Ernst & Whinney study, covered in Chapter II.

In the consumer part of the response-analysis survey conducted among households earning $20,000 a year or more—there are fifty million such households in the United States—20% have no insurance agent for auto insurance, 28% have no agent for homeowners insurance, and a whopping 42% have no insurance agent for life insurance!

Imagine the impact of those numbers. This means that 10 million households seek to buy their auto insurance through other means; 14 million find some other source from which to purchase homeowners insurance; and a staggering 21 million households look for some other distribution channel from which to purchase life insurance.

The research continues with some other interesting facts concerning consumers and direct marketing techniques. Of the consumers who have purchased insurance, 36% have done so via direct marketing methods—and with a high degree of satisfaction. Of consumers purchasing by mail, 82% are very or quite satisfied with their purchase. And, of those who have purchased via telemarketing, 94% are very or quite satisfied.

In addition to providing you with some interesting facts concerning the place of direct marketing in the overall insurance-marketing mix, these data are cited as an example of the kind of *reality* research can unlock.

Research delivers knowledge. And, equipped with this knowledge, the insurance direct marketer can save time and money, achieve a competitive edge, define a strategy, and create irresistible tactics.

Now, according to *Webster*, research is "studious inquiry: usually critical and exhaustive investigation or experimentation, having for its aim the revision of accepted conclusions in the light of newly discovered facts."

Certainly, it is the purpose of direct marketing research to develop new facts. And Webster's definition gives the methodology for doing so. But direct marketing research has another purpose—which expands the definition. Direct marketing research is the *organized* investigation of qualitative and quantitative data leading to *improved profitability.*

In fact, the direct marketing research functions are relatively new.

Years ago the pioneer insurance direct marketers were satisfied with in-market testing.

In-market testing produces the most powerful research tool of all—a very measurable response. The trouble is that today it may be very expensive to mount such a testing program—especially in insurance direct marketing.

Bringing a new product on stream is a very expensive undertaking. We are not speaking about a "copycat" product, but a truly inventive, *new* product that satisfies the perceived needs and wants of consumers to whom you intend to market.

It is not unusual—when all expenses are totaled—for an in-market, new-product test to exceed a *quarter of a million dollars!* It isn't the promotion expense that is the culprit—although it is high, but the time and effort expended by the company to develop the product, file it, set up administrative systems to handle it, create unique fulfillment material, and a host of other costs.

Today's insurance direct marketer needs a great amount of information:

O Information that helps determine what products consumers want and need to purchase.

O Information to identify prospects' buying intentions and characteristics.

O Information leading to an understanding of the marketing environment critical to strategic planning.

O Information to help creative people upgrade offers, develop copy platforms and graphics *before* incurring production and media costs.

O Information about which elements of the programs are working—and why.

O Information about how the market's perception of the product or service is changing *over time.*

In-market testing doesn't deliver.

Today, sophisticated direct marketers are using research techniques that have long been standard among our general advertising brethren. These applications are unlocking a continuous stream of marketing secrets that are changing the face of the direct marketing system.

Research is not marketing elegance. It is marketing necessity.

The post-World War II development of the marketing concept and its partner, technological revolution, as we have explored in Chapter II, shaped the movement toward direct marketing research.

To these elements add one more—competition.

36

Two dozen years ago there were few insurance companies willing to risk an *invitation to contract* by mail. Today there is a host of companies doing so. Insurance direct marketing has become a growth industry. Increasing competition means that each company seeks an "edge." Honing the edge means finding the right niche in the marketplace. And that takes effective and timely information, intelligence, and research.

Available applications from disciplines like psychology, sociology, economics, and statistics impact on the daily working patterns of today's marketers. These applications, combined with ready access to computers that perform routine research calculations and advanced quantitative routines, allow marketers to consider research as a nearly routine direct marketing function.

There are two generic types of research: *qualitative* and *quantitative.*

Qualitative research generates ideas and formulates hypotheses. Characteristically:

1. *It is exploratory*, investigating the reasons consumers buy products, what they might like to buy, how they might use what they buy, and what they like or dislike about what they buy.

2. It is usually conducted among a *relatively small group* of people.

3. It is often conducted through *group sessions*, although it can be conducted via in-depth interviews.

Perhaps the most familiar form of this research type is the *focus-group interview*. Prescreened, prequalified participants, about eight to twelve, attend a two-hour session led by a professional group moderator. Sessions are usually conducted in four to six geographically dispersed regions.

Focus-group interviews help the marketer to understand consumer language and attitudes, uncover underlying motivations and attitudes relating to the product or service being sold...or that the marketer is *contemplating* selling. Frequently, focus-group interviewing provides the marketer with valuable insights into the consumer's purchase decision-making process.

One of the more fascinating examples of the art of focus-group interviews and how this research application impacts on marketing is the Avon Products story.

Beginning in 1976, Avon Products, in partnership with Monarch Life Insurance Company, began investigating the prospect of selling life and health insurance to Avon representatives—one of the largest affinity groups in the United States...numbering almost one million prospects.

Preliminary marketing studies conducted by Avon clearly indicated that a dynamic market existed for the sale of insurance. But, equally, it was apparent that no one had attempted to sell to that market in an organized way—too, there was a lot the company did not know.

Avon retained the consulting firm of Frank Kennedy & Associates to get the needed information. The firm conducted "clinics" (focus groups) among hundreds of Avon representatives. These women represented middle America in every way, and they were alike in that they needed some form of extra income.

The research firm investigated the attitudes these representatives held toward insurance, and tried to determine if they would be willing to make purchase decisions on their own—without consulting their spouses. The interview groups were held in a number of states, including Ohio, Iowa, Minnesota, Nebraska, New Jersey, and Virginia.

The results of the research were startling! Much of the current theory, held by insurance companies, regarding the women's market was contradicted.

First, among the surprises, was the women's attitude toward agents. The insurance agent was perceived as a "con man"—untrustworthy. They placed the agent five steps below a used-car salesman. Strange attitudes—since 95% of the women had never been contacted by an insurance agent!

Second, it was discovered that the women had their own ideas about how they wanted to pay premiums, choosing bank drafts and quarterly payments over monthly or annual bills.

Third, and what might have been the most valuable finding, women—at least, women in this group—make insurance decisions without their husbands...and *they make them on the spot*!

Fourth, women are far and away much more common-sense buyers than men; they are not nearly as emotional.

Finally, it was discovered that, to these women, low cost was much more important than high benefits.

Armed with the information from these focus groups, Avon performed in-market testing, which confirmed the results of the research. By the beginning of 1980, 150,000 Avon representatives had "signed up." Every product was guaranteed issue with no medical examinations. And the policyowner distribution was amazing: 35% of the policyowners were under 35 years of age; only 15% were over 50!

Ultimately, Avon formed its own insurance company, The Great Oak Insurance Company. In February 1980, it shared the elements of its marketing success with the insurance community through an article in *Best's Insurance Management Reports.* AND, NO ONE PAID ATTENTION! *Every program directed at the women's market has used shelf products, high benefits, and higher premiums—billed in monthly modes.*

For Avon, research unlocked reality and provided a startling example of the power of the focus-group interview as a research technique.

A second type of qualitative research is the *in-depth interview.* This research technique is most frequently used when there is a great deal of detailed information you need from a geographically dispersed market.

Moreover, any data you are accumulating needs to come from people who have little to do with each other—limited affinity—and who might have some difficulty answering questions in a group environment. In-depth interviewing generates discussions that are extremely complex and very technical. The technique is time consuming and expensive—far more expensive for the direct marketer than that person is, in all probability, willing to pay.

Remember, qualitative research is used to generate ideas or to develop hypotheses. The next step is to test the hypotheses in a quantitative environment.

Quantitative Research has its own set of characteristics:

1. It generally follows the qualitative stage of research.

2. It is well structured, seeking answers to questions like: Is the product easy to use? Is it timesaving? Is it a good value?

3. It is conducted among a relatively large number of respondents... from 100 to 1,000, or more.

4. It can be conducted by personal interviews or micro/macro mathematical analysis.

5. Quantitative research measures behavior and attitudes. It places statistical data in historical perspective, and *it delivers information.*

*   *   *

Remember, *research unlocks reality.* It answers three critical questions for the marketer: What consumers want to buy, who buys, and why they buy. Then comes product development, market development, and advertising and marketing strategy.

Quantitative research helps assemble the data. Personal interviewing techniques include:

Door-to-door interviewing This uses complex questionnaires and presents respondents with a variety of concepts—perhaps the product itself. It is expensive and time consuming.

Intercept interviews   If you frequently walk through a large shopping mall, it is likely that you have been "intercepted" by an on-site interviewer. These interviewers screen research candidates to make sure they are "qualified," and those who qualify are interviewed in a mall facility.

Telephone survey   Perhaps you've answered your phone recently and participated in this economical research technique. It lends itself to very close supervision and is fast. It is particularly effective when conducting a study among a select group—association members, for example.

Mail survey   The least expensive research technique has strengths and weaknesses. One strength: It is anonymous, lending itself to statistical analysis. One weakness: Even with a free gift, response is relatively low. You must be sure that your mail survey delivers enough response from a defined universe to provide you with statistically valid data. In fact, our mail-order entrepreneur may make the claim that he is conducting a mail survey each time he mails anything going to a substantial number of actual or potential policyholders.

*   *   *

Truthfully, every time we conduct a direct marketing program, we accumulate an enormous amount of information about our market and our customers. Too frequently, however, marketers do not sit down and analyze results. They don't discover what secrets the results reveal. Statistical analysis helps define and focus a marketer's thinking. Analysis provides a basis for research continuation. It reveals program elements that not only help us save money, but help us make money, as well.

Recall one part of our definition...*profit is our motivation*! Today, nothing is more critical to producing profit for our companies than the basic statistical tool of direct marketing, the DATABASE.

Your database is the genetic code of your strategic planning. It tells you who has purchased your insurance products. It examines persistency and helps you understand why some folks pay and some lapse. It tells you about folks who buy riders to your policies, and about the people who buy other types of coverages from you. It defines demographics—age, gender, geography, marital status, and frequently, family composition. The addition of file enhancement overlays, using systems like ACORN, PRIZM, and Cluster-Plus, indicates income, education, lifestyle, attitudes, and buying behavior—all through geodemographic analysis.

This historical information is so basic it is a company's "rosetta" stone.

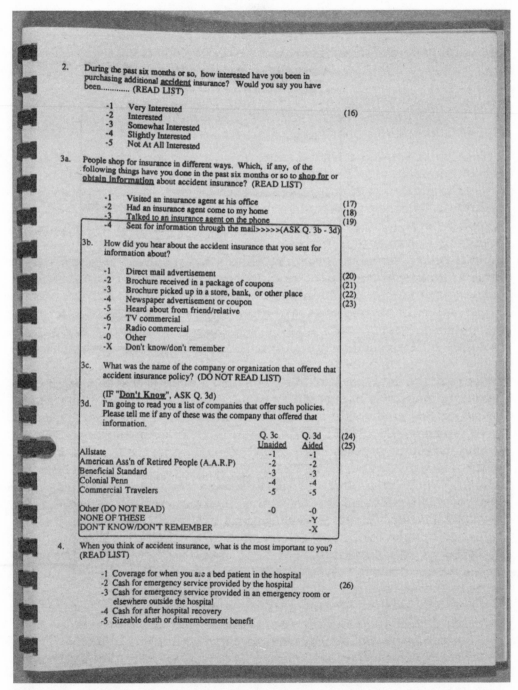

2. During the past six months or so, how interested have you been in purchasing additional accident insurance? Would you say you have been............. (READ LIST)

    -1 Very Interested   (16)
    -2 Interested
    -3 Somewhat Interested
    -4 Slightly Interested
    -5 Not At All Interested

3a. People shop for insurance in different ways. Which, if any, of the following things have you done in the past six months or so to shop for or obtain information about accident insurance? (READ LIST)

    -1 Visited an insurance agent at his office   (17)
    -2 Had an insurance agent come to my home   (18)
    -3 Talked to an insurance agent on the phone   (19)
    -4 Sent for information through the mail>>>>>(ASK Q. 3b - 3d)

3b. How did you hear about the accident insurance that you sent for information about?

    -1 Direct mail advertisement   (20)
    -2 Brochure received in a package of coupons   (21)
    -3 Brochure picked up in a store, bank, or other place   (22)
    -4 Newspaper advertisement or coupon   (23)
    -5 Heard about from friend/relative
    -6 TV commercial
    -7 Radio commercial
    -0 Other
    -X Don't know/don't remember

3c. What was the name of the company or organization that offered that accident insurance policy? (DO NOT READ LIST)

    (IF "Don't Know", ASK Q. 3d)

3d. I'm going to read you a list of companies that offer such policies. Please tell me if any of these was the company that offered that information.

	Q. 3c Unaided	Q. 3d Aided	
Allstate	-1	-1	(24)
American Ass'n of Retired People (A.A.R.P)	-2	-2	(25)
Beneficial Standard	-3	-3	
Colonial Penn	-4	-4	
Commercial Travelers	-5	-5	
Other (DO NOT READ)	-0	-0	
NONE OF THESE		-Y	
DON'T KNOW/DON'T REMEMBER		-X	

4. When you think of accident insurance, what is the most important to you? (READ LIST)

    -1 Coverage for when you are a bed patient in the hospital
    -2 Cash for emergency service provided by the hospital   (26)
    -3 Cash for emergency service provided in an emergency room or elsewhere outside the hospital
    -4 Cash for after hospital recovery
    -5 Sizeable death or dismemberment benefit

igure 4-1: A typical format for a telephone survey

It points to future direction, translating what has been to what can be. Database development can be the single most important key to unlocking profitability in your insurance direct marketing operation.

SECRET No. 6

Start today to build a professionally designed, relational DATABASE for your insurance direct marketing operation.

You will be startled at what it can do for you! And your database will form the foundation for the next statistical technique, simulation modeling.

Simulation modeling is a controversial state-of-the-art, pretesting technique. What it does is build a mathematical equation from survey or response data—a model—that translates the acquired information into a prediction of in-market response.

In a rather simplistic overview, simulation modeling has two parts. First, a number of alternative mailings are assembled, for example, for a particular product, each mailing using a different copy platform or offer. These alternative mailings are then exposed to target consumer respondents. Respondents answer very detailed questions about the mailings, including a variety of purchase-intent options and overall rating scales, focusing on appeals.

Second, the data generated is quantified and subjected to a statistical technique known as regression analysis. From the analysis, a formula is developed that predicts future response with, theoretically, great accuracy.

According to Bob Stone, Allstate Insurance Company has been using a similar technique successfully for quite some time. He reports that Allstate saves money on test packages by using dummies (hand-designed direct-mail kits) on a pre-production basis. It saves money when the test goes "live" by mailing smaller test cells. And the company finds it particularly appealing because this method allows product pretesting, without having to file each product with the various state insurance commissioners.

Research unlocks reality.

Knowledge delivers power. If your goal is marketing power, it makes sense to extract research dollars from your marketing budget.

Research helps you identify your target market.

Research helps you identify what to say to your target market.

Research helps you identify what to sell to your target market.

Research helps you unlock the secrets of increased profitability that lie hidden in your own files, in the minds of consumers, in their lifestyles, and in their buying habits.

Sophisticated insurance direct marketers are leveraging the quantum technological advances available today to leap beyond brainstorming and in-market testing to increase response. While the research and development function is relatively immature in the insurance direct marketing system, it is a critical step for your company to take, if it hopes to focus on a profitable future in the decades ahead.

SECRET No. 7

Never close your mind to possibilities.

The possibilities are endless. Keep in mind that direct marketers must be adept in lateral thinking as well as focused in vertical thinking. Since the system is essentially linear, a clear understanding of the composition "sets" that structure the system is enormously enhanced by an ability to creatively develop solutions and techniques that take advantage of situations, environments, and possibilities.

One of these possibilities has an enormous potential impact on the insurance direct marketing community—lifetime policyowner value.

More frequently than not, acquisition allowance—that sum of money you can afford to spend to acquire a new policyowner—is based on a profit-study projection for that product. The profit study normally does not consider what happens after the policyowner is in your file. In fact, the normal actuarial position is that, once acquired, the policyowner becomes a liability, not an asset.

It costs money to maintain the policyowner on the file. It costs money to pay the policyowner's claims. It costs money to collect premiums. The only asset, managers may reluctantly admit, is the interest earned on the policyowner's unearned premium.

For years, direct marketers have realized that their existing customer base is the best prospect for future sales. And, for years, they have used calculations that allowed them to offer merchandise to their customers for little or no up-front profit. Book clubs offer their customers 4 books for $1; record clubs offer 10 records free with membership; and merchandisers offer discounts and free gifts with each offer.

Why?

A simple fact—the future value to you of your customers is far greater than the money you spent to acquire them.

Applying this fact to insurance product development by treating your policyowners as a producing asset, and a very valuable one, will alter the financial foundation of your company. It has been so for most companies in the direct marketing business.

The concept of lifetime value will be revisited frequently as we journey through the insurance direct marketing system. It has many possibilities in product and market development—and is an exceedingly valuable management tool. Let us give LTV a definition: THE LIFETIME VALUE OF A POLICYOWNER IS THE PRESENT VALUE OF A FUTURE STREAM OF NET CONTRIBUTION TO OVERHEAD AND PROFIT.

Its determination is a function of research. First comes an examination of the historical data. Then comes the creation of a predictive model. Continued enhancement of the historical data derived from your database follows. Then comes the continued refinement of your predictive model.

Lifetime value is the foundation from which products grow. In fact, keen product development is one of the success keys to your direct marketing operation. After research, the next step in the insurance direct marketing system is the development of appropriate products.

Historically, in most insurance companies, product development was the sole sanctuary of the actuary. Today, however, the actuary is a member of a product-development team. Mortality and morbidity tables are important—and obviously form the foundation of product pricing.

But, there is more. A great deal more.

V

The Secrets of Product Development

Product development in direct marketing insurance is more a process than an event. It is a complex business. Actuaries don't disappear into a room, mumble a spell, and reappear after an appropriate time with all the elements of a new product clearly defined and rated on otherwise clean white paper.

Therefore, as a marketer, it is absolutely essential for you to clearly understand the process, its mathematical basis, its rationale, and how you can help.

To start: *All successful insurance direct marketing products are market driven!* They are created by detailed market analysis and based on consumer-perceived needs.

In fact, any type of insurance product can be distributed (sold) through the direct marketing system. That includes the intricate investment-oriented products. Products like single-premium deferred annuities, interest-sensitive whole life, and universal life.

These products, for the moment, are the exception—not the rule—in insurance direct marketing. So, the focus of this chapter is on the more traditional insurance products sold through the use of mail-order techniques. However, the basic principles remain the same for other product types.

Here's a key point: Successful product development is a team effort, embracing competent actuaries, marketers, data processors, and operations people, all of whom clearly understand the elements of the insurance direct marketing system, working together to build products. See the model in Figure 5-1.

In the past, companies developed their product portfolio for sale to consumers through the agency/brokerage distribution channels. Two decades ago, when a company decided to try to jump on the "mass marketing" bandwagon, its marketers simply dusted off one of these products and offered it through the mail. It didn't work then. And, that approach certainly will not work today.

The basic procedures of direct marketing insurance product development closely parallel, if not duplicate, the techniques normally associated with the creation of new insurance products developed for other channels of distribution. However, there are some concepts that are unique to the mail-order distribution channel, which are equally applicable to life, health, accident, and property and casualty coverages.

SECRET No. 8

Successful insurance direct marketing products are guaranteed issue, or require minimum (simplified) underwriting.

It is essential that they be designed to fit the market you are targeting.

SECRET No. 9

Successful insurance direct marketing products are simple!

They cover easily definable risks with advantageous consumer benefits...lending themselves to total disclosure in a marketing environment...and most frequently considered *supplements* to major forms of insurance protection. The obvious exception is the auto and homeowner area.

SECRET No. 10

Successful insurance direct marketing products are "priced right," have a high "perceived value," and carry premiums that are affordable, budgetable, and—wherever possible—represent conquest rates.

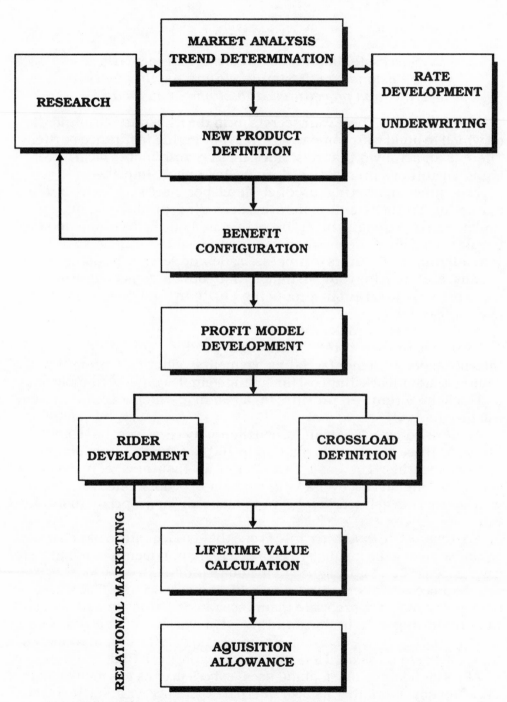

Figure 5-1: Product development model leading to acquisition allowance. Note the relational marketing elements.

Chapter V

SECRET No. 11

*Successful insurance direct marketing products
are designed with simple claims requirements,
verification procedures, and payment methods.*

Taken together, these four secrets form the indisputable foundation on which to build your company's direct marketing insurance portfolio. There is an acronym that describes these requirements clearly: KISS. Using an author's prerogative: Keep It Startlingly Simple!

The direct marketing product developer needs to help out his marketing brothers and sisters by delivering products that can be explained easily to consumer prospects. Simplicity helps the compliance people internally. It helps when you file the policy forms. Also, it helps your administrative units to process, issue, and service the policyowner.

Most of all, it helps your customer. And, your customer will grow to be the most important profit-producing entity in your insurance direct marketing system.

Again, the key word is *profit.*

Every insurance direct marketing product contains the same internal expense elements: claims payments, policy fees, premium tax, administration, marketing cost (including commissions where applicable), and most important—it provides for a residual, which we appropriately call profit.

At the risk of oversimplifying, when the product developer has completed his work, these six elements add up to 100% of the premium collected.

Consider this: The basic function of an insurance contract is to spread a common risk over a large number of people. Once the risk you want to cover is defined, you begin to make an "appropriate insurance rate."

An *appropriate insurance rate* is one that is adequate to pay claims, is equitable among the insureds, meets all legal requirements, is adequate to cover expenses, and is designed to include a profit.

The process of rate making is part art and part science. The actuarial ability to create an appropriate insurance rate is a study in balances and understanding—an understanding of a variety of factors which influence our daily lives. Most of the process is based on assumptions, and these are based on as hard a reality as the actuary can find.

At its foundation, rate making uses "experience" as a principal factor. The company uses either its own internal experience, or published tables that offer quantitative data on mortality and morbidity. Initially, this process identifies the claims situation which the actuary feels the company will face on the defined risk for the particular class of business. This is the claims part of the formula.

The premium tax is a provision for satisfying state requirements. For the moment, the tax is usually pegged at 2.5% of *earned* premium.

Administrative expenses are next. These include elements such as policy issuing, data processing support, premium billing and collection, customer service, policy maintenance, and other operational expenses. Portions of administrative expenses are frequently offset by a policy fee. The purpose of the policy fee is to equitably distribute the fixed expenses each policy incurs, so that each policy sold bears its fair share of such expenses.

Marketing cost is next. In setting this expense, you must consider what portion of premium you can afford to spend to sell your policy. Total marketing cost includes a provision for commissions, normally expressed as a percentage of *collected* premium for the first year and each renewal.

Finally, margin is added to the formula. *Margin* is the amount of money the company wants to make on the product. Yes, you guessed it ... profit.

Profit in any direct response insurance product is exceedingly sensitive to actual marketing cost. Obviously, the lower the marketing cost, the higher the profitability. This statement assumes that all other elements are at optimal levels.

According to Jay M. Jaffe, a leading direct marketing actuary, product profitability is expressed in four different ways.

- X% of premium
- Breaking-even by policy year n
- Return on investment of p%
- $X surplus after n years

Where: X is a stipulated or experienced number.

  n is a stipulated or experienced number of years beyond the starting time.

  p is a stipulated or experienced percentage.

Generally accepted accounting principles (GAAP accounting) requires insurance companies, according to Jaffe, to match up income and expenses as to accounting periods. This requirement has made companies more conscious of profit as a percentage of premium. But, other measures of profitability are more or less equally valid and comparable.

For example, increasing the return-on-investment objective usually lowers the permissible acquisition allowance assigned to the product.

Equally, increasing the desired ROI tends to reduce the number of years necessary for the product to break even.

These elements represent the *basic* rate-making considerations. Different products require additional considerations. But there is a general assumption that underlies the process. This is an important principle for you to understand.

Premiums are considered paid at the beginning of each policy year. Claims are considered paid at the end of each policy year, and they are considered to be distributed evenly throughout the policy year. This understanding is important, because insurance direct marketing products are not like a hard-goods single product sold by mail.

Insurance direct marketing products are like a continuity program. Once an applicant has paid a premium and become a policyowner, his policy will have an average life of perhaps 20, 40, 60, or more months on your books. In simple terms, once you've gotten a policyholder, he tends to stay awhile. This concept, called *persistency*, is at the heart of the insurance direct marketing system—as well as in many other insurance operations.

In fact, since policyholders (read this as *policies*) have an "average life," the term itself implies the basic concept of persistency. Essentially, it means that you will collect premium over a long period of time, say, ten years or twenty years—sometimes more. This speculation is displayed in a profit study.

A *profit study* is a mathematical model that identifies deterioration of premium and expense flow over some period of time. It is created by using assumptions for income and expenses. Then—through simple addition and subtraction, some multiplication and division—you arrive at profitability and return on investment over such period of time.

Because consumers, when they become policyowners, persist—stay on your books a length of time, you collect far more money for your marketing dollar than you would collect from the sale of a gold chain, or some other catalog item. *In insurance direct marketing, it is important to treat marketing cost as an investment,* as opposed to pure expense. Therefore, your marketing dollars must return some level of financial gain.

Interestingly, in GAAP accounting, that is the way marketing cost is treated. But regulators demand *statutory* accounting, as well. Here, marketing cost is treated as an expense when incurred and, therefore, gives a cloudy picture of a company's operations.

The logical way to express this unique function is to charge your marketing dollars each year in proportion to the money you earn each year.

The GAAP method appropriately expresses the relationship of your marketing dollars to income, and clearly indicates the first year "strain" on surplus. *Strain* is simply first-year loss. Normally, you spend more dollars in the first year of product life than you take in. Figure 5-2 displays a profit study with marketing cost expressed on a GAAP basis. You will find specific formulas for the calculation of profit studies in Chapter XVI.

To the marketer, an understanding of this process goes a long way in explaining how actuaries assign a marketing allowance to a product.

The *marketing allowance* (or allowable acquisition allowance) is the portion of first-year and renewal premium which the marketer is allowed to spend to sell the product, while maintaining the targeted profitability and return on investment. As noted, marketing allowances have enormous impact on product profitability. In fact, most direct marketing actuaries "solve" their initial equations for marketing allowance first. Historically, actuaries and marketers have a tug-of-war over marketing allowances.

The marketer wants the maximum amount of money he can get to put policyowners on the books of the company.

The actuary, on the other hand, wants to maintain the structural integrity of the product. To reach and sustain the calculated profitability and return on investment, he insists, there is no room for "maneuvering."

When you consider the situation, it is really silly to argue over marketing allowances. Direct marketing actuaries clearly understand the marketing problem. One of their clearest understandings relates to conquest rates. A *conquest rate* is one that overcomes consumer resistance against purchasing the product. It directly relates to the consumer's perception of the benefits offered by the protection, frequently referred to as the price/benefits ratio.

The direct marketing actuary understands that, to successfully market an insurance product, the proposed rates must make the product attractive to the consumer, easy on his pocketbook, and as competitive as possible, while protecting the company from unreasonable, if any, loss. There is a variety of devices he can use to do so. Years ago the *deviated premium* was the key.

A *deviated premium* was simply a bargain basement price—one arbitrarily charging, say, a quarter or a dollar for the first month of coverage, then the appropriate (higher) premium for the remainder of the contract.

It is still used by some companies today. There are other means. Conquest rates can be achieved by step-rated premium schedules; folks pay more for coverage as they move from one age band to another.

MODEL PROFIT STUDY--DIRECT MARKETING HEALTH INSURANCE GAAP BASIS

SCREEN VALUES (INPUT DATA + AUTOMATIC CALCULATION)

```
PRODUCT   HIP/TV     LAPSE(1)   0.36    ULTCLAIM   0.52    RESERV(1)   0.15    INFORCE-1   1000   PRESVAL      46,991.96
AARP      $285.20    LAPSE(2)   0.23    CLAIM(1)   0.60    RESERV(2)   0.10    INFORCE-2    640
ISSUES/M   45.59     LAPSE(3)   0.18    CLAIM(2)   0.75    RESERV(3)   0.05    INFORCE-3    493
CICR(M)    21.93     LAPSE(4)   0.18    CLAIM(3)   0.40    RESERV(4)   0.05    INFORCE-4    404
MC/M    12864.19     LAPSE(5)   0.12    CLAIM(4)   0.40    RESERV(5)   0.03    INFORCE-5    331   LTV            $46.99
TMC    282171.30     PREMTAX   0.025    CLAIM(5)   0.45                        INFORCE-6    292   ALLOW         107.40%
T/MC        1.01     INT.RATE   0.06    CLAIM(6)   0.45    N           1.00    INFORCE-7    257   COLFACT        79.49%
COMMISFY       0     MODPAYFAC          CLAIM(7)   0.45                        INFORCE-8    226
COMMISREN      0     :PAY/N    12.00    CLAIM(8)   0.45    POLCYFEE  $10.00    INFORCE-9    199   ACQUSITION    $306.31
ADMIN(1)    0.10     YEARS     10.00    CLAIM(9)   0.45                        INFORCE-0    175   ALLOWANCE
ADMIN(RE)   0.06     ROI    15.00%      CLAIM(10)  0.45
```

PROFIT STUDY (AUTOMATIC CALCULATION)

YEARS	COLPREM	CLAIMS	ADMIN	COMMISS	TMC	PREMTAX	RESERVES	TOT/RESEV	INT	INCOME	EXPENSE	P(L)	PROFIT%	ACQALLOW
1	226,714	135,575	22,671	0	56,973	5,668	34,007	34,007	2,628	229,342	254,894	(25,552)	-11.14%	80.46
2	174,569	130,718	10,474	0	43,869	4,364	17,457	51,464	3,977	178,547	206,882	(28,335)	-15.87%	50.06
3	143,147	57,242	8,589	0	35,973	3,579	7,157	58,621	4,530	147,677	112,539	35,138	23.79%	150.14
4	117,381	46,938	7,043	0	29,498	2,935	5,869	64,490	4,984	122,365	92,282	30,082	24.58%	150.47
5	103,295	46,462	6,198	0	25,958	2,582	3,099	67,589	5,224	108,518	84,299	24,219	22.32%	136.67
6	90,899	40,887	5,454	0	22,843	2,272	(13,518)	54,071	4,179	95,078	57,938	37,140	39.06%	135.87
7	79,992	35,980	4,799	0	20,102	2,000	(13,518)	40,554	3,134	83,126	49,364	33,762	40.62%	135.07
8	70,393	31,663	4,224	0	17,690	1,760	(13,518)	27,036	2,089	72,482	41,818	30,664	42.31%	134.27
9	61,945	27,863	3,717	0	15,567	1,549	(13,518)	13,518	1,045	62,990	35,178	27,813	44.15%	133.47
10	54,512	24,519	3,271	0	13,699	1,363	(13,518)	0	0	54,512	29,334	25,178	46.19%	132.68
TOTALS	1,122,846	577,846	76,439	0	282,172	28,071	(0)		31,791	1,154,637	964,528	190,109	16.46%	1,239.18
%		51.46%	6.81%	0.00%	25.13%	2.50%								

Figure 5-2: Model profit study on a GAAP basis. Note that total marketing cost is allocated on the basis of collected income.

Conquest rates can be achieved by limiting coverage during the first few years the policy is in force—for example, excluding an additional payout by the company for death benefits during the first two years of a life insurance contract.

Conquest rates can be achieved by benefit limitations, say, $25 per day hospital cash benefit instead of $50 per day. And there are other methods. In fact, the method of delivering a conquest rate to the marketer is limited only by the imagination of the actuary.

There has been some controversy over the years on what drives an insurance sale. Consumer price sensitivity is certainly part of the equation. Keep in mind, for instance, the Avon research, which we covered earlier. And, competitively, it is always to your advantage to enter a marketplace with the lowest price.

Moreover, it is true that most direct marketing insurance products must be "sold." Perhaps Medicare supplement protection is an exception. This coverage is surely needed by people over 65. Mandated coverages such as automobile insurance is another exception. Truthfully, selling at the lowest price you can is far easier than fighting the uphill marketing battle caused by having the highest rate on the block.

Nonetheless, the marketer must keep in mind that rates are only part of the picture. No direct marketer would think of entering the marketplace without price-testing hard goods or most service products. It is equally true, however, that an insurance direct marketer, for the most part, cannot.

Because the insurance industry is regulated, product price testing is out. Conventional wisdom postulates that no insurance commissioner would approve several different rates for the same benefit levels in the same product, unless the discriminatory rates were developed for different circumstances. Oddly enough, regulation does not prohibit rate discrimination under this type of circumstance.

Consider the issue of the nonsmoker vs. the smoker. The nondrinker vs. the drinker. The steeplejack vs. the office worker. Price testing might be achieved by creatively segmenting the market, or by creatively dif-ferentiating product features.

However, this price-testing concept is somewhat advanced for the average company getting into the business. That makes the conquest-rate idea all the more important. It is a "take-your-best-shot" philosophy. And, for the moment, it recognizes the stark reality that it is the system within which you must live.

Remember, though, *you can test different rate levels for a product through your research function*, before your product development rate making is completed and the material is filed for approval by the insurance commissioner.

The two most important questions an actuary can ask a product development team are: 1) "How much can the market afford to pay?" and 2) "How much do you want to charge?"

Technically, when you file rates with insurance commissioners, they must be substantiated in order to be approved. Included in the filed pricing are such factors as mandatory minimum loss ratios and allowable cost assumptions. Now, you have two choices to get the answer to those two critical actuarial questions: You can conduct research to get the answers. Or, you can guess.

If you guess, based on gut feeling, experience, or even what the competition is charging for the same or similar product, you are increasing the risk you are willing to take with your program. Because, after all is said and done, and you have filed product approval, the program simply might not work.

Testing prices and price resistance among people populating your target market just might end up saving you a bundle in product-development expenses. Or, it might deliver a most pleasant surprise—the fact that you can charge more than you guessed.

Now, in addition to the "science" part of your product development team's ruminations, they have a lot of "art" to consider.

Insurance contracts are designed to fulfill certain aspects of human needs. Basic subsistence has long been recognized as the primary human need and goal.

In the United States, we've developed far beyond that particular goal. Other needs are ascendent today. And these needs—real or perceived—by consumers are the ones direct marketing insurance products seek to satisfy.

The hierarchy of human needs generally accepted in the insurance industry include:

1. Psychological needs

2. Safety needs

3. Love and acceptance needs

4. Esteem needs

5. Self-fulfillment needs

Insurance direct marketers seek to sell to consumers by identifying which of these needs the product fulfills. As a point of comparison, according to Andi Emerson, direct marketing copywriters, for decades, have identified eight basic human needs used to motivate direct marketing purchases by consumers:

- Making money and saving money
- Winning praise
- Helping children and/or family
- Self improvement
- Having fun
- Saving time and effort
- Impressing others
- Avoiding loss

Remarkable list, isn't it?

The similarity of the psychological motivators with the industry-accepted hierarchy of human needs clearly focuses attention on the basic elements that must be built into a new insurance product to help it sell.

The simple fact is, as you develop an insurance product for this system, you must understand that you are not selling an *insurance* product in the traditional sense. You are attempting to sell a *perceived need.*

Insurance, conceptually, provides protection against defined risks. Since it provides protection and must be purchased, it is clearly an economic action. Economic actions are designed to satisfy needs.

Economic security plays an extraordinarily important role in the lives of most Americans. Economic security is achieved by control over economic goods. Fear of loss, therefore, becomes a compelling reason for the purchase of insurance.

While this reasoning may supply the answer as to why people buy insurance, the question extended as to why people buy insurance *by direct marketing methods, without agent intervention,* is more complex. Specific research into this question is covered in Chapter IX.

It has already been demonstrated, in Chapter IV, that substantial percentages of the consuming public do not care to purchase protection from an insurance agent. In the case of life insurance, if you recall, it is estimated that 42% of the population prefers to purchase protection directly, rather than through an insurance agent.

It is also *convenient* to do so, because the prospect neither has to leave his own home, nor have a stranger in the house.

As well, people tend to believe the written word more than they believe what is said orally. Almost all insurance direct marketers make product offers in writing.

Perhaps, what is most important is the fact that, to a large extent, insurance direct marketing product purchases are event driven. It has long been recognized, and research confirms, that life events drive purchasing patterns. The birth of a child generates the purchase of life insurance. Turning 50 might do the same. A friend's hospitalization, or the loss of a job, stimulates the purchase of a hospital indemnity coverage. Richard C. Miller, an internationally known direct marketing consultant, labels these events "need awareness points."

Fear of a physical examination, or the findings of such, may account for the purchase of graded death-benefit coverage. A home purchase stimulates a need for guaranteed-issue decreasing-term protection.

The point to this is that the process of product development requires you and your development team to think through the reasons why folks want or think they need the protection—and whether they will buy a particular coverage. This intellectual sifting, combined with aggressive research support, will help you create successful products.

A whole raft of successful products have been developed over the years, using the above techniques:

Health Products

Hospital indemnity: Daily benefits for hospital confinements.

Scheduled surgical benefit: Dollar indemnification for specific surgical procedures.

Convalescent facility care: Daily benefits for confinement in a convalescent care facility (usually triggered by the number of days of preconfinement hospitalization).

Disability income: Paycheck replacement, usually STD (short-term disability).

Excess major medical: A dollar tie-in based on percentage of incurred excess hospital expenses.

Medicare supplement: Benefit structure pays what Medicare parts A & B do not...can also be a basic-care plan eliminating first-dollar benefits. However, this will be changing in the future.

Nursing-home care: Daily indemnification based on intermediate or long-term nursing-home care.

Riders: Double daily benefits or some other percentage of base indemnification for intensive care confinement, cancer, heart attack or stroke, emergency care, extra care-major medical, and outpatient care.

Cancer care: A stand-alone protection offering daily indemnity and scheduled benefit payments in the event of cancer.

Return of premium (ROP): An interesting concept that offers to return all premium paid if no claims are filed during a certain period...three, five, seven, or ten years.

Life Coverages

Term Life: In amounts from $10,000 to $100,000—generally using a short four-question underwritten application.

Whole life: Underwritten in amounts from $500 to $10,000...most frequently as "burial insurance" or birthday life programs.

ROP (return of premium) life: An endowment coverage—relatively new to the industry.

Guaranteed-issue, decreasing-term: Usually sold in units of coverage based on face amount or monthly premium rate, benefits payable for natural causes on a schedule of face amount for the first two or three years, and 100% of face amount for accidental death. Either, benefits decrease with age or premiums increase with age.

Guaranteed-issue, graded death benefit: Similar to GIDT (just above), but a whole-life coverage, with very moderate cash values. Frequently marketed as "burial" insurance.

Guaranteed-issue, level-term life: A term coverage that does not decrease with age, also sold in units of coverage, with similar benefit restriction periods.

Accident

Accidental death benefit (ADB): Usually high-limit, low-cost, 24-hour coverage for accidental death.

Accidental death & dismemberment: Same basic coverage as above with the addition of dismemberment benefits. Has a lot of appeal to younger ages.

AD&D stack: A Sears favorite...small-base, all-risk AD&D benefit... then a large auto/pedestrian benefit...and on top a whopping common-carrier benefit.

Hospital accident protection: Similar to hospital indemnity, but the daily benefits are payable only for hospital confinement due to accident.

Scheduled surgical benefit (accident only): Same as the health coverage, but limited to surgery performed as the result of an accident.

ADB Riders: A terrific device for increasing benefits. Can be added to a life or health product to increase advertised benefit levels. Different rules apply depending on the basic coverage to which you are adding the protection—life or health.

Property & Casualty Coverages

Automobile insurance: Property & casualty products are interesting, because—for the most part—they are state-mandated *need* products. That means a lot of different forms for each of the states in which you want to market. The real key here is *price*. The lower the price and the better the claims payment procedure, the more business you're going to do. GEICO is very big in this business, as well as USAA. Years ago Colonial Penn pioneered, through NRTA and AARP, special auto coverages for folks over 55. Basically, the two-step auto insurance procedure offers both physical-damage coverage as well as liability coverage. The coverage is almost always on the vehicle, not on the driver.

Homeowners insurance: Again, a strong-need product made up of highly regulated "forms." Protection is offered against physical-damage loss to the property, as well as liability benefits. Homeowners coverages are highly price-sensitive and subject to a variety of complex rating and underwriting elements. But, it is being sold successfully to consumers through direct marketing techniques—including one of the newest— telemarketing.

Umbrella liability: This is an *excess* protection, offered to consumers to protect them against serious liability judgments. Usually starting at $250,000 and going up to, perhaps, $10 million. It is excess, because benefits are not paid until liability limits are reached in the required underlying coverages—auto and homeowners.

And a host of other products: Baggage insurance, trip-interruption coverage, credit-card protection, flight insurance, credit life, A&H, and disability, even prepaid legal services.

* * *

It is apparent from this list, possibly incomplete, of 39 direct marketing insurance products that there has been a lot of work done in this area over the last twenty-five years or so.

It's also worth noting that these successful insurance direct marketing products have been spawned by products sold through more traditional distribution channels. In other words, in every existing insurance product there is an "acorn" from which a direct marketing product "oak" can grow.

Remember, each product began with an idea. A concept that led the insurance direct marketing product development team to unravel criteria based on experience and the four product development secrets stated above. To restate briefly:

1. Product must be designed simply—capable of being understood in a relatively short period of time.

2. Product must have affordable premium rates, as low as allowable for the coverage offered.

3. Products must be easy to order, and the prospect must be given a period of time to examine it without obligation.

4. Product application forms must be designed simply, easy to complete, and contain no questions—or, if questions are necessary, be kept to a minimum number.

These criteria are going to have an enormous impact on both the under-writing and actuarial process in direct marketing insurance product development. Remember, the direct marketing system supports the concept, "The Consumer is King." It is market driven, and therefore very different from agency/broker product development. While it may be true that insurance companies exist to pay legitimate claims, it is also true that we are dealing with a business, designed to make a profit.

Now, let us turn our attention to controlling RISK in direct marketing product development.

Controlling risk is, essentially, the process by which the claims expense portion of the product profitability curve is limited.

The first major problem the actuary and underwriter face is anti-selection. It is well known, for example, that term life insurance experiences a mortality rate about 15% higher than permanent insurance in the agency marketplace. The cause is probably the result of anti- (or adverse) selection.

Anti-selection is the process by which impaired risks seek the protection offered by the company, thereby skewing the general tables used to calculate rates.

How to control it—that's the question. In life insurance the "law of large numbers" plays an important part, from the traditional company's viewpoint, in controlling the problem.

The law of large numbers states that as the number of protected lives increases, the actual mortality—within the group of lives considered—moves closer to expected mortality.

This underlies the concept of group life insurance. However, the law of large numbers was "made" for insurance direct marketing, because the distribution system issues policies in volume—marketing shorthand for "large numbers."

As important as the law of large numbers may be, there are other means of limiting risk.

Benefit limitation: As a general rule, direct marketing life insurance policies limit the benefit amount on any one life. This retention limit is an important risk control that limits the harmful extent of claims exceeding the number anticipated. Usually no more than $100,000 in term life benefits are offered. And limits of $15,000 to $20,000 of face amounts are usually associated with guaranteed-issue life products.

Grading periods: A grading period limits benefit payments for some specific period of time—usually the first two or three years a policy is in force. Benefits can be stipulated, or they can be expressed as a percentage of face amount. For example, 20% of face during the first year, 40% in second year, 100% in third year.

Short-form underwriting: Most frequently associated with term life offers, short-form underwriting simply asks some generalized questions about the applicant's health history. Moreover, the applicant normally gives permission on a short-form application for the company to investigate his answers. This allows the underwriter to apply some general principles, which can be carried out by a computer, and permits him to request an "MIB" report from the information bureau that stores health information on almost everyone. As well, the underwriter can request an APS—attending physician's statement, referring to a particular illness or state of health situation.

Substandard criteria: And why not? Assuming the prospective insured does not meet the underwriting criteria, offer him a lower face amount for the same premium. You may marginally increase the risk of loss, but you get an "appropriate" insurance rate for it.

There's still more:

Including *guaranteed renewability*, that gives you the ability to raise rates over a whole class of business in the event your loss experience exceeds what the rate anticipated. *Exclude* war risks, flying as a pilot, self-inflicted injury, drug use, and alcohol-related mortality. Exclusions are a normal part of an insurance contract. Thus, they should be used effectively. After all, it's your business.

One important note: Do not let your financial management talk you into a thing called a *commercial contract*. While that is the most desirable form of contract, from an underwriting point of view, it is the least desirable from a direct marketing view. A commercial contract simply allows your company to cancel the policy or raise rates any time it wants to. This is bad direct marketing business.

Pre-solicitation underwriting: This is the process by which risks are selected...hopefully the best ones. Good risk selection is absolutely basic and critical to guaranteed-issue products. And, here is where the partnership—made up of marketer, actuary, underwriter, data processor, and administrator—is critical.

There are many sources for statistical data relating to market segments. Defining—up front—what market you intend to penetrate is of help in limiting risks and setting rates. For example, if you decide to offer accident insurance to steeplejacks, your rates are going to be higher than if you plan on offering accident insurance to young marrieds, assuming they are not steeplejacks.

If credit union members are better risks than vets, you can find out. If homeowners offer better risks than airline stewardesses or nurses, you can find out. If people over 55 have fewer and less costly automobile accidents than people under 21, you can find out.

Let's look at graded death-benefit insurance coverage, for example. If you offer the coverage to people over 50, the limited face-amount benefit period of two years works in your favor. Technically, the logic flows, substandard or declinable risks have lower mortality ratios at the older ages. As people grow older and survive, the chances increase that they will move toward standard mortality tables.

The same theory is applicable to morbidity as to health insurance. In principle, you build into your hospital cash product a *pre-existing exclusion*. You are stipulating that for a certain period—now one year—health conditions that are manifested during the exclusionary period are not covered for one year from the policy effective date.

Elimination of certain pre-existing health situations allows people who normally cannot obtain protection to apply for, and be issued, an insurance contract that internally eliminates a portion of the overall risk for a period of time. This can be done at an appropriate insurance rate.

The declaration: The final potential control factor is one that is frequently overlooked by direct marketers, but it is worthy of serious consideration. Every insurance contract, as part of its "general conditions," eliminates benefit payments relating to any sort of fraud. It is the ultimate protection for the insurance company. And, at least in theory, prevents applicants as well as agents from foisting horrid risks—deathbed applications, for example—on an insurance company. It's simple—lie and you've lost your benefits.

Therefore, why not ask the question on an application? How about a statement that in effect says "to the best of my knowledge I'm OK? I don't have anything wrong with me, and I haven't been in a hospital for a dog's age."

It may give a lawyer some pause, but if the applicant doesn't tell the truth, it seems apparent that the benefits aren't payable. You return the premium and keep the interest it has earned. Simple and clean. Lately, some courts have challenged the "misstatement or fraud" protection concept. However, so far, it appears appropriate to refuse to pay a claim on a policy in which a material declaration, later found to be untrue, was used as an inducement to issue a policy. This can be successful in helping control risk.

Finally, while it is more a part of the tactical elements of marketing programs than product development, the limited enrollment period helps in risk control. By limiting the time period during which a prospect can apply for the coverage offered, you have succeeded—for the most part—in limiting or eliminating the deathbed application.

The consumer prospect cannot apply for the offered protection *at his convenience*. So, the prospect does not rush home after hearing the bad news from his doctor and send in his application.

As a marketer, you can see how much you can contribute to the process of risk control. Be assured that there's a lot more.

Successful product development requires the marketer to have an acute sense of the persistency concept introduced above. It is the single factor that most affects profitability and return on investment for any single insurance product.

PERSISTENCY is the rate at which a policyowner continues to pay the premium on a given policy form beyond the first period of coverage.

This is the concept that gives such a long average life to a policy and makes an insurance direct marketing program such an attractive *investment.*

Direct marketing product lapse rates display a significantly different pattern than for traditionally sold products. Overall, traditionally sold products exhibit a more level lapse rate than products sold by direct marketing. The lapse curve is much steeper in the first several years of a policy's existence for the direct marketed product. Thereafter, renewal lapse rates can be lower for direct-response products than for traditionally marketed products. When you translate that into dollar volume, the difference is enormous!

Following are some principles you may find useful to apply, plus several more secrets.

Lapse rates are highly sensitive to the general marketing environment. Broad-market business lapses at a higher rate than endorsed-market business, for example. Lapse rates also are sensitive within the specific business category. Strong affinity associations lapse more slowly than S&L-endorsed business. S&L-endorsed business lapses more slowly than created-consumer associations. And, business billed to credit cards lapses the least of all!

The basic principle to apply in examining lapse rates is that the higher the affinity, the lower the lapse rate. But, there are several other general principles relating to lapse rates.

SECRET No. 12

Direct marketing life insurance products persist better than direct marketing health insurance products.

SECRET NO. 13

Guaranteed-issue life insurance products persist better than underwritten term life insurance products.

SECRET NO. 14

The lower the age of a policyowner, the higher the lapse rate.

As you can see, a great many factors influence efficient persistency—including age. Turning Secret No. 14 around, the older the policyowner, the lower the lapse rate.

Since most direct marketing policies are sold in the over-age-40 group, it is important to understand something about the state of mind of the people in such group.

The consumer in the 40-, 50-, or 60-year-old age group has a lot of things on his mind. One thing…when he thinks about it…is the idea of insurability—or, its opposite, uninsurability. At these ages, the consumer has collected a lot of health baggage.

These years see consumers entering or just leaving their peak earning years. They have acquired property, savings, and economic life equity, as well as a family and a host of friends. A man who wants to protect all of this, as well as to create the highest-value life estate he can, begins to perceive his insurance needs in terms of what he can afford and the amount of protection he can acquire.

Once he has the protection, he is not apt to allow it to go away so quickly. It is a tendency, but it is the foundation of our business.

This leads, logically enough, to one of the most critical secrets in insurance direct marketing:

SECRET No. 15

POLICYOWNER LIFETIME VALUE IS THE FOUNDATION OF INSURANCE DIRECT MARKETING EXPANSION, PROFIT, AND RETURN ON INVESTMENT.

Customer valuation has long been a staple of direct marketing practices. But, for some reason, it has been generally overlooked by the financial services industries, and most particularly by the insurance direct marketing industry.

Let's explore the mysteries of this secret in Chapter VI.

VI

The Secrets of Policyowner Lifetime Value

Quantifying the *value* of a customer to the insurance company is absolutely essential in the modern insurance direct marketing environment. Without knowing the value of a policyowner, it isn't possible to know how much you can afford to spend to acquire one.

Calculating LTV (lifetime value) assists you in a variety of applications for product development, market development, media selection, and more.

Relatively speaking, policyowner lifetime value is a concept new to insurance direct marketing. At the moment, only three organizations are known to use LTV calculations as part of their marketing efforts. Several others use modified methods of valuing customers, without the specifics. LTV is based on an inflexible rule that achieved general recognition and acceptance in the direct marketing community decades ago.

Here is a fact of *great importance: Your own customers are your best prospects for future sales.*

By logical extension, therefore, the more sales you make to your own customers, the more profit you will make from those individual purchasers.

In fact, the percentage of profit you make on continued sales to your own customer base is consistently higher than the profit made on the original sale.

Each of your customers, then, delivers an income stream and a stream of profit that far exceed the value of the original purchase.

65

All of this implies that it is necessary, in today's real world of insurance direct marketing, to determine what a policyowner is worth to your company in the long term. In determining this, it *is necessary to consider the original product you've marketed plus all the other products you intend to market over a period of time.*

The technique is familiar to, and used by, book and record clubs, continuity programs, and catalog marketers. A book-club membership solicitation, for example, offering four books for one dollar is not going to make much of a profit on the initial response. Profit is dependent on downstream purchases by the book-club member.

The fundamental architecture and nature of an insurance product acts in a similar way. Income streams, as explained in Chapter IV, contribute cash flow in terms of years for any single product. This income is similar to the downstream purchases made by book-club members. But the fact is there is no *new* purchase. The income is generated by the initial solicitation purchase.

In insurance, rates and acquisition allowances are normally determined by examining assumptions about income and expenses—including the impact of persistency—over a relatively long period of time, say, ten to twenty years. But, the product acquisition allowance assigned for you to use when you go to market is for that one product. Your product acquisition allowance is treated as if it is the only product you will sell to that policyholder.

Most insurance financial people have gone this far and stopped there. However, there is more to calculating acquisition allowance—much more.

In Chapter IV, policyowner lifetime value was defined as the present value of a future stream of net contributions to overhead and profit expected from the policyowner.

Your profitability, in the long term, will be the result of two factors. First, there is the difference between the acquisition allowance developed using policyowner lifetime value and policyowner acquisition cost. Second, the number of policyowners that can be acquired at an acceptable investment cost determined by their lifetime value expands your policyowner base. More policyowners mean more policyowner sales. More sales mean more net contribution to overhead and profit.

If you have the courage and conviction to understand LTV—its application and its rationale—undoubtedly it will alter the character of your business, allowing you to continuously view it as a strategic whole. LTV gives you a foundation for tactical decision making and stimulates a host of possibilities that may be obscured by your present accounting methods.

Since policyowner marketing is a mainstay of most insurance direct marketing companies, a considerable amount of time and talent is devoted to it. Response rates from the policyowner base are far higher than response rates on first-time mailings; therefore, marketing efficiency is higher.

But, it usually stands alone. Policyholder marketing profit is not counted in determining an overall acquistion allowance for an initial sale.

It is the source solicitation—the one that attracts the policyowner for the first time—that is assigned the job of handling the first-year strain on capital. It is isolated—as if nothing else is going to happen.

The calculations for the source solicitation product profit study may deliver an acceptable profit and return on investment *for that product alone.*

That technique is shortsighted. By separating the future income stream of a policyowner from the current income stream, significant limitations are placed on the marketer and his company relative to policyowner acquisition.

This is true because: Policyowner acquisition is less a function of a single solicitation event than it is a function of a related string of solicitation events, all of which—taken together—produce profit and return on investment.

This is the basic concept of *relational marketing.* It is applicable to every direct marketing program, every base product. It is absolutely essential to the success of your insurance direct marketing operations! By following a relational marketing strategy combined with policyowner LTV, you provide a financial foundation for six key management decisions:

1. *Assigning an acquisition allowance for policyowner acquisition* The more detailed the calculation, the more products included in the marketing program. The more of that, the more you will enhance your acquisition allowance. In other words, you will have more money to spend to acquire the new policyholder in the first place, while maintaining a predetermined profitability and return on investment.

2. *Developing rates for insurance products* You will be able to achieve the most profitable and attractive initial price for your products with the least impact on overall profitability and return on investment.

3. *Setting selection criteria for policyowner marketing* You are helped by identifying those policyowner segments most likely to respond in the desired pattern and the desired profitability.

4. *Allocating distribution channels, media, promotions, and offers*

for initial policyowner acquisition These are designed to produce the targeted financial objectives.

5. *Investing in reactivation of former policyowners* This is carried out by identifying segments most likely to produce desired profitability and return on investment targets.

6. *Assigning an asset value to your policyowner base* Since policyowners are valuable, they are part of your company's asset base. Lifetime value calculations quantify the value and provide more credible, supportable monetary unit asset value—enhancing the overall value of the company to its shareholders and/or policyholders.

* * *

Keep firmly in mind, however, that lifetime value is not the "second coming." It is a management tool that recognizes a future value. Since it is built on assumptions, it is a potential house of cards that can reduce itself into a scattered deck—*if the assumptions are not constantly tested.*

When you consider the principle, it isn't a bad one to follow in all product development. It is not enough for your actuaries to give you prices. The two of you together must constantly examine—perhaps on a quarterly basis—the reality of the marketplace.

What's really happening to those actuarial assumptions? Are policyowners acquired at the assumed marketing allowance? Are claims coming in at a predictable rate and pattern? Are administrative expenses being contained?

To a large extent, insurance direct marketing product development is a high-risk game of "what if?" In order to succeed—at some point—you have to answer the questions.

Moreover, actuaries are uncomfortable with numbers that are less than statistically reliable. So, too, should be the marketer. The marketer needs a constant stream of data on which to base judgments and on which to make adjustments. In fact, this is the whole point to database marketing.

It is in your best interest to accumulate real marketing data on a product as soon as it is available. Share the data with your product development and financial partners on a continuing basis. Following this procedure means that adventuring into the complexities of the lifetime value concept is less apt to produce consternation and more apt to produce profit.

All of which leads to our next secret:

SECRET No. 16

Constantly test your product-development assumptions against the marketing realities you are experiencing.

This idea is more understandable when you come to realize that lifetime value is similar to a brick wall. Each "product" in the calculation is one "brick." The basic-product "brick" is the foundation—that's the one responsible for attracting the policyowner initially.

All the rest of the bricks are laid one on top of another to form the wall. Now, the foundation bricks have to be pretty solid. Equate your foundation—perhaps to a hospital-cash product. The next layer of brick represents the riders to that product. Historically, riders counter lapsation (improve persistency), and increase the average annualized premium, as well as cash flow, of the base product 15% to 25%. Figure 6-1 displays this idea.

When you start crossloading—selling life products to the hospital-cash policyowner—you are simply building up the wall. This is *relational marketing* in action. Relational marketing is very profitable because of the ratio between premium collected currently and marketing cost spent. It is, as well, fundamental to the database marketing concept.

Now, policyowner lifetime value is determined by examining the income and expense streams you can expect from your policyowners. You know that the sale of a single insurance product produces income over a long period of time. Figure 6-1 shows the income and expense stream, over a ten-year period, for a $50-a-day hospital indemnity plan, generated by a television inquiry campaign and fulfilled with a three-effort conversion series.

The total collection of premium from this hypothetical 1,000 policyowners reduces each year. This element—"persistency"—equates to the lifetime value notion of sales decay. In reality, a profit study projection is the actuarial way of demonstrating sales decay. The bottom line is that the profit indicated in the last column of the illustration, obviously, does not fall into your hands in the first year of solicitation. It comes to you over a period of time. Therefore, to give this profit a current value, the actuary calculates the present value of that amount of cash.

Please note that the market cost to total annualized renewal premium ratio (MC/TARP) for this initial source solicitation is $1.00 to $1.01. For every marketing dollar spent, you receive back $1.01 in annualized premium.

Figures 6-2 through 6-8 show what happens next. These profit study projections reflect, in a cash flow model format, what happened to five

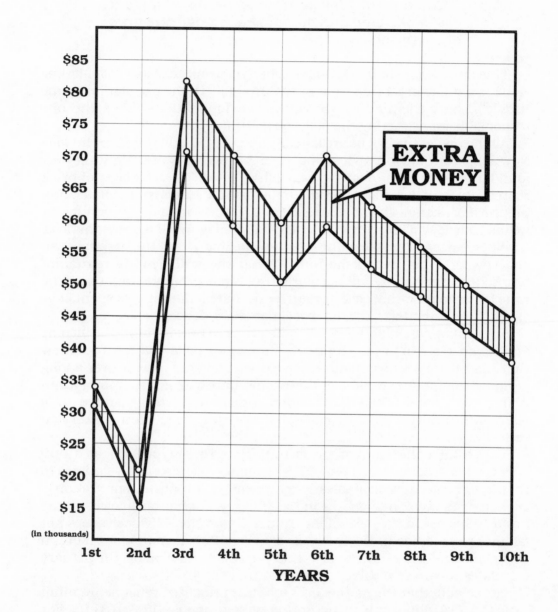

Figure 6-1: Based on Figures 6-2 through 6-8. The screened area represents the extra cash generated by relational marketing.

```
SCREEN VALUES (INPUT DATA + AUTOMATIC CALCULATION)

PRODUCT  HIP/TV      LAPSE(1)   0.36  ULTCLAIM     0.52 RESERV(1)   0.15 INFORCE-1   1000  PRESVAL    46,992.13
AARP     $285.20     LAPSE(2)   0.23  CLAIM(1)     0.60 RESERV(2)   0.10 INFORCE-2    640
ISSUES/M   45.59     LAPSE(3)   0.18  CLAIM(2)     0.75 RESERV(3)   0.05 INFORCE-3    493
CICR(M)    21.93     LAPSE(4)   0.18  CLAIM(3)     0.40 RESERV(4)   0.05 INFORCE-4    404
MC/M    12864.19     LAPSE(5)   0.12  CLAIM(4)     0.40 RESERV(5)   0.03 INFORCE-5    331  LTV          $46.99
TMC    282171.30     PREMTAX   0.025  CLAIM(5)               N           INFORCE-6    292  ALLOW       107.40%
T/MC       1.01      INT.RATE   0.06  CLAIM(6)     1.00        1.00       INFORCE-7    257  COLFACT      79.49%
COMMISFY      0      MODPAYFAC        CLAIM(7)                           INFORCE-8    226
COMMISREN     0      PAY/N            CLAIM(8)    12.00  $10.00 POLCYFEE  INFORCE-9   199  ACQUSITION  $306.31
ADMIN(1)    0.10     YEARS     10.00  CLAIM(9)    10.00                  INFORCE-0    175  ALLOWANCE
ADMIN(RE)   0.06     ROI              CLAIM(10)  15.00%
```

PROFIT STUDY (AUTOMATIC CALCULATION)

YEARS	COLPREM	CLAIMS	ADMIN	COMMISS	TMC	PREMTAX	RESERVES	TOT/RESEV	INT	INCOME	EXPENSE	P(L)	PROFIT%	ACQALLOW
1	226,714	135,575	22,671	0	282,171	5,668	34,007	34,007	2,628	229,342	480,092	(250,750)	-109.33%	80.46
2	174,569	130,718	10,474	0		4,364	17,457	51,464	3,977	178,547	163,013	15,534	8.70%	50.06
3	143,147	57,242	8,589	0		3,579	7,157	58,621	4,530	147,677	76,566	71,111	48.15%	150.14
4	117,381	46,938	7,043	0		2,935	5,869	64,490	4,984	122,365	62,784	59,580	48.69%	150.47
5	103,295	46,462	6,198	0		2,582	3,099	67,589	5,224	108,518	58,341	50,177	46.24%	136.67
6	90,899	40,887	5,454	0		2,272	(13,518)	54,071	4,179	95,078	35,095	59,983	63.09%	135.87
7	79,992	35,980	4,799	0		2,000	(13,518)	40,554	3,134	83,126	29,262	53,864	64.80%	135.07
8	70,393	31,663	4,224	0		1,760	(13,518)	27,036	2,089	72,482	24,128	48,354	66.71%	134.27
9	61,945	27,863	3,717	0		1,549	(13,518)	13,518	1,045	62,990	19,611	43,380	68.87%	133.47
10	54,512	24,519	3,271	0		1,363	(13,518)	0	0	54,512	15,635	38,877	71.32%	132.68
TOTALS	1,122,846	577,846	76,439	0	282,171	28,071	(0)		31,791	1,154,637	964,528	190,109	16.46%	1,239.18
%		51.46%	6.81%	0.00%	25.13%	2.50%								

Figure 6-2: Basic profit-study model for a "source solicitation." This case considers 1,000 policyowners generated by a hospital indemnity TV inquiry campaign.

```
SCREEN VALUES (INPUT DATA + AUTOMATIC CALCULATION)

PRODUCT    UPGRADE    LAPSE(1)   0.36   ULTCLAIM   0.52   RESERV(1)   0.20   INFORCE-1   180     PRESVAL     4,048.69
AARP       $60.00     LAPSE(2)   0.23   CLAIM(1)   0.60   RESERV(2)   0.15   INFORCE-2   115.2
ISSUES/M   180        LAPSE(3)   0.18   CLAIM(2)   0.75   RESERV(3)   0.08   INFORCE-3   89
CICR(M)    1.00       LAPSE(4)   0.18   CLAIM(3)   0.40   RESERV(4)   0.05   INFORCE-4   73
MC/M       800        LAPSE(5)   0.12   CLAIM(4)   0.40   RESERV(5)   0.03   INFORCE-5   60      LTV         $22.49
TMC        800        PREMTAX    0.025  CLAIM(5)   0.45                      INFORCE-6   52      ALLOW       107.81%
T/MC       13.50      INT.RATE   0.10   CLAIM(6)   0.45   N           1.00   INFORCE-7   46      COLFACT     64.00%
COMMISFY   0          MODPAYFAC  12.00  CLAIM(7)   0.45                      INFORCE-8   41
COMMISREN  0          PAY/N      N      CLAIM(8)   0.45   MOS/COL     10     INFORCE-9   36      ACQUSITION  $64.68
ADMIN(1)   0.10       YEARS      10.00  CLAIM(9)   0.45                      INFORCE-0   31      ALLOWANCE
ADMIN(RE)  0.06       ROI        15.00% CLAIM(10)  0.45
```

PROFIT STUDY (AUTOMATIC CALCULATION)

YEARS	COLPREM	CLAIMS	ADMIN	COMMISS	TMC	PREMTAX	RESERVES	TOT/RESEV	INT	INCOME	EXPENSE	P(L)	PROFIT%	ACQALLOW
1	6,912	4,133	691	0	800	173	1,382	1,382	107	7,019	7,180	(161)	-2.29%	16.95
2	6,387	4,782	383	0		160	958	2,340	181	6,568	6,283	284	4.33%	10.64
3	5,237	2,094	314	0		131	419	2,759	213	5,450	2,958	2,492	45.72%	31.75
4	4,294	1,717	258	0		107	215	2,974	230	4,524	2,297	2,227	49.23%	31.82
5	3,779	1,700	227	0		94	113	3,087	239	4,018	2,134	1,883	46.87%	28.93
6	3,326	1,496	200	0		83	(617)	2,470	191	3,516	1,161	2,355	66.98%	28.72
7	2,927	1,316	176	0		73	(617)	1,852	143	3,070	948	2,122	69.13%	28.52
8	2,575	1,158	155	0		64	(617)	1,235	95	2,671	760	1,911	71.55%	28.32
9	2,266	1,019	136	0		57	(617)	617	48	2,314	595	1,719	74.31%	28.11
10	1,994	897	120	0		50	(617)	0	0	1,994	449	1,545	77.48%	27.91
TOTALS	39,697	20,314	2,658	0	800	992	0		1,447	41,144	24,765	16,379	39.81%	261.68
%		51.17%	6.70%	0.00%	ERR	2.50%								

Figure 6-3: An "upgrade" profit model study showing what happens with a $10-a-day upgrade, offered as a rider.

SCREEN VALUES (INPUT DATA + AUTOMATIC CALCULATION)

PRODUCT	SURG		LAPSE(1)	0.52	RESERV(1)	0.20	INFORCE-1	200	PRESVAL	4,983.87
AARP	$68.00	LAPSE(2)	0.23	CLAIM(1)	0.60	RESERV(2)	0.15	INFORCE-2	128	
ISSUES/M	200	LAPSE(3)	0.18	CLAIM(2)	0.75	RESERV(3)	0.08	INFORCE-3	99	
CICR(M)	1.00	LAPSE(4)	0.18	CLAIM(3)	0.40	RESERV(4)	0.05	INFORCE-4	81	
MC/M	800	LAPSE(5)	0.12	CLAIM(4)	0.40	RESERV(5)	0.03	INFORCE-5	66	LTV $24.92
TMC	800	PREMTAX	0.025	CLAIM(5)	0.45			INFORCE-6	58	ALLOW 107.56%
T/MC	17.00	INT.RATE	0.06	CLAIM(6)	0.45	N	1.00	INFORCE-7	51	COLFACT 51.20%
COMMISFY	0	MODPAYFAC	0.10	CLAIM(7)	0.45			INFORCE-8	45	
COMMISREN	0	PAY/N	12.00	CLAIM(8)	0.45	MOS/COL	8	INFORCE-9	40	ACQUSITION $73.14
ADMIN(1)	0.10	YEARS	10.00	CLAIM(9)	0.45			INFORCE-0	35	ALLOWANCE
ADMIN(RE)	0.06	ROI	15.00%	CLAIM(10)	0.45					

PROFIT STUDY (AUTOMATIC CALCULATION)

YEARS	COLPREM	CLAIMS	ADMIN	COMMISS	TMC	PREMTAX	RESERVES	TOT/RESEV	INT	INCOME	EXPENSE	P(L)	PROFIT%	ACQALLOW
1	6,963	4,164	696	0	800	174	1,393	1,393	108	7,071	7,227	(156)	-2.21%	19.14
2	8,042	6,022	483	0		201	1,206	2,599	201	8,243	7,912	331	4.02%	11.97
3	6,595	2,637	396	0		165	528	3,127	242	6,836	3,725	3,111	45.51%	35.89
4	5,408	2,162	324	0		135	270	3,397	263	5,670	2,893	2,778	48.99%	35.96
5	4,759	2,141	286	0		119	143	3,540	274	5,032	2,688	2,345	46.59%	32.68
6	4,188	1,884	251	0		105	(708)	2,832	219	4,407	1,532	2,875	65.24%	32.47
7	3,685	1,658	221	0		92	(708)	2,124	164	3,849	1,263	2,586	67.19%	32.26
8	3,243	1,459	195	0		81	(708)	1,416	109	3,352	1,026	2,326	69.38%	32.05
9	2,854	1,284	171	0		71	(708)	708	55	2,909	818	2,090	71.87%	31.84
10	2,511	1,130	151	0		63	(708)	0	0	2,511	635	1,876	74.71%	31.63
TOTALS	48,248	24,540	3,173	0	800	1,206	(0)		1,633	49,882	29,719	20,163	40.42%	295.91
%		50.86%	6.58%	0.00%	ERR	2.50%								

Figure 6-4: Scheduled surgical benefit rider profit model

SCREEN VALUES (INPUT DATA + AUTOMATIC CALCULATION)

```
PRODUCT   UPGRADE2   LAPSE(1)    0.52   RESERV(1)   0.36   ULTCLAIM            INFORCE-1   0.20    160  PRESVAL      3,342.86
AARP      $60.00     LAPSE(2)    0.60   RESERV(2)   0.23   CLAIM(1)            INFORCE-2   0.15   102.4
ISSUES/M  160        LAPSE(3)    0.75   RESERV(3)   0.18   CLAIM(2)            INFORCE-3   0.08     79
CICR(M)   1.00       LAPSE(4)    0.40   RESERV(4)   0.18   CLAIM(3)            INFORCE-4   0.05     65
MC/M      800        LAPSE(5)    0.40   RESERV(5)   0.12   CLAIM(4)            INFORCE-5   0.03     53  LTV          $20.89
TMC       800        PREMTAX     0.025                     CLAIM(5)   0.45     INFORCE-6            47  ALLOW       107.32%
T/MC      12.00      INT.RATE    0.06   N           1.00   CLAIM(6)   0.45     INFORCE-7            41  COLFACT      38.40%
COMMISFY  0          MODPAYFAC   0.10                      CLAIM(7)   0.45     INFORCE-8            36
COMMISREN 0          PAY/N       12.00  MOS/COL     6      CLAIM(8)   0.45     INFORCE-9   6        32  ACQUISITION  $64.39
ADMIN(1)  0.10       YEARS       10.00                     CLAIM(9)   0.45     INFORCE-0            28  ALLOWANCE
ADMIN(RE) 0.06       ROI        15.00%                     CLAIM(10)  0.45
```

PROFIT STUDY (AUTOMATIC CALCULATION)

YEARS	COLPREM	CLAIMS	ADMIN	COMMISS	TMC	PREMTAX	RESERVES	TOT/RESEV	INT	INCOME	EXPENSE	P(L)	PROFIT%	ACQALLOW
1	3,686	2,204	369	0	800	92	737	737	57	3,743	4,203	(459)	-12.27%	16.82
2	5,677	4,251	341	0		142	852	1,589	123	5,800	5,585	215	3.70%	10.49
3	4,655	1,862	279	0		116	372	1,961	152	4,807	2,630	2,177	45.29%	31.58
4	3,817	1,526	229	0		95	191	2,152	166	3,984	2,042	1,942	48.75%	31.65
5	3,359	1,511	202	0		84	101	2,253	174	3,533	1,897	1,636	46.30%	28.74
6	2,956	1,330	177	0		74	(451)	1,802	139	3,095	1,130	1,965	63.48%	28.58
7	2,601	1,170	156	0		65	(451)	1,352	104	2,706	941	1,765	65.24%	28.41
8	2,289	1,030	137	0		57	(451)	901	70	2,359	774	1,585	67.20%	28.25
9	2,014	906	121	0		50	(451)	451	35	2,049	627	1,423	69.42%	28.08
10	1,773	797	106	0		44	(451)	0	0	1,773	497	1,275	71.94%	27.91
TOTALS	32,829	16,587	2,117	0	800	821	(0)		1,020	33,849	20,325	13,524	39.95%	260.51
%		50.53%	6.45%	0.00%	ERR	2.50%								

Figure 6-5: A second $10-a-day upgrade rider profit model

```
SCREEN VALUES (INPUT DATA + AUTOMATIC CALCULATION)

PRODUCT   CONVELS     LAPSE(1)   0.36   ULTCLAIM   0.52   RESERV(1)  0.20   INFORCE-1  160    PRESVAL     3,796.47
AARP      $70.00      LAPSE(2)   0.23   CLAIM(1)   0.60   RESERV(2)  0.15   INFORCE-2  102.4
ISSUES/M  160         LAPSE(3)   0.18   CLAIM(2)   0.75   RESERV(3)  0.08   INFORCE-3  79
CICR(M)   1.00        LAPSE(4)   0.18   CLAIM(3)   0.40   RESERV(4)  0.05   INFORCE-4  65
MC/M                  LAPSE(5)   0.12   CLAIM(4)   0.40   RESERV(5)  0.03   INFORCE-5  53     LTV         $23.73
TMC       800         PREMTAX    0.025  CLAIM(5)   0.45                     INFORCE-6  47     ALLOW       107.08%
T/MC      14.00       INT.RATE   0.06   CLAIM(6)   0.45   N          1.00   INFORCE-7  41     COLFACT     25.60%
COMMISFY  0           MODPAYFAC  0.10   CLAIM(7)   0.45                     INFORCE-8  36
COMMISREN 0           PAY/N      0.10   CLAIM(8)   0.45   MOS/COL    4      INFORCE-9  32     ACQUSITION  $74.96
ADMIN(1)  0.10        YEARS      10.00  CLAIM(9)   0.45                     INFORCE-0  28     ALLOWANCE
ADMIN(RE) 0.06        ROI        15.00% CLAIM(10)  0.45
```

PROFIT STUDY (AUTOMATIC CALCULATION)

YEARS	COLPREM	CLAIMS	ADMIN	COMMISS	TMC	PREMTAX	RESERVES	TOT/RESEV	INT	INCOME	EXPENSE	P(L)	PROFIT%	ACQALLOW
1	2,867	1,715	287	0	800	72	573	573	44	2,912	3,446	(535)	-18.37%	19.54
2	6,623	4,959	397	0		166	993	1,567	121	6,744	6,516	228	3.39%	12.14
3	5,431	2,172	326	0		136	434	2,001	155	5,586	3,068	2,518	45.08%	36.75
4	4,453	1,781	267	0		111	223	2,224	172	4,625	2,382	2,243	48.50%	36.82
5	3,919	1,763	235	0		98	118	2,342	181	4,100	2,213	1,887	46.01%	33.43
6	3,449	1,551	207	0		86	(468)	1,873	145	3,594	1,376	2,217	61.71%	33.26
7	3,035	1,365	182	0		76	(468)	1,405	109	3,143	1,155	1,989	63.27%	33.08
8	2,671	1,201	160	0		67	(468)	937	72	2,743	960	1,783	65.00%	32.91
9	2,350	1,057	141	0		59	(468)	468	36	2,386	789	1,598	66.96%	32.74
10	2,068	930	124	0		52	(468)	0	0	2,068	638	1,430	69.16%	32.56
TOTALS	36,867	18,495	2,327	0	800	922	0		1,035	37,902	22,543	15,359	40.52%	303.24
%		50.17%	6.31%	0.00%	ERR	2.50%								

Figure 6-6: A convalescent care rider profit model

SCREEN VALUES (INPUT DATA + AUTOMATIC CALCULATION)

PRODUCT	EMERGEN	LAPSE(1)	0.36	ULTCLAIM	0.52	RESERV(1)	0.20	INFORCE-1	100	PRESVAL	2,680.54
AARP	$85.00	LAPSE(2)	0.23	CLAIM(1)	0.60	RESERV(2)	0.15	INFORCE-2	64		
ISSUES/M	100	LAPSE(3)	0.18	CLAIM(2)	0.75	RESERV(3)	0.08	INFORCE-3	49		
CICR(M)	1.00	LAPSE(4)	0.18	CLAIM(3)	0.40	RESERV(4)	0.05	INFORCE-4	40		
MC/M	1000	LAPSE(5)	0.12	CLAIM(4)	0.40	RESERV(5)	0.03	INFORCE-5	33	LTV	$26.81
TMC	1000	PREMTAX	0.025	CLAIM(5)	0.45			INFORCE-6	29	ALLOW	106.84%
T/MC	8.50	INT.RATE	0.06	CLAIM(6)	0.45	N	1.00	INFORCE-7	26	COLFACT	12.80%
COMMISFY	0	MODPAYFAC	0.10	CLAIM(7)	0.45			INFORCE-8	23		
COMMISREN	0	PAY/N	12.00	CLAIM(8)	0.45	MOS/COL	2	INFORCE-9	20	ACQUSITION	$90.81
ADMIN(1)	0.10	YEARS	10.00	CLAIM(9)	0.45			INFORCE-0	17	ALLOWANCE	
ADMIN(RE)	0.06	ROI	15.00%	CLAIM(10)	0.45						

PROFIT STUDY (AUTOMATIC CALCULATION)

YEARS	COLPREM	CLAIMS	ADMIN	COMMISS	TMC	PREMTAX	RESERVES	TOT/RESEV	INT	INCOME	EXPENSE	P(L)	PROFIT%	ACQALLOW
1	1,088	651	109	0	1,000	27	218	218	17	1,105	2,004	(899)	-81.41%	23.64
2	5,027	3,764	302	0		126	754	972	75	5,102	4,945	157	3.07%	14.63
3	4,122	1,648	247	0		103	330	1,301	101	4,222	2,328	1,894	44.86%	44.50
4	3,380	1,352	203	0		84	169	1,470	114	3,493	1,808	1,686	48.25%	44.60
5	2,974	1,338	178	0		74	89	1,560	121	3,095	1,680	1,415	45.72%	40.46
6	2,617	1,177	157	0		65	(312)	1,248	96	2,714	1,088	1,626	59.91%	40.28
7	2,303	1,036	138	0		58	(312)	936	72	2,376	920	1,456	61.28%	40.10
8	2,027	912	122	0		51	(312)	624	48	2,075	772	1,303	62.79%	39.91
9	1,784	802	107	0		45	(312)	312	24	1,808	642	1,166	64.49%	39.73
10	1,570	706	94	0		39	(312)	0	0	1,570	528	1,042	66.39%	39.54
TOTALS	26,891	13,385	1,657	0	1,000	672	(0)		668	27,559	16,715	10,844	39.35%	367.39
%		49.78%	6.16%	0.00%	ERR	2.50%								

Figure 6-7: An emergency care rider profit model

	COLPREM	CLAIMS	ADMIN	COMMISS	TMC	PREMTAX	RESERVES	TOT/RESEV	INT	INCOME	EXPENSE	P(L)	PROFIT%	ACQALLOW
BASIC	1,122,846	577,846	76,439	0	282,171	28,071			31,791	1,154,637	964,528	190,109	16.46%	1,239.18
RIDER1	39,697	20,314	2,658	0	800	992			1,447	41,144	24,765	16,379	39.81%	68.00
RIDER2	48,248	24,540	3,173	0	800	1,206			1,633	49,882	29,719	20,163	40.42%	295.91
RIDER3	32,829	16,587	2,117	0	800	821			1,020	33,849	20,325	13,524	39.95%	260.51
RIDER4	36,867	18,495	2,327	0	800	922			1,035	37,902	22,543	15,359	40.52%	303.24
RIDER5	26,891	13,385	1,657	0	1,000	672			668	27,559	16,715	10,844	39.35%	367.39
CRSLOAD1														
CRSLOAD2														
CRSLOAD3														
TOTALS	1,307,379	671,167	88,372	0	286,371	32,684	0	0	37,593	1,344,973	1,078,595	266,378	19.81%	2,534.21
				80%	60%	50%								
PRESENT VALUE:	65844.56													
LIFETIME VALUE:		65.84		52.68	39.51	32.92								
ACQ.ALLOW		626.42		501.13	375.85	313.21								
Cost/App		282.17		282.17	282.17	282.17								

Figure 6-8: Finally, a summary of the basic coverage and the four riders offered during the first year

77

riders you offered to the basic program.

Figure 6-2 reflects a $10.00-a-day benefit upgrade to your HIP product, offered two months after the business is in force. Now the MC/TARP ratio is $13.50.

Figure 6-3 reflects a surgical rider, offered four months after the basic policy is in force. The MC/TARP ratio is $17.00.

Figure 6-4 reflects a second $10.00-a-day benefit upgrade, offered six months after the basic policy is in force. In this case, the MC/TARP ratio is $12.00, down slightly from the first-cycle offer.

Figure 6-5 reflects a convalescent care rider, offered eight months after the basic policy is in force. The MC/TARP ratio is $14.00.

Figure 6-6 reflects an emergency services rider, offered ten months after the basic policy is in force. The MC/TARP ratio is $8.50.

As you can see, each offer has resulted in a substantially greater MC/TARP ratio than the original source solicitation.

Figure 6-7 summarizes the performance of the basic product and the five riders you offered during the first year. You can now see the value of relational database marketing. The lifetime value of a policyowner from the original profit study was $46.99. By adding the lifetime value of the five riders, it is now $65.84—a 40% increase over the the base LTV.

As well, note what has happened to the acquisition allowance for your product. The original profit study created an acquisition allowance of $306.11. In the summary, the acquisition allowance (remember, that's the sum of money you can afford to pay to acquire a policyowner) has more than doubled. It is now $626.42.

The reason is simple. Each time you market a new product to your policyowners, you enhance the lifetime value of each. As you will see later, the higher the lifetime value of a policyowner—the more money you can spend to acquire that policyowner.

Now, let's examine how to create a policyowner lifetime value model.

The first thing to understand is that the past dictates the future. So, there are two LTV models.

The first is historical—an examination of what has happened in the past, by product. The second is predictive. Based on what is discovered as a result of the historical perspective, an attempt is made to predict what will happen in the future under similar circumstances.

Step one in the historical re-creation of "what happens" to a basic product—the first brick—in an examination of LTV is the creation of a cash-flow profit study projection. Remember, Figure 6-1 re-creates such a profit study projection for the hospital-cash product. It is based on a view of 1,000 policyowners.

Using a spreadsheet analysis program (LOTUS 1-2-3, Visicalc, PFS Plan or Deskmate Worksheet, or whatever you happen to be working with), you create a data-input screen.

Each "cell identity" in the screen carries on identifiable value that you will use later in creating what is essentially a sales decay analysis for the HIP product.

Elements of the screen (screen values)

Project identification: The source of your data. In the example, HIP/TV inquiry-conversion program.

Next, AARP: Average annualized renewal premium, or average annualized premium. This is the average of annualized premiums paid by all of the 1,000 policyowners in the group during the first full year their policies are in force. Annualization is the process of assuming all premium is paid when the coverage is issued. In insurance direct marketing, if working on a pre-policyowner basis, average annualized premium is most commonly calculated by multiplying monthly premium by 12. Total annualized *renewal* premium is then calculated by multiplying the average annual premium by the number of policyowners within the model. It is not necessary to have a separate entry for TARP in the model screen values, although it will be used to make a calculation later on.

Next, come the elements of marketing expense. In this example, for every 1,000 inquiries received from TV, 45.59 policies were issued and paid for (issues/M). In order to produce 1,000 policies, it was necessary to generate 21,930 inquiries (circ/M). Each inquiry cost slightly more than $12.86. Therefore, marketing cost per thousand (MC/M) is $12,864.19. The total marketing cost (TMC) to produce the 1,000 policyholders in the model was $282,171.30—or $282.17 per policy.

To calculate the MC/T ratio, the next cell on the screen, you divide TARP by TMC. MC/T is a basic measure used by insurance marketers to determine the success, or failure, of a marketing program. By achieving the MC/TARP ratio, or exceeding it, your marketer has a successful program.

MC/T is frequently reversed to T/MC and is expressed in "dollars and cents." Remember that it means, for every marketing dollar you have spent, you have brought in so many annualized premium dollars ($1.00 : $X.XX).

Commissions (the next two cells) are expressed as first year and renewal. If your profit study is being conducted for a third-party account, you will have these expenses, both expressed as a percentage of collected premium. Remember, if you pay commissions, they must be included in total marketing cost.

Administrative expenses: You need two lines on your screen to express administrative expenses. There are first-year expenses and renewal-year expenses, both expressed as a percentage of collected premium.

In terms of fixed dollars, administrative expenses are variable, changing inversely with the volume of policies handled. The larger the volume, the lower the expense per policy should be. Remember, administration includes fulfillment (policy issuing) expenses, data processing entry and maintenance expenses, premium billing and collection, and customer service.

Lapse rates: This number is expressed as a decimal, and measures the number of policyowners who flow off the book of business by year. The reciprocal of lapse is persistency, which measures the number of policyowners who continue to pay premium and remain on the books, by year.

Normally, about the fourth year your book of business is in force, a pattern begins to emerge. The highest lapse rates for this product occur in years one and two, then the rate settles down. In this case, we have entered lapse rates for 5 years, assuming the rate remains the same in years 6 through 10 as in year 5. We have, as well, entered the lapse-rate reciprocals by year in a separate column to calculate the number of policyowners remaining on the books, by year.

Premium tax: In this case it is 2½% of collected premium.

Interest rates and reserves: It is necessary to set aside some portion of the premium dollars you collect to pay future claims. Usually these dollars are part of the investment a company makes in marketing a product. There is a "strain," so to speak, that the marketed product places on the asset base of the company. The good news is, the interest your reserves earn "counts" toward a product's profitability.

Remember, it is *assumed* that all the dollars you collect come through the door on the first day of the policy year, and all the claims are paid on the last day of the policy year. That means you earn interest all year.

To offset reality, the assumed interest rate built into a product is normally moderate—regardless of what level of interest is being paid by your local bank. Each company has its own policy regarding how much of the premium is reserved, and when those reserves are released to offset claims. These items are governed by reserving requirements, set by law, in each state.

In the example in Figure 6-1, reserves are allocated for five years, then released during the second five-year period.

Claims: Like lapse rates, claims are a decimal expression of loss ratios. These sums of money paid out in benefits are expressed as a percentage of *collected premium.*

Claims are highest in the first several years the book of business is in force. Again, similar to lapse rates, a pattern will emerge. What you are seeking is the "ultimate" loss ratio—the percentage of sales that will be, or has been, paid out in claims benefits relative to the total premium you have collected. For HIP, the ultimate loss ratio will fall in the 50% to 65% area.

Reinsurance: Although not displayed in Figure 6-1, some risks are extremely volatile—accident risks for example. Most companies require some form of reinsurance to protect themselves against "one bad year." Essentially, reinsurance is simply the sharing of the risk with another company.

The reinsurer guarantees to pay some portion of the benefit in return for receiving some portion of the premium—whatever the reinsurer stipulates is an "appropriate rate" for the risk. Usually there is a difference between what an insurer pays to a reinsurer and what the insuring company collects.

The trick is to avoid a proportional reinsurance "treaty"—for example, 60% of the risk for 60% of the premium. In a profit model assumption, you express reinsurance as an expense. However, remember—if you incur a reinsurance expense—you will pay less money out in claims, since the reinsurance company pays a portion of the claims. Thus, you have to make that adjustment.

Payment factor (MODPAYFAC): This element expresses the concept of modalization. Most direct marketing insurance policies offer four modes of payment: annual, semiannual, quarterly, or monthly. You have two choices here. You can divide your premium into expected modal percentages, or you can express collected premium in one mode.

To err on the conservative side is the better way. Therefore, all premium in this example is considered paid monthly. That makes the *period* of payments (PAY/N): 12. And, since the profit study is based on 10 years, that is the "years" input.

Next, you identify the return on investment (ROI) which you need to achieve. In this case it is 15%. As well, you will normally add into your calculations a policy fee. Years ago, in the A&H business, a policy fee was a commission enhancement kept by the agent. Today, a policy fee is used to cover the fixed expenses of doing business. Normal everyday operating costs that, in theory, should be shared by all the policyowners of the company.

Insurance policies are normally designed in units of coverage. In this case, rates are based on $10.00 per day of daily indemnity. So, a $50.00-a-day policyowner has five units of coverage. To illustrate the policy-fee concept, each unit of coverage costs approximately $4.58 per month, using the numbers developed in this model. That makes the average monthly premium for the coverage $22.93 and the average annualized premium $275.20. Now, we add the $10.00 policy fee and get the AARP of $285.20. The policy fee is about 3.5% of the average annualized premium.

But, what if some folks purchase fewer than five units of coverage? Assume they take three units for a $30.00-a-day benefit level. At the same monthly rate, $4.58, their bill is $13.74 per month, or $164.88 per year. When you add the $10.00 policy fee to each annualized premium, it is now $174.88. Now, the policy fee is about 5.7% of annualized premium.

The idea is that, the larger the policy, the lower the share of fixed costs. Put another way, the larger the policy, the lower the cost per unit.

Your profit study screen is now set up. You are ready to use these factors to calculate profitability and return on investment over a ten-year period. Figure 6-1 displays these calculations in the lower half of the illustration.

Now, comes the elegant part. When you have calculated the expected profit over the ten-year period, you ascertain the present value of that profit.

Since a total of 1,000 policies has been used as the base for this calculation, simply dividing the present value of the anticipated future profit by 1,000 gives you the lifetime value of a policyowner, who purchases your HIP product.

And that's just the beginning.

Next, you iterate a separate profit study projection for each of the other types of products—in this example, the five riders—you have offered to this list of names. Now, as to the number of months during the first year in which you expect to collect premium, remember that each iteration is a cash flow model. This is an attempt to reflect what really happened.

Finally, you summarize the result of each iteration. This is displayed in Figure 6-7.

Now, how to use the number.

One way of using the lifetime-value number created by these various iterations is to determine what we could have spent to acquire a policyowner while maintaining a specific return on investment. Remember, when the present value calculation was made on each of these profit studies, the required ROI was 15%.

Normally, the first thing a direct marketing actuary does in product development is solve for acquisition allowance. There are two ways, using the data developed so far, to do so. First is the *iteration method*. Use the following formula, which has been used to calculate the individual acquisition allowances in the illustration figures:

AA = Acquisition Allowance

$$AA = \sum_{N=1}^{10} \left(\frac{\text{Annualized}}{\text{Premium}}\right) \bullet \left[1 - \text{loss \%} - \text{expense \%} - \frac{\text{Premium}}{\text{Tax \%}}\right] + \left(\frac{\text{Investment}}{\text{Income}}\right) \frac{1 - \text{lapse \%}}{(1 + I)^N}$$

Set I to target rate of return.

You need to make separate calculations for each of the ten years you are examining. Then the present value is taken to determine acquisition allowance. You will find a model using this technique in Chapter XVI.

A second, more precise method, is the *LTV method*. It uses *LTV* to solve for acquisition allowance.

   AA (acquisition allowance) = solicitation cost (in $/M) /required sales (in $/M).

The first step is to find out exactly what the "required-sales" figure is. The formula for required sales (RS) is:

   RS in $/M = c/1 - a - b + LTV/A

Where:

   LTV = $65.84 (from the summary sheet)

   A = Actual sales per thousand, $1,307.38 (Income/1000)

   a = Cost of sale (ultimate claims) 51.3% (claims/collected premium)

   b = Variable operating expenses—administration, premium tax, etc., 9.25% (administrative expense + premium tax/collected premium)

   c = Actual solicitation cost/M, $17,064.19 (the sum of the actual solicitation cost per thousand for each effort)

By substitution, required sales in $/M + $38,355.11.

Return to your original formula to determine acceptable solicitation cost.

   AA = $17,064.19/$38,355.11 = 44.49 %

This calculation reveals that you could have spent 44.49% of total sales in order to maintain a 15% return on investment.

The model shows that we have spent only 21.90% of sales to produce the customer (TMC/Income from Figure 6-8). Each application actually costs you $286.37. And, you could have spent, according to this formula, $581.65.

If you'll note, the acquisition allowance for this program, using the iteration method, has been pegged at an assumptive $626.42. The difference is accounted for by the formulas used to arrive at the number, and the details included in the model. See Chapter XVI for the details.

The point is: In both cases, the amount of marketing dollars you could have spent to acquire the policyowner is greater than the amount you actually spent!

The application of the lifetime value concept clearly indicates, irrefutably, that policy acquisition allowance can no longer be based on a profit study for the initial product alone.

It is up to the insurance direct marketer to lead the way in this regard. A corporate strategy that myopically views policyholder acquisition as a single event is *doomed* in the modern insurance direct marketing environment!

Here is another big "BUT": When you deal in projections, it is critically important to properly assess the amount of risk you care to take.

Figure 6-8 shows three levels of risk evaluation: 80%, 60%, and 50%. A profit study projection is based on a series of assumptions, rather than on experience.

Assuming a lower LTV than that which is projected by your various iterations makes good business sense. Since this is conservative, it provides a safety net in the event your program does not perform as you project it will.

Remember, the higher the LTV percentage, the more risk you are willing to assume. These calculations are math elegance. As you know, LTV is based on assumptions to determine how much you can spend per paid application. *Therefore, employing it at 100% is dangerous.*

What happens if you use the lower LTVs? In every case you can afford to spend more than you spent to acquire the policyowner!

Now, for the what-ifs.

Since you know you could actually, by using lifetime value, spend more money than you did to acquire a policyowner, you might speculate about rates. What would happen if you lowered rates to meet the amount of money you spend? The change would be in the AARP column in your screen. The theory is, the lower the premium, the more prospects will purchase.

Or, what if you increased benefits?

Or, what if you used a little of all three options? Perhaps you could achieve a different balance to your product, all the while maintaining the profit and return on investment requirements your model has produced.

Certain benefits will accrue to your company, if it does the following:

a. Adopt the above method of calculating acquisition allowance.

b. Commit to *relational marketing.*

c. Actually spend an enhanced marketing allowance to acquire policyholders.

Doing the above things allows you to penetrate marginal lists more deeply, solicit marginal portions of endorsed-marketing accounts, remain on television longer, and accept as few as one or two paid applications per thousand and still have a successful insurance direct marketing program!

Clearly you can see the lifetime value concept is a critically important addition to your ability to go to market.

In this age of database marketing, downstream sales can no longer be separated from the initial policyowner-acquisition sale. Moreover, mathematical modeling is a necessary tool in the modern insurance direct marketing world.

Perhaps, as these models show—from a financial point of view—today's measure of success in insurance direct marketing is the total relational values of long-term profit, return on investment, or internal rate of return.

Lifetime value is the key that opens those doors.

Consider this: If the marketer in the model program had been allowed to spend $581.65 to acquire a policyowner, several interesting things would have happened.

First the MC/TARP ratio would have dropped to $.55. The company would have been able to stay on television much longer, thus increasing the number of leads generated. The increased number of leads would have resulted in approximately double the number of policyowners put on the books. Doubling the number of policyowners means the company would have doubled its policyowner sales.

And please keep the following in mind: The illustrations you have seen reflect the first year of marketing activity to these policyowners. Policyowner marketing and relational marketing continue year after year. Therefore, the volume of profit dollars as well as the percentage of profit yielded by the policyowner base grows year after year. Not in initial profit dollars, but in *long-term profit dollars!*

By doing the following, you may discover revealing secrets about solicitation sources of business:

1. Apply even finer segmentations.

2. Calculate the LTV for:

a. Every list you use

b. Every TV station on which you run

c. Every endorsed-marketing account you solicit

What appears to be a failure, may in fact be startlingly successful . . . and vice versa.

Remember, first develop historical perspective, then a predictive model, then test your assumptions to ensure they are solidly based.

It is apparent that this chapter and the previous one have approached product development from a marketer's perspective. Calculation of profit and loss in an insurance environment is complicated. Successful product development is complex. Yet the problems facing the insurance direct marketing industry today demand the total participation of marketers. We mention the following: declining response rates, product wear-out, crowded air waves, consumers rights, and increased regulatory awareness. All of these make creative, inventive participation by every member of the insurance direct marketing team imperative. The leader of the team is the marketer.

Now let us pull together what we've seen.

The Final Touch

In preparing for effective product development, one of the most important functions a marketer needs to carry out is communications. Assuming all product development is market driven and assuming you are involved in a "team environment," the following format is suggested:

New Product Development Format

Product—What it is

Description—The risk that is covered, generic type

Type—Underwritten/guaranteed issue

Eligibility—Those who can buy it—whether group or individual

Benefits—Outline specifically

Distribution—Response rates as a % of total sales for each benefit offered

Premium—The desired premium which you feel will successfully sell in the marketplace

Gender—Distribution by gender—xx% male, xx% female

Est. AARP—Based on desired premium

Payment options and distribution—Direct bill, credit card, check-o-matic

Acquisition allowance—Based on your LTV calculations—that sum of money you can afford to spend to acquire a policyowner

Administrative allowance—Expressed as a % of first-year and renewal premium

Premium form—Actual mode of payments available

Modal distribution—% of premium collected monthly, quarterly, semi-annually, and annually

Collected factor—% average annual premium estimated to be collected

Reinsurance data—Averages, net retention, reinsurance expense as a % of AARP

Underwriting/Actuarial Considerations

Age distribution

Pre-solicitation underwriting factors (limits on anti-selection)

Exclusions, limitations, and reductions

Anticipated claim rates

Anticipated lapse rates

Historical experience with similar product

Marketing

Outline and definition of markets

Impact of seasonality on response

General demographics—target markets

Competitive product information

Target Date—When development needs to be completed to go to market

* * *

The more complete the information you provide, the more effective your product development team will be.

The life blood of any insurance direct marketing operation is effective product development. To synthesize every rule into a few words is, at best, difficult.

Yet, the secrets and the concepts shared here will focus your attention on the principal elements of the process. In a marketing environment, market-driven product development is critical. It is, in fact, the keystone of strategic planning. Insurance direct marketing, today, demands creativity in every element of the system.

Effective strategic thinking is no exception. Market planning, in a macro sense, identifies the windows of opportunity that propel corporate growth. Strategic planning hides its own secrets. Revelation follows.

VII

The Secrets of Strategic Planning

Albert Einstein once wrote: "When I examined myself, and my methods of thought, I came to the conclusion that the gift of fantasy has meant more to me than my talent for absorbing positive knowledge."

The gift of fantasy—its importance has no limit.

SECRET No. 17

Imagination, lateral thinking, and holistic orientation are the handmaidens of successful insurance direct marketing strategic planning.

There has never been a more motivating challenge to the marketer's creativity than the development of a strategic plan. Here, in one assignment, you find all the wonder-generating, intellectual stimulation that direct marketing can provide.

The most successful insurance direct marketing planner will possess characteristics of originality, invention, and inspiration that have been common to thinkers from Aristotle to Zola:

    o To see in new ways, transferring the familiar to the strange, viewing the commonplace with new perception

    o To challenge assumptions, accepting little at *face value*, always questioning accepted truths

89

o To recognize patterns by focusing on sameness or differences in events, ideas, and perceptions

o To make connections, bringing together seemingly unrelated ideas, events, or objects

o To take risks, daring to try new ways with no guarantee of results

o To recognize chance—the ancient Greek concept of "Tyche"; and be prepared, always, to take advantage of the unexpected; to recognize, and accept, the extraordinary value of "accident"

Finally, the most effective insurance direct marketing planner constructs *networks* among peers for the exchange of ideas, perceptions, and encouragement.

These networks function internally and externally, relative to the corporate environment—with the external relationships most often having greater impact. The reason is simple. It is extremely difficult to look at ourselves from a purely objective viewpoint. All too often we become wedded to procedures that have worked in the past, but are unlikely to work efficiently in the present or in the future.

These need to be changed.

Enter the corporate iconoclast. The challenger of cherished corporate belief—the effective planner. In a sense, it is the *intrapreneur—one possessing an entrepreneurial spirit but working in the corporate environment*—who seems to be so sought after by corporations today.

Now, that is not to say there are no rules. Just as the scientific and social scientific communities have their *scientific method*, so, too, does the strategic planner have his.

Undisciplined speculation has no place in a profit-making organization. Yet, for the company that combines the essential ingredients of creativity with the vertical disciplines of implementation, the future is there for the taking. The possibilities are endless.

And, essentially, that is what strategic planning is all about. It is the organized examination of the profit-making possibilities available to the company, plus the planning and directing of the whole operation, combined to achieve that profit. The strategic plan is the quintessential management tool. It provides a blueprint to success on a macro level.

Your strategic plan will be theoretical, not operational. It will be descriptive, not executional. It will be general, not specific. It will be broad, not detailed. It will provide a set of guidelines, not implementation procedures.

It seeks to latch onto the 20% of your resources that produce 80% of your results. It provides the criteria for the employment, management, and expansion of those resources.

SECRET No. 18

No insurance direct marketing operation can succeed without a focused, penetrating, effective strategic marketing plan!

To succeed in insurance direct marketing, there are three *absolutely indispensable* ingredients for effectiveness:

First, a superior product portfolio; second, an efficient, professional organization; and third, the strategic plan.

One of the critical purposes of the plan is to make certain all the relevant facts are known to everyone in the organization.

From the facts, emerges a clear view of the problems, the opportunities, and the possibilities for your company. On the basis of these discoveries, a set of realistic and specific objectives is compiled. Then, a broad plan of action is created to overcome the problems, exploit the opportunities, and develop the possibilities in such a way that the plan objectives are met—profitably.

These are five principal purposes the strategic planning process achieves for any insurance direct marketing organization.

First, the act of accumulating data on every element of the plan requires a reasonably complete knowledge of the facts. As a result, the likelihood that critical considerations might be overlooked is greatly reduced. The act of putting the plan on paper requires tighter thinking than an oral presentation which dances from idea to idea and from mouth to ear.

Second, the plan evaluates alternatives. Intelligent management decisions need to be justified. Information needs to be accurate. Credibility needs to be established.

Evidence is not limited to jurisprudence. It is as much a part of the business environment as of the legal environment. Alternatives accepted for execution and corporate policies that are established by the planning group represent the best thinking and a consensus of the group.

The result is a strategy that is executed by the company as a whole, thereby eliminating, to a large extent, those pockets of resistance that can cause the best-laid plans to go astray.

Third, the plan promulgates policies based on expected profits. It contains, hopefully, lucid and concise financial data that support estimates of profits, sales, and expenses.

Fourth, it produces a unified and cohesive statement of purpose, thus allowing line managers to achieve the stipulated objectives with as much latitude—room for growth—as possible within the corporate environment.

Fifth, and finally, the strategic plan determines if the information concerning products, markets, delivery and fulfillment systems, and administrative techniques are adequate to achieve the stated objectives. If they are not, the plan provides the framework in which special programs can be developed to overhaul the shortcomings.

Now...the format. There is a variety of formats in which a strategic plan can be presented. An important point to keep in mind is that no strategic plan can be omnidirectional. It must be monodirectional and be aimed at the primary decision maker of your company, most frequently the chief executive officer.

He is the "captain" of the team—the one person responsible for the ultimate decisions regarding the plan. Therefore, the format must be logical, hence the following:

1. Executive Summary
2. Introduction
3. Environment
   a. External
   b. Internal
4. Assumptions
5. Objectives
6. Marketing Strategy
   a. Research & development
   b. Product
   c. Marketing
7. Financial Strategy
8. Administrative (Operations) Strategy
   a. Fulfillment
   b. Data processing
   c. Premium billing and collection
   d. Underwriting
   e. Claims

f. Customer service

g. Legal & regulatory

9. Short-Term Tactical Strategies

10. Long-Term Strategic Implications

Specific Considerations of Strategic Planning

1. *Executive summary* In a concise overview of each part of the plan, you summarize the conclusions, policies, and objectives you have planned. More than a table of contents, this exercise forces the planners to reduce explanation to specific synthesis of the ideas the plan supports. It tells the chief executive officer, and perhaps the board of directors, what you propose to accomplish, what resources you intend to employ, and—broadly—how you intend to manage those resources to achieve your goals.

2. *Introduction* Here is the beginning...the function and scope of your strategic plan. The introduction brings into focus an evaluation of "what's happening now." It defines the present situation. For example:

o Decline in sales or market share

o Business as usual

o A new, promising product or products

o A static, unsatisfactory situation

o Unusual action or inaction by competition

o Inadequate growth in sales or market share

The list of appropriate situations is limited only by the reality you face each day. Most frequently, situations are complex...with more than one factor influencing your current business. Try to parse your current situation to its root. Then analyze the "why" of the "what" you discover.

3. *Environment* Whatever you choose as your situation, it is likely you did not arrive at it in a vacuum. You were helped by internal and external factors. Your environmental analysis focuses on those factors that contributed to your situation. In this section, you examine the history, competition, business sources, markets, strengths, and weaknesses that you bring to the business table.

For example, a static, unsatisfactory situation might be the result of internal accounting procedures, poor product development, or the inability of management to recognize the value of your policyowner base.

On the other hand, it might be the result of competitive pressures. A competitor may be limiting your exposure on television by dominating time buys, or introducing an innovative product—one not in your portfolio.

By dividing the environmental elements into internal and external factors, you start to isolate the things that require "fixing"—anything from product pricing to fulfillment material design.

When examining your internal history, for instance, be specific and objective. Look at programs, response rates, marketing philosophies, accounting, fulfillment, and premium billing and collection—all in a broad context. Perhaps, going back only two or three years will indicate previously unnoticed trends.

Response rates in certain business lines will be declining. Lapse rates will be increasing. Profitability will be falling...perhaps only by tenths of a point. But, by taking this "overview" of your business, these trends will become apparent. Remember you are looking at the "forest," not individual trees.

Once you have defined your situation and your environment, you evaluate your strengths and weaknesses.

Strengths are the things you will want to emphasize, and they come in all sizes and shapes. They may range from highly trained personnel, to wonderful relations with endorsers, to dominance in TV, to terrific premium billing material, and to a state-of-the-art data processing system.

Weaknesses are the things you need to remedy. They, too, come in all sizes and shapes. Here's a hint regarding critical weaknesses. There is a generally accepted hierarchy of marketing values for successful businesses:

    a. Price advantage

    b. Benefit advantage

    c. Service advantage

It is interesting to learn that the weakest companies in the insurance direct marketing business believe absolutely that they render to their clients and their customers a superior level of "service."

Yet, in the hierarchy of marketing values, service is the least important of the three advantages. It is true that each company must seek a balance between these values. It is equally true that the most successful direct marketing operations will seek and achieve either price or benefit advantage—perhaps both. However, when service is combined with either price or benefit advantage, relational marketing possibilities expand enormously.

The fact is clear: A *service* advantage simply cannot stand alone in today's competitive environment.

    4. *Assumptions* After emerging from the examination of your

situation and the environment in which you work, certain logical assumptions that underlie the rest of the planning process will become apparent.

One of the factors that will become clear from your analysis is where your company stands in the business of insurance direct marketing—what stage of maturity you have reached.

There are four such stages, almost self-explanatory: embryonic, growing, maturing, and aging.

Each stage dictates its own unique assumptions relative to the strategies you are in the process of developing. If your company is in the *growing* stage, it may dictate aggressiveness as a macro-strategy. If it sits in the *aging* stage, it may dictate conservativeness as a macro-strategy.

Simply remember, assumptions are macro in nature. You may have built your plan around:

○ An assumption of continued economic growth at current rates

○ A decrease in aggressive regulatory environments

○ A decline in the prime rate of interest, therefore generating decreasing capital costs

○ The expansion over the next five years of the 50+ marketplace in the United States

* * *

Furthermore, in addition to these types of assumptions, you probably will assume that your strengths will continue and your weaknesses will be fixed—some even turning into strengths.

Keep in mind, as well, that your assumptions form a foundation for your objectives.

5. *Objectives* Probably you are already aware that goal setting is difficult. Yet the objectives you establish in the strategic-planning process are critical to your company and its future.

In general, objectives need to be specific and achievable. They need to be established for every department and for every function in the insurance direct marketing system.

Start again with macro-objectives:

○ To increase sales by $X.XX, share of market by XX.X%, profits by $X.XX.

○ To stop a decline in sales or market share

o To take advantage of competitive weakness or opportunity

o To maintain business as usual

o To respond to competition, by protecting or maintaining a product against it

o To introduce and make profitable a new product

o To increase total sales through increasing the market

Remember, your managers are going to be working toward the objectives you establish in the strategic plan. It is critical to give them clear direction. If you seek a 16% profit and a consistent 15% return on investment for every product in your portfolio, your marketing managers must set up their tactical planning to produce the appropriate levels of response necessary to meet that objective.

On the other hand, if profit and return on investment vary by generic product line, calculate a specific objective for each product.

The same concept is applicable in the support areas. If your fulfillment people don't know that you are going to try to expand the business by adding 500,000 new policyowners, the line managers will not be prepared to fulfill that many new policies.

After setting the macro-objectives, it is a good idea to clearly establish where you expect the business to go—on every level. It is also a good idea to separate your marketing objectives from your financial objectives. It simply makes them easier to comprehend and recall.

Goal setting requires a remarkable amount of attention to detail. But, as you and your planning group define the objectives you seek to reach, strategies for reaching the objectives begin to take shape.

A final note. As your strategic-plan objectives accumulate, and you and your planning group begin to establish priorities in order to achieve the objectives, you will recognize that a good deal of functional data begins to come on stream.

All of this lends itself to an organizational chart that answers a "what-why-when" type formula. *What* tasks need to be accomplished? *Why*, that is, what is the purpose of the task? And, *when* does it need to be done?

In a sense, you are creating a PERT type chart—a program evaluation review technique. In a general way, your objectives begin to sort themselves, and can be classified as follows:

a. Those that can be achieved quickly

b. Those that require prerequisite activity—certain changes that need to be achieved first

c. Goals that need to be achieved over the course of the plan's time period—one year or so

This *task* orientation creates a ready-made control document for the management group to monitor the activity of the plan.

6. *Marketing strategy* This is the heart of the strategic plan. Creativity is critical in the development of your plan, but perhaps no more critical than in the concept of how to get the job done.

And, in a direct marketing company, *marketing is paramount!* Marketers have their fingers in every part of the direct marketing system's pie. The idea is to pull out as many "plums" as possible. Realize, however, that plums are elusive! Nonetheless, it is the marketer's job to develop the strategies that will successfully meet the outlined objectives.

The development of marketing concepts that lead to marketing strategies is similar to panning for gold. The small nuggets...the business-as-usual type...are in the stream. Logical analysis and linear thinking help the marketer to capture enough small nuggets to keep things going. But, the demand is greater than that.

Here is Einstein's "fantasy." That single moment of insight—of illumination—when the marketer knows...knows for sure that the idea he is forming is a big winner...the twenty-pound nugget.

When that glorious, blinding flash of brilliant understanding strikes, most often it is preceded by linear examination. But it is created by thinking "outside the nine-dot square." Thinking that does not violate fundamentals is needed, the type that displays an intense grasp of a possibility, perhaps never before considered.

Such conceptualizing cannot happen in a production line environment. It cannot happen on demand. It can happen only in the right atmosphere—an atmosphere of unbridled curiosity, piercing questioning, and lateral thinking. Sometimes, it is the result of sheer accident—stumbling across a set of facts, a trend, or an idea overlooked in the past.

The trick is to recognize it.

So, marketing strategies are, essentially, ideas in motion. Concepts that are compelling and capable of continued growth.

The development of effective and efficient marketing strategies addresses three basic elements: research and development, products, and markets.

In *research and development*, a strategy might be birthed to employ corporate resources to develop a sophisticated database to support an objective of increasing policyowner marketing profitability by 15%.

Another...to engage in focus-group interviewing in order to develop three new health products, supporting the objective of increasing the health product portfolio income by one million dollars, and profit by 5%.

Notice the macro-nature of the strategy. *Strategies* are the alternatives chosen for the employment of resources to achieve a planned effect.

So, too, for *products*. This section deals with your entire portfolio. Concise definitions of each product—new and old—are included, as well as an identification of the role you expect each to play in achieving the objectives.

List the features of the products and the profitability of each product—either in terms of objective T/MC ratios, or actual profit margins.

Then stipulate broad strategies. For example, a product strategy might be to offer guaranteed-issue term life insurance to meet the objective of increasing life insurance sales by 20% during the next year, and to increase overall persistency of the policyowner base by 3%.

Marketing considerations provide the triggers for the strategic planning process. In general, this part of the planning process identifies the markets you are penetrating, and those you intend to penetrate in order to achieve the plan's objectives. In broad terms, your first step is to identify each market you intend to solicit in support of the plan.

The following outline may prove helpful:

Market Specification Outline
_____

Identification Generic type (broad, endorsed, policyowner, association, club, etc.)

Total universe An estimate of the total number of consumers, households, or members represented in the market selected

Market composition A look at who populates the market, a narrative of its members, and specific characteristics of the members (i.e., conservative vs. liberal, wealth rating "A" vs. wealth rating "B," etc.)

Demographic characteristics A definition of age, gender, income, etc.

Media The media available for reaching your target market: direct mail, space advertising, telemarketing, television two-step, print inquiry/conversion

Affinity An estimate of the market's affinity—how the members of the market "hang together"—member of a group, club, or association, bankcard holders, trusted group

Payment options An important consideration, how the members

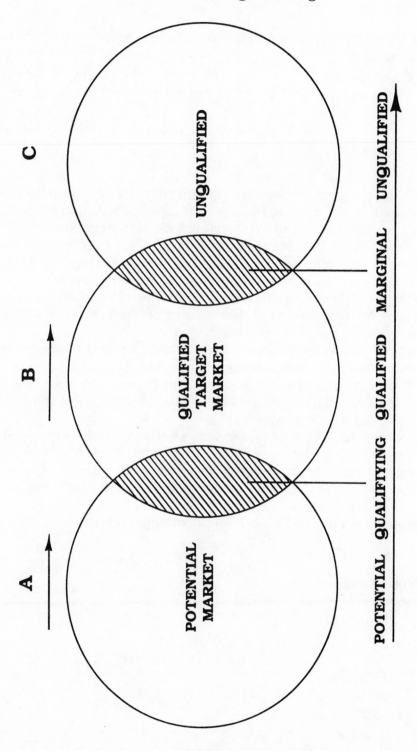

Figure 7-1: Markets are dynamic with populations moving through eligibility stages.

of your target market desire to pay premium—credit card, direct bill, or check-o-matic

Organizational relationships Any outstanding relationships with brokers, agents, other broad organizations—for example, credit card issuers

Remarks Other pertinent data worth commenting on relating to the specific market

* * *

By defining the markets you are planning to solicit, you begin to examine the bridges from objectives to strategies and the obstacles and advantages of each. You are looking for the levers that unlock the particular markets.

Be assured that this search is not an easy one. In July 1984, LIMRA undertook a research study in an effort to discover exactly who buys insurance directly. The results are illuminating. When the report was released, the results became very controversial. But, in a very preliminary way, the results provide clues concerning the character of direct marketing insurance buyers.

Direct life insurance buyers Of the total, 37% were headed by persons 35-49 years of age; 41% were parents with children present in the households.

Direct health insurance buyers In this group, 76% were headed by persons age 50+; 67% had incomes under $20,000; 82% had less than a college degree; 50% were not employed.

Direct auto, home/renter insurance Of the total, 40% were headed by persons with a college degree or more; 31% had income of $35,000+.

Whole life insurance represented 35% of the most recent purchases, 54% term insurance, and 11% other. Median policy size was $20,000 term life, and $6,000 whole life.

What was the purpose for life insurance bought directly?

	Policy Size		
	To $10m	$10m-$19m	$20m+
Final Expenses	81%	60%	47%
Security	21	40	66
Mortgage	2	2	17
	Income		
	To $20m	$20m-$35m	$35m+
Final Expenses	75%	53%	41%
Supplement	18	29	25
Mortgage	3	8	17

	Age			
	To 35	35-49	50-64	65+
Final Expenses	56%	49%	73%	81%
Security	54	48	26	38
Mortgage	15	6	5	0

Here is a good example of how research unlocks reality. Perhaps these results confirm your own experience. What may be even more interesting to a marketer are the reasons recent purchases were made directly, as opposed to buying from an agent:

Less expensive	50%
Policy meets needs	13
Convenient, easier	12
Advertising	7
Company reputation	6
Endorsed by association	4
Other	8
	100%

There's more:

What are the reasons respondents gave for buying consumer goods directly?

	Bought Directly		
	Life	Others	Non-Buyers
Convenient	85%	87%	78%
Saves time	65	66	60
Product available	56	60	59
Advertisements	36	37	29
Less expensive	34	32	31
No salesmen			
Will call	40	35	29
To deal with	32	27	23

What did respondents consider very important when deciding on a direct purchase?

	Bought Directly		
	Life	Others	Non-Buyers
Explanations	88%	93%	90%
Ease of purchase	64	67	68
Toll-free number			
To purchase	58	68	68
Make claims	79	82	81
Other service	81	84	81
Use of credit card	18	16	23
No agent will call	40	41	29
No physical exam	38	40	34

Among respondents, what percentage would consider buying directly?

Life insurance	66%	23%	11%
Hosp/med	40	50	14
Auto	30	50	16
Home/renters	24	37	11

As you can see, the insurance direct marketing buyer is elusive—as elusive as the "plums" the marketer needs to pull out of his pie. But, by integrating the right research and development assignments with the right products to the right markets... *voila—a plum!*

Say you have examined your markets and your products and done the research you need to do. Now, you are prepared to examine marketing strategies. Take a look at a few examples.

Most companies are interested in growing... and controlled growth strategies are common in insurance direct marketing.

At the moment, it appears that the market for direct marketing insurance products is finite. That is, the number of people who will consider purchasing insurance protection by mail is limited to about 5 to 6% of the 80 million, or so, households in the United States.

That does not mean the market is not expandable. It is. It simply means that, at this stage in the market's growth, insurance direct marketers are going to have to work harder to achieve deeper penetration.

Nonetheless, in examining a marketing strategy of growth there are several choices in which to invest:

a. New policyowner acquisition

b. The development of new media for offer presentation

c. New, innovative insurance products, or other services

d. The expansion of the policyowner marketing programs to increase the number of times policyowners are contacted.

e. Technological innovation that creates new access to key market segments

Chances are, if your company decides on a marketing strategy of growth, there will be some interrelationships among these specific strategies. These interrelationships depend in large part on the specific financial goals and specific financial strategies your company chooses to employ.

7. *Financial strategy* It is foolish to believe that marketing is separate from finance.

The financial-strategy part of your plan should outline specifically how each of the three areas of marketing—endorsed marketing, broad marketing, and policyowner marketing—will contribute to the financial objectives outlined in Section 5.

What about those financial objectives? There are four basic financial goals a company pursues in its operations:

First, it might seek to maximize sales. *Size* frequently equates with *success*. To the outside world, the larger your sales volume, obviously, the smarter you are. Big numbers mean big profits. The substance of neither of these statements is necessarily true. An expansion marketing strategy certainly supports a financial objective of increased sales, especially when supported by relational marketing and LTV.

Second, your company may seek to maximize profits. This greatly affects the financial thinking of an organization—especially if it is owned by one person. Volume frequently is sacrificed in favor of higher profits. Even if your company is owned by many persons, increased profit per share is a particularly attractive goal and strategy. It is less appropriate to a marketing strategy of growth.

Third, maximizing your profit as a percentage of sales may be the goal. This speaks to a balance between volume and profitability. As a goal and strategy, this is particularly appropriate, if your company needs to raise money from investors, outside financial institutions, or others.

Fourth, maximizing return on investment is clearly the most sophisticated approach to financial planning—and perhaps most appropriate for a relatively mature marketing company. This technique simply demands certain predetermined levels of investment return for each marketing dollar spent, on a unit-for-unit basis.

Fundamental to each of these goals and strategies is the concept of lifetime value and relational marketing.

Since policyowner marketing delivers the highest profitability and highest return on investment for the insurance direct marketing organization, it follows that the more responsive your policyowners, the better your results will be.

To attract those policyowners, you must invest your solicitation dollars in high-yield markets. You must increase sales. When you increase sales, you increase the number of available policyowners to resolicit. When you resolicit your policyowner base, you increase your profits and return on investment. This is syllogistically sound!

An insurance direct marketing strategy of growth satisfies almost all the basic requirements of the insurance direct marketing system. It is the soundest reason to be in the business in the first place. Remember the system!

While you develop your goals and strategies to deliver the profit you have defined, there are seven critical support areas in which strategies must be developed in support of your proposed programs.

8. *Administrative (operational) strategy* This is discussed by category:

Data processing strategy develops the support systems necessary for getting information from applications into the masterfile. The DP function propels the direct marketing system.

Fulfillment is the fundamental consumer contact with your company. The design of your fulfillment material clearly communicates how you feel about your new policyowner. Fulfillment material must be attractive, informative, simple to understand, and compelling. You need to make an *impression* on your new policyowner—an impression that fulfills the promises you made in the solicitation material.

Here's an important point: It doesn't matter whether you fulfill with printed material, personal visit, or a telephone call. *You need to make the best impression possible on your new customer!*

Premium billing and collection is another critical function, without which a company would not survive very long. This is a DP-driven function. You must constantly seek improvement, reinforce buying decisions, and force paying decisions.

Underwriting, claims, and customer service strategies deal not only with the service functions of the direct marketing system, but with the policyowner marketing programs as well. You seek the *satisfied* customer. There is no one to intervene on your behalf. There are no agents, yet you know a happy customer will buy and buy again.

Finally, *legal and regulatory* strategies are necessary to keep you out of trouble and in the marketplace.

Good insurance regulatory relations with each of the fifty state departments, and the strategic implications thereof, are essential for everything from product filings to advertising approval. It is true that your lawyers must be no less sales-minded than your marketers.

Operational strategic development is a difficult, attention-to-detail business. It is in this area that the concept of home office is discarded—and appropriately so.

A marketing company must pay as much attention to its "backroom" operations, and frequently more, than it does to its "front-end" marketing.

9. *Short-term tactical strategy* Your strategic plan clearly is developed on a macro-basis. However, in its development, certain tactical considerations become apparent.

Perhaps, for example, there is a short-term marketing opportunity, lasting for only 30, 60, or 90 days, which needs to be addressed. It should be, and it should be addressed in a special section of your plan.

While such an opportunity may never recur, it needs to be as fully developed as possible, as part of the strategic planning process. In fact, a variety of tactical factors may need to be addressed as a matter of policy. You should address them here.

10. *Long-term strategic implications* This section deals with the co-ordination of your plan with senior management's long-range planning. Your plan must mesh with the setting of overall corporate goals and your company's mission statement. Both define what the company wants and hopes to be in three, five, seven, or as long as ten years in the future.

In terms of direct marketing, it is almost impossible to speculate so far into the future. Windows of marketing opportunities usually slam shut within a relatively short time.

Marketplace dynamics are hard to predict anywhere near ten years ahead. Technology changes so rapidly that the DP system you are using today—even if relatively new—may well be obsolete in three years.

However, on a corporate level, certain generic objectives and broad policy guidelines can be developed. It is important to insure that your strategic planning serves those corporate goals.

SECRET No. 19

The development of the most effective insurance direct marketing strategic plan is a team effort, in which every system function has a representative on the team. It is a thoughtful, provocative, provoking, synergistic procedure, which demands the best from every member of the planning group.

The processes of strategic planning have come a long way since Arthur DeMoss counseled a "research-test-explode" philosophy of marketing. Yet, even with the sophistication of a functional, effective strategic plan supporting your insurance direct marketing operations, his idea is a good one. And, one that direct marketers employ every day.

Let's see how research-test-explode works in the four marketing environments of the insurance direct marketing business, starting with endorsed marketing.

VIII

The Secrets of
Endorsed Marketing

Few secrets of insurance direct marketing are as well hidden as the key to third-party, or endorsed, marketing. Most frequently, companies entering the business pursue this class of business...purposely or by accident.

Because of long-standing business relationships—usually with brokers—targets of opportunity crop up that are mouth watering to companies that have engaged in the true group business. This may lead to the company's charging into an area about which it knows little. Usually, the most successful third-party insurance organizations develop their expertise through many years of experience—some effective and some otherwise.

Now, *third-party marketing*, in insurance direct marketing terms, is simply a communication by an organization—not necessarily affiliated with the insurance company—to its members or customers, recommending that they purchase the offered product.

In theory, and frequently in practice, the credibility of the endorsing organization is such that the recommendation will be followed by a significant number of people. Therefore, response rates are higher, persistency is greater, and there is more profit to share with the endorsing organization.

The secret of response rates ranging from 5 to 30 issued apps per thousand is *affinity*.

SECRET No. 20

The stronger the affinity among the endorsing organization's customer base, the more successful an endorsed insurance direct marketing program will be.

Undoubtedly, some of the highest response rates in third-party marketing have been experienced by groups such as American Association of Retired Persons, Catholic Golden Age, Bankcard Holders of America, Avon Representatives Group Insurance Trust, American Legion, Veterans of Foreign Wars, Overseas Discount Shopping Service, Dreyfus Fund shareholders, credit unions, and similar organizations. These are examples of classic third-party or endorsed marketing opportunities.

One of the most difficult jobs of the endorsed marketer is to evaluate a third-party opportunity in an effort to determine how well a program might do. The following checklist may be helpful:

Opportunity Ratings for Affinity-
Group, Third-Party Sponsorship Offers

A. Size of Market (number of persons)   Value Rating

    Over 500,000 ....
    250,000 - 500,000 ....
    100,000 - 250,000 ....
    50,000 - 100,000 ....
    25,000 - 50,000 ....
    Under 25,000 ....

B. Affinity Evaluation (type of group)

    Employer-employee ....
    Consumer association ....
    Special purpose ....
    Labor union ....
    Credit union ....
    Commercial bank/credit-card issuer ..
    Private label credit card ....
    Fraternal ....
    Social ....
    Religious ....
    Consumer medical organizations ......
    Business/professional/honorary ....

Value Rating

Travel & expense cards ....
Mail-order buyer lists ....
Utilities ....
Telephone companies ....
Groups limited/no natural affinity .....

C. Endorsement Rating

Endorsement assures complete confidence in product and serious consideration by recipient ....

Endorsement carries a great deal of weight and is meaningful. The recipient has confidence in the capabilities and purpose of the sponsoring organization and will react favorably to recommendation ....

Endorsement has some meaning and offers an advantage over a cold approach. The recipient may feel that the endorser will profit from his involvement, yet it would not give the recommendation unless it felt offering was a good one ....

Endorsement carries minimum weight or there is a low transferability of referrer image with regard to insurance product ....

D. Demographic Information Available

1. Age/gender/income/education/ previous mail-order buyer/occupation/home ownership/ car ownership/family size ....

2. Age/gender/occupation/income/home ownership/family size ....

3. Age/gender/occupation/income .....

4. Age/gender/income ....

5. For any one element ....

6. For no available demographics ......

E. Group Communications

109

Possible means of communicating with group:

Value Rating

    1. Monthly newsletter/magazines ....

    2. Quarterly (or less) newsletter/
magazine ....

    3. Billing notices ....

    4. Periodic letters ....

    5. Regular visits ....

    6. Regular meetings ....

    7. Other ....

    8. None ....

F. Do group members make periodic
   payments?

    Yes ....

    No ....

G. Growth of Group in Last Three Years

    100% or more ....

    50% - 100% ....

    25% - 50% ....

    10% - 25% ....

    Under 10% ....

H. Premium-Payment Possibilities

    1. Payroll deduction ....

    2. Deduction from automatic payments

    3. Personal collection ....

    4. Credit card ....

    5. Other automatic payment ....

    6. Payment book ....

    7. Direct bill (affinity 80+) ....

    8. Direct bill (affinity $<$ 80) ....   _____

    Total Rating Points.......................   ========

    Total from line above/8 = Rating ....   ========

In general, the more desirable characteristics appear in descending order (highest at top). You can assign your own rating points to each characteristic (on a scale of 1 to 10, from 1 to 100, or A to Z).

Most organizations have some experience with evaluating potential third-party accounts. This checklist helps to focus on what is important in determining affinity and potential response.

What you are looking for are distinguishing features which help break down into *success* possibilities. You want to assign a high opportunity, good opportunity, marginal opportunity, or low opportunity rating to the third-party or endorsing organization.

Basically, you are seeking the degree of risk you are willing to assume when marketing to the third party.

Once you have evaluated a prospective third-party account and have decided to solicit its customer base, you are faced with another difficult task—compensation.

The whole question of third-party compensation is a critical one, and will influence the success of your program enormously. Normally, endorsers are compensated in standard commission arrangements—a certain percentage of collected premium first year and renewal.

However, in all jurisdictions an entity must be licensed to receive commissions. This requirement tends to complicate commission payments. Consequently, the industry has turned to the present-value-compensation (PVC) scheme to uncomplicate the regulations.

PVC payments are determined by looking at the premium income stream anticipated from the account, discounting its value, and paying the endorser on the basis of so many dollars per thousand names mailed.

The problem with PVC payments is that no matter what the results of the program are—good or bad—you've paid for the endorsement up front. And, no endorser is going to return your dollars, if things don't work out.

Intervention might be the answer—bringing in a broker or agent to act as an intermediary. You pay commissions to the intermediary and the intermediary works out compensation agreements with the endorsing organization. For example, New York State allows licensed agents and brokers to compensate non-licensed list owners for insurance solicitation to their lists on a commission basis.

Whatever compensation scheme you choose, you must set up an effective *service agreement* with the endorsing organization. In some cases, this requires a "participation" agreement in a group-insurance master contract. In others, this agreement simply takes the form of a contract with the endorsing organization.

The key here is that a service agreement is needed to provide both parties with the details of how the program is going to work and what the obligations are. Moreover, it provides compensation ground rules and establishes the relationship between the parties.

An effective third-party relationship is one where there is free communication between or among the parties—underwriter, endorser, and (if present) the intermediary. Communication means helping each other. It means cooperating with each other. It means telling the truth— about anticipated response rates, projected compensation, mailing dates, and results of the program.

Absolutely the worst thing a third-party insurance marketer can do is *overestimate* the response rates and the compensation a third party can receive. Nothing can destroy a relationship faster.

And, today, effective third-party marketing must seek to establish long-term relationships. In fact, the degree of investment for third-party marketing—not just in marketing cost, but in staffing, administration, and systems, as well—requires a longer view than has been common in the past. This is because:

SECRET No. 21

The most effective relationship, leading to successful third-party insurance direct marketing programs, is one where the endorser and the underwriter agree to a long-term, multiple-product, joint-venture program.

This is a relatively skillful solution to the complicated opportunities to make third-party endorsements work. The reason concerns not only compensation to the third party; it involves one of the most basic rules of direct marketing—one frequently overlooked by companies going into the third-party markets.

SECRET No. 22

Never…never…never, under any circumstance, mail an endorsing organization's entire customer file until you have tested for response!

What seems apparent to the direct marketer, sometimes appears obscure to the inexperienced third-party insurance direct marketing company—and even more obscure to the endorsing organization.

After all, the third party wants to generate income from its customer base. So, too, the underwriter wants to generate income from the customer base. What could be more natural than to mail an entire file of 50,000, 100,000, or 200,000 names. However, in seven out of ten cases, the solicitation will fail! It will not meet its financial criteria.

Now, response testing need not necessarily be in-market (actual-mailing) testing. However, mailing ten thousand pieces of direct mail on an "Nth" name basis is better than no testing at all.

There are research techniques available to determine market-response indications. But, in fact, the larger the endorser's marketing universe, the more opportunity there is for in-market testing and research.

This marketing attitude requires a great deal of skill on the part of your sales force. However, testing justifies your investment in the endorser's market. And it is clearly beneficial to the endorsing organization—for it will maximize the endorser's income over a long period of time.

If you are committed to third-party marketing, it is a good idea for you to separate *sales expense* from *marketing expense* in your endorsed-marketing activities. Sales expense includes those expenses associated with acquiring the endorser. Marketing expense includes those expenses associated with acquiring the policyowner. Which leads to:

SECRET No. 23

Assign to your sales efforts a client-acquisition budget (a sales expense budget) that is separate from your company's endorsed marketing budget.

The result of such policy is that your sales force will have maximum competitive compensation possibilities to allocate to the most promising third-party opportunities. Yes, they can "buy" the business. Moreover, they have the capability to make the most palatable deals for allowing your marketers to test.

The marketers, on the other hand, now have the opportunity to meet realistic financial goals in their marketing efforts. What about those marketing efforts?

Too frequently, marketers fail to remember direct marketing requirements, techniques, and attitudes, when soliciting endorsed-marketing accounts.

Endorsed-marketing accounts represent definable market segments with distinguishable characteristics, just as any market segment does.

The elements that drive third-party market response are exactly the same elements that drive market response for rented lists—with an important difference. When soliciting the third-party market, the marketer expects a response "lift" because of the credibility of the endorser. In fact:

SECRET No. 24

The strength of your response is directly proportional to the third party's willingness to express the endorsement throughout the solicitation material. The higher the endorser visibility in the material, the higher the response.

Therefore, it seems reasonable that compensation to third parties needs to be tied to their participation in the solicitation. While endorsers normally have some hesitancy regarding the strength of their endorsement, it is necessary to obtain the strongest endorsement possible. This is limited, in general, by regulatory considerations.

Several years ago, California limited the use of endorsements for insurance products among Savings & Loan Associations. The result was that mailings made to well-established, responsive California S&L accounts yielded response rates roughly 50% less than before the regulation was passed.

This is a dramatic example of unwarranted intrusion on the part of regulators—and perhaps a testament to the strength of the agents' lobby, as well. Nonetheless, it is an equally persuasive illustration of the power of the third party's endorsement.

While affinity drives successful third-party marketing, it is a two-edged sword. For the most part, endorsed markets are static markets. When the market arrives at relative maturity, there is minimal growth. It becomes finite.

The organization may become a victim of its own affinity. That is what makes the concept of multiple-product, multiple-year marketing arrangements so important.

Single-product marketing agreements severely restrict the marketer's ability to penetrate the third-party market. Since the marketing universe is relatively static, single-product mailings quickly skim the cream, the "responders," from the marketing base. What is left are "non-responders," people who—for whatever reasons—have no propensity to respond to direct marketing offers received through the various direct marketing media available to the marketer.

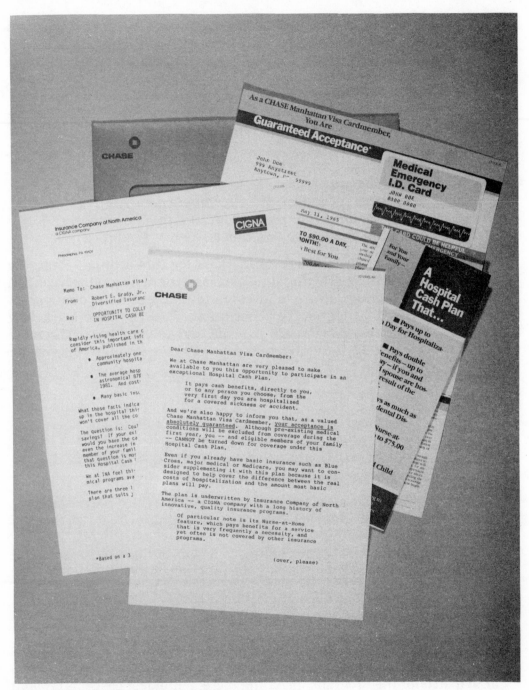

Figure 8-1: From "lift letter" to OSE, endorser identification is critical.

Product variation, in the course of a marketing year, may well help to penetrate the "non-responders." In theory, those non-responders who, though uninterested in a hospital cash plan, may be attracted by a term life plan.

To the marketer, these non-responders are enormously important, because in every instance non-responders represent the majority of the marketing universe available. Therefore:

SECRET No. 25

In third-party, joint-venture marketing, market penetration is critical. That is why agreements that allow for multiple-product marketing are more desirable than those that don't.

There are some obvious substantiations for this attitude. First, the longer the term of the marketing agreement and the more products you can offer, the more willing you are to invest in in-market testing and market research. Second, the higher the penetration of the endorsed-marketing universe, the more policyowners you will add to your base. The more policyowners you add, the more profit you will make through policyowner marketing. So:

SECRET No. 26

The most successful endorsed-marketing joint ventures allow the marketing company to crossload and add additional policyowner products through policyowner marketing programs.

Once you have arrived at the agreement with the third-party client, the marketers move in to execute the marketing programs. To do so, they will create a tactical marketing plan.

The tactical marketing plan, or program plan, outlines in considerable detail the steps necessary to execute the program. It includes:

1. *Program Objectives* Marketing objectives, financial objectives, and testing objectives

2. *Product* A complete description of the product to be offered

3. *Financial Projections* Total expense and income streams anticipated for the program, including incremental test costs and rollout expenses, plus response projections

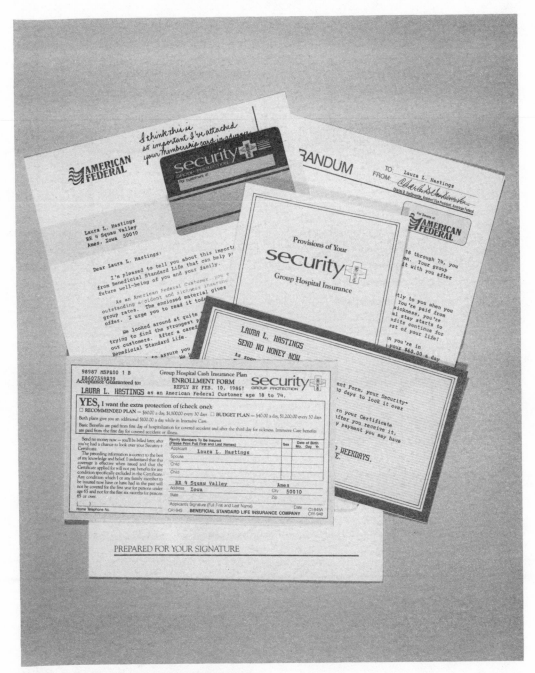

Figure 8-2: New formats are necessary to overcome static markets. Personalization can frequently give material a big boost.

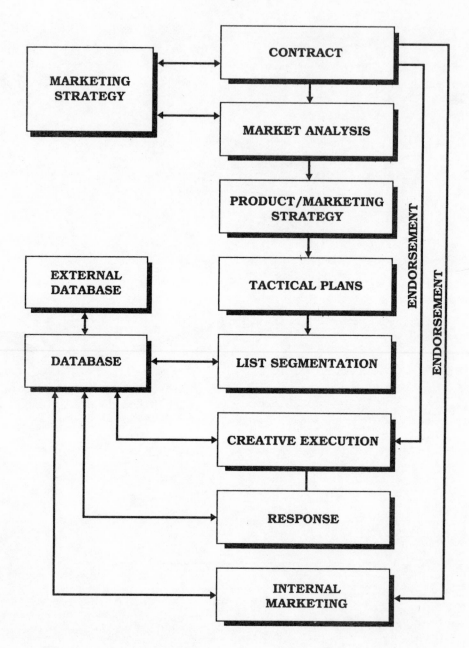

Figure 8-3: Endorsed (or third-party) marketing model. Note the use of the database *and* internal marketing to enhance revenues for both endorser and company.

4. *Segmentation Techniques* From file information, through overlays, by file appending, or by use of other segmentation methods

5. *Media Matrix* Selection of media to solicit the market—most frequently direct mail or telemarketing, but can include support advertising in newspapers, on television or radio, "take-one" boxes, billing inserts, and telemarketing support

6. *Tracking Data File* Keying information, by specific market segment to track each element of the program within the test matrix

7. *Solicitation Marketing Considerations* Offer structures, creative material to be used, and premium-payment options

While the outline of the plan is self-explanatory, there are some unique considerations relating to endorsed marketing that are worth examining. The first:

SECRET No. 27

First-time, endorsed-marketing mailings deliver response rates approximately 25% higher than subsequent mailings to the same file in markets under 750,000 net names.

One of the elements that influences what kind of results your marketers get is the condition of the third-party list. It is remarkable that endorsers generally don't keep their lists in very good shape—unless, of course, the list is generated using direct marketing techniques.

Especially, is this surprising, when you consider that the most successful endorsers are usually billing their members on some periodic basis. Savings & loan associations seem to be prime offenders in this area.

Frequently, information critical to the insurance direct marketer is not captured by the endorsing organization. This is most often true about age. Since insurance direct marketing products are developed to attract different age segments of the general marketplace, it becomes critical to know the ages of third-party market members. Without it, successful product selection becomes difficult. With it, your chances of success are greatly enhanced.

There are three primary means of finding age for files without the data available.

The first is the *overlay method.* Using census-table data or some other geo-demographic database, the endorsed-marketing file is matched against overlay file. What emerges are age clusters, sometimes identifiable down to zip levels. The overlay method in endorsed marketing is not wonderfully effective, but somewhat better than nothing.

Second is the *age-appending method*. Here a database of individual records, all with date-of-birth or actual-age information, is matched against the endorsed-marketing list. Usually the match rate—or "hit rate"—is about 40 to 50%. However, the larger the individual-record database, the higher the "hit rate."

Finally, a unique system for age segmentation was developed around 1983 based on social security numbers. This means can be referred to as the social-security-number (SSN) method. It began on the premise that individuals 65 and over can be segmented within a given file, based on the fourth and fifth digits of their social security number. Using a simple "if, then" algorithm, the fourth and fifth digits of the SSN are matched against a "table" of two-digit numbers first issued by the Social Security Administration at the program's inception in 1936.

Basic to the premise is the assumption that individuals were at least 18 years old in 1936 when issued their SSN. When applied to certain S&L files, the technique produced response rates for Medicare supplement products that clearly indicated the system worked.

The problem with the system is that it is finite. There are only "X" number of permutations of the Social Security I.D. numbers available. There will come a time when these numbers will be recycled and given to younger individuals.

In fact, it may already be starting. Refinements developed at the University of Delaware, and tested against known-age databases, indicate that the system can be used to identify age segments of individuals in the 21-65 band, with significant probability of accuracy.

The perfect solution to the *age* problem is to have the endorsing organization capture the information at the outset. In a joint-venture environment, you can help them do it.

There are several more observations regarding the condition of the endorsing organization's list. Frequently, you will discover a considerable degree of *duplication* of list records.

It will pay dividends for you to "de-dupe" the list before mailing. It is likely that you will lose up to 25% of the records through this process. But, at today's per-thousand mailing cost, you can end up saving a bundle.

Finally, the more recent the list is run, the higher the response rate is likely to be. Recency of a name, frequency of purchase, and volume of dollars are helpful in selecting lists. The *old* recency-frequency monetary formula is still applicable today. In a service environment such as banks, S&Ls, and credit-card issuers, frequency of purchase can be replaced by frequency of transactions. Nonetheless, you should consider applying this formula whenever possible.

In general:

SECRET No. 28

Effective segmentation techniques are critical to successful third-party marketing programs. The more segmentation possibilities are explored and implemented, the more successful the endorsed program will be.

This is especially true when you consider product customization for individual third-party accounts. Obviously, it is almost useless to offer an insurance direct marketing product designed for people over the age of 50 to a list of customers or members aged 25 to 45.

However, if the list can be segmented into a group over age 50, and another under age 50, two products can be offered—each appropriate to the specific age segment.

That is "the obvious." What may not be so obvious are the demands of the client population.

In true-group situations—employer/employee markets, for example—product demand is primarily for basic and major medical coverages, group life coverages, long- and short-term disability coverages, and some of the more complicated forms of P&C coverages. Some product configurations are not particularly suited to the demands of simplicity required by the system.

Association groups demand major medical, accident and disability, and P&C product configurations. Several specialty companies offer these—designed in a relatively simple way—to the membership bases.

Consumer markets, such as consumer associations, banks, S&Ls, credit unions, credit-card issuers, and mail-order buyer lists, are more apt to accept the supplementary coverages specifically designed for the direct marketing system.

If products are designed in a modular way, the natural demand of the endorsing organization, for customization, can be satisfied. For example, in a hospital cash plan (HIP), you have some options in configuring a specific product to your endorser's market. These may include a variety of daily indemnity benefit levels, first- and third-day payments, selected riders like ICU (intensive care), cancer, heart attack and stroke, and convalescent care.

Flexible benefit levels, inventive riders, and price advantages in endorsed-marketing products allow you to match products to markets in a logical way.

In fact, these same elements are absolutely critical to a process essential to endorsed-marketing program success: *the structure of offers.*

Offer structures are driven by the product and the marketing strategy associated with the program. In insurance direct marketing, offers are what attract consumers' attention—and, hopefully, force the ultimate purchase.

Offers can affect response rates by 25, 50, 75, even 100 percent or more. And the manner in which your offer is presented can have an equally dramatic effect. Consider these offers:

1. Buy two books for $1.00, get two books FREE!

2. Choose any 4 books for $1.00.

3. Choose any four books...25¢ each!

Essentially, the offers are exactly the same. But, #2 has been the standard book-club offer for years. Obviously, it was the winner.

For years, one of the most effective offers in insurance direct marketing was the deviated premium. The first month's coverage is offered for a quarter or a dollar. In fact, some companies still use it. The idea was to attract the maximum number of prospective insureds, and then convert them to full-premium-paying policyowners.

Today, that offer has changed to "free information," particularly on television, in the hope of achieving the same objective.

While Chapters IX and XII explore "offer structure" in detail, there is a particular consideration which is appropriate to examine here. That is the concept of price.

SECRET No. 29

The lower the price of your product, the greater chance your product has to succeed in the market. In short, the higher the response rate.

After years of offering deviated premiums and underpriced products, insurance direct marketers started to fool themselves into believing that products had to be "sold," and were not price sensitive.

Nonsense!

It is true that insurance direct marketing products must be sold. So must financial services, book clubs, record clubs, and hard goods be sold. This applies absolutely to any product offered through the direct marketing system.

But, consider this: In the LIMRA research displayed in Chapter VII, the principal reason people gave for purchasing was that the product was less expensive! Decisions were based upon PRICE. Nothing else even came close. In fact, association endorsement as a reason for purchasing was a dismal 4%, compared to 50% for price.

Remember, too, that Chapter IV reported the results of the Avon focus-group interviews. *To those women, low cost was much more important than high benefits!*

The evidence appears persuasive that, in structuring your offers, one of your principal considerations must be the prices you are charging. This applies the concept of conquest rates.

In addition to offer structures, solicitation strategy is critical in endorsed marketing. Possibly the first thing you should consider is the use of cash-with-application vs. send-no-money offers. *It is always better to receive cash with your applications.* The question: Is it appropriate for every market?

The answer is... *test!*

In fact, this is one of the first in-market tests you should run against any endorsed market. Front-end response will always be higher with a send-no-money offer. With an effective conversion program, you may increase your issue rate by as much as 2 applications per thousand.

But, be careful. Historically, one of the enormous advantages of endorsed marketing over broad marketing is the persistency of the policyowner. *Endorsed-marketing policyowners persist better than broad-market policyowners.* You must examine lapse rates carefully against send-no-money offers, to ensure that lapse rates do not increase compared to lapse rates of the cash-with-app policyowners.

Policyowner persistency is also an important consideration when deciding on premium-payment options. It is always true that *automatic premium payments are better than direct-bill premium payments.*

In fact, the persistency rate for the following forms is 20% to 40% better than direct-bill premium payers: automatic premium payers, pre-

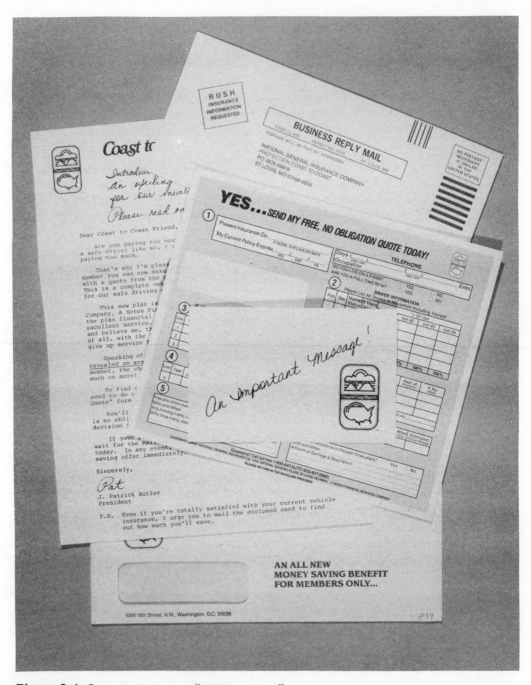

Figure 8-4: Group auto uses a "saving money"
theme to generate RFQs—request for quotations.

authorized checking, credit cards, and automatic deductions.

Remember, the trick to insurance direct marketing profitability is to keep *as many* policyowners as possible paying premiums *as long* as possible. Persistency increases product profitability. And, it certainly increases policyowner lifetime value. Both are highly desirable conditions.

Another aspect of solicitation strategy is media considerations. Most endorsed marketing depends on direct-mail solicitation as a principal media strategy. It is part of your marketing strategy and tactics—after looking at the market—to determine how much you can afford to spend to obtain a policyowner.

You will run into situations where the expense of solo direct-mail efforts simply cannot be effectively recovered, because of the mini-market problem. Usually mini-markets deliver under 100,000 net name circulation.

Consider syndications.

A *syndication* is simply making available prepared direct-mail solicitation material for a specific product or service to a list owner for mailing to his own list, with a minimum amount of endorser personalization.

In the endorsed-insurance markets, technology exists today that can provide quite a lot of personalization—laser fill-in techniques, for example—that makes this solicitation method practical and cost effective in developing the smaller-circulation marketing opportunities. The problem, of course, is that the endorser has minimum input to the material.

This method, in fact, is particularly effective in a marketing environment which few insurance direct marketers consider: the agency and brokerage markets.

Logic tells us that an insurance agent goes to quite a lot of trouble in making a sale on a one-to-one basis. History also shows us that once a sale is made, minimum effort is expended in following up the sale. Yet, what is true in general direct marketing terms—your own customers are your best prospects for future sales—must be true for agents and brokers, as well.

It is equally true that few agents or brokers can possibly handle a volume business—sales in the thousands, for example. But, there is an affinity to the customer relationship. Trust is one of the foundations of the agent's sales. Exploiting that relationship makes sense. Syndication is the way to do it cost effectively.

And, it has been done successfully in the past. AIG ran a successful broker syndication in the early 1970s. So did AID Insurance Services and at the same time. The technique was successfully exported to Europe, with

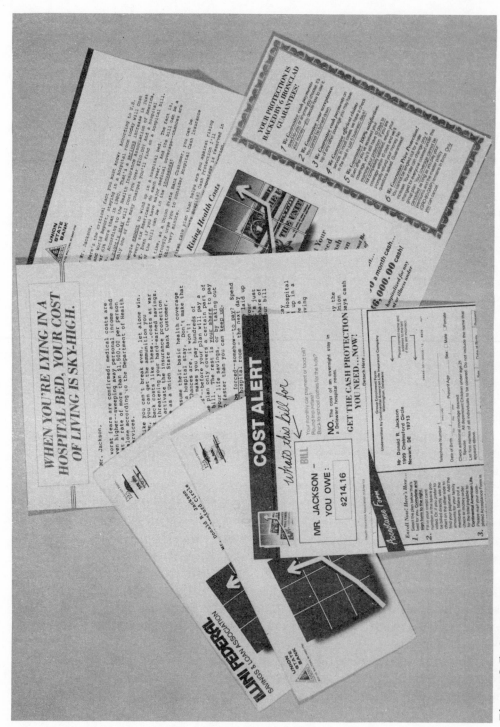

Figure 8-5: Syndication, using personalization, allows you to stabilize successful creative while tailoring the material to the endorser.

marvelous results in the Netherlands and France, where response rates achieved double digits!

Today, several companies are soliciting major insurers with large agency forces to test the technique. It is certainly a concept worth exploring in any direct marketing environment.

Lastly, some observations regarding third-party insurance marketing.

Effective endorsed-marketing programs require a great deal of work. An element is introduced into the direct marketing equation that does not exist in broad marketing. That difference is the client.

The third-party client comes in all sizes and shapes and a variety of emotional postures—understandably so. Client sensitivity is acute. After all, you will be soliciting the client's bread and butter—his list of customers. Notwithstanding the "deal," probably the most important thing to realize is that the first growl of discontent from your client's customers lands you in his doghouse.

Obviously, you must be careful. On the other hand, you cannot lose control of the account. Every client believes his market is different, better, and unique. And, while that may be true, you have the marketing expertise and experience to make your joint-venture insurance program work.

Frustration is your constant companion in third-party marketing. Learn to handle it and you can build a dynamic, exciting, profitable business. A business that can form the foundation—as has been done by companies before—can have a tremendously magical insurance direct marketing adventure.

Frustration is a less constant companion in the world of broad marketing. Unendorsed insurance direct marketing programs aimed at the American consumer are almost totally controllable. And, while broad marketing may be less frustrating, it is detail ridden, and demands continuously the absolute best the marketer can offer.

Mistakes here can result in huge, unrecoverable losses. Capital intensive, insurance broad marketing offers mouth watering opportunities and possibilities, coupled with serious risk taking.

Let's take a look at some of the secrets that can help you succeed.

The Secrets of
Broad Marketing

"Small opportunities are often the beginning of great enterprises..."

The truth of Demosthenes' statement aptly describes the world of insurance broad marketing. Programs begin small. And successful programs turn into significant endeavors. The marketing philosophy of Art Demoss—*research-test-explode*—is the basic rule of broad marketing, which is corporately-controlled market access.

Your marketers select market segments appropriate for your marketing strategy and focus on them alone. Because there is no endorsing organization to depend on, broad marketing is more flexible than third-party marketing. It is akin to general direct marketing. Figure 9-1 shows a broad-market model.

Governed by general direct marketing principles, broad marketing is an exciting, entrepreneurial operation carried on within the corporate environment. The successful marketer needs to be concerned with every aspect of the system. Because, in a profit-center management organization, the broad marketer makes decisions that commit millions of marketing dollars to generate many millions of premium dollars.

SECRET No. 30

The objective of a broad-marketing program is to

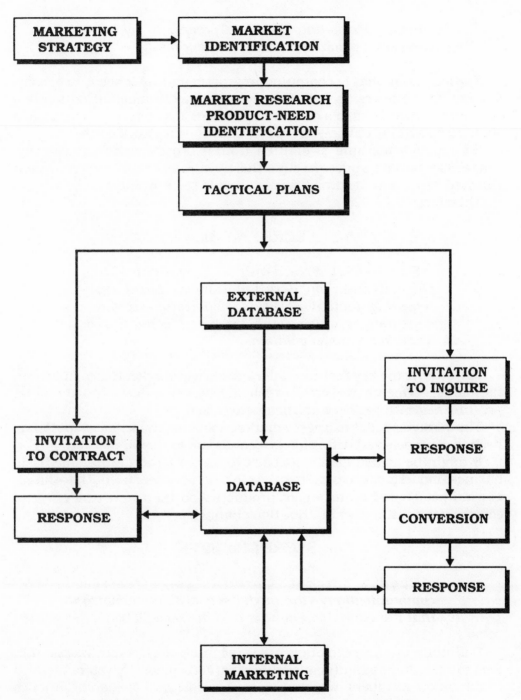

Figure 9-1: Broad-market model. Database/relational marketing is a critical necessity to make programs successful.

create a marketing "loop"—a process in which a successful program repeats itself endlessly.

The loop is familiar to computer programmers, and it needs to become familiar to marketers, as well. The idea is to pay as much attention to a marketing program as to a computer program. If a step is omitted from a computer program, chances are pretty good it won't work correctly.

So, too, if something is omitted from a broad-marketing program, chances are it won't work correctly either. And, considering the investment required to get into the broad market, that is to be avoided.

Therefore:

SECRET No. 31

Successful broad-market programs are characterized by detailed tactical planning—requiring logical patterns of activity—and are dependent as much on the "back end" of the system as on front-end solicitation.

Planning is the key that can unlock the broad-market riches hidden in the market segments you intend to solicit. Now, where does a broad-market program begin? It begins with the market itself.

The marketer needs to target a market segment. Any segment that lends itself to diagnosis and definition is a candidate for broad marketing.

It might be a good idea to go back to basics for a minute. The basic business model for success: There has to be a consumer need. There has to be a market. There have to be good products. And, there have to be effective communications in your distribution channel.

SECRET No. 32

Need ... market ... products ... effective communications—the model seems so elementary that it's worth the reminder and the secret label.

Defining a market segment is not very hard to do, if you think about it. For example, grandparents constitute a market segment, or veterans—also credit union members, working women, credit-card holders. Catholics constitute a market segment, as well as do government employees, homeowners, Blue Cross/Blue Shield subscribers, etc. Notice that these groupings do not mention age, marital status, or gender. Those are demographic distinctions.

Defining a broad-market segment is seeking to define an affinity.

Years ago, it was enough to invite people to purchase your product simply by advertising it. Today, thanks to the information explosion of the seventies, we know considerably more about people than we did in the fifties and sixties. With that knowledge, came the discovery:

SECRET No. 33

Broad-marketing programs work best when directed at groups having a definable affinity. (2)

When you think about it, the broad market is a cross section of people from 18 to 100. Certainly, we can postulate that the eighty million or so households in the market need life insurance or health insurance, But, looking at the numbers...it does not take a cognitive genius to recognize that the market defined in such macro terms is unmanageable.

And, while it might be catchy to have a United States Population Group Insurance Trust, it probably would run into all kinds of difficulties.

To mail a solicitation to such a list and say "buy our product" is not nearly as effective as mailing to an appropriate segment of the population base and proposing: "As a credit union member, you are eligible to buy our product."

Once you have decided on a market segment, your work is just beginning. If your company has decided on a strategy of expansion— investing in new policyowner acquisition or investing in the development of new media—then your task is somewhat simplified. Insurance broad-marketing programs are extremely sensitive to strategy.

Expansion strategies support broad-based, aggressive marketing programs. Profit-maximization strategies demand more conservative, aggressively managed programs.

Assume for the moment that you have selected homeowners in the United States as your affinity market. Investigating the universe, you will discover, according to the census, that there are approximately 51 million of them. That's the start.

Your next task is to begin to segment this macro market into manageable subsegments. The first step in that process is to go into your database. Profile your current policyowners to determine their particular characteristics.

Profiling is the process by which you attempt to determine the characteristics of your buyers—or policyowners—from actual responses and issued policies.

If you are fortunate enough to have an enhanced database, you will discover quite a lot about your buyer profile.

You will learn, for example, that your buyer median age is 52. Your buyer is employed and earns in excess of the $20,000-a-year median U.S. income. You will discover your buyer is married, with children—between 14 and 19 years of age—living in the household.

Perhaps you will know that 50% of your buyers have a bank credit card, and 44% hold department-store credit cards. Half, you may discover, entered into a credit transaction in the past ninety days, and the outstanding balance of debt is a number...like $1,000.

You may discover that your buyer lives in a single-family dwelling and owns a car. You may also discover your buyer is a traditional direct marketing buyer.

By analyzing these buyer characteristics, you will set up a file that is relational to the source of the business and that reflects a hierarchy of response.

Normally, this is placed in deciles. In a certain sense you are developing a generalized AID (automatic interaction detector) analysis, seeking to isolate the past market segments that have responded best to your offers.

Then, you examine the characteristics of the American homeowner. Perhaps from the census or from *Simmons Syndicated Studies*, you will discover that homeowners tend to be married, have a median age of 51, a median home equity of $24,000, are credit-worthy, bank credit-card holders, employed, owning one or more automobiles, and with children in the household at a median age of 14.

By comparing the data from your database with the generalized statistics from your marketing-characteristic analysis, you will come up with a demographic profile of the American homeowner most likely to respond to your offer.

The most important thing you've done is to reduce a 51-million-name marketing universe to more manageable numbers. Perhaps you've cut the number of names in your universe in half.

Next, by investigating one of the important characteristics of your buyers—*the propensity to purchase by mail*—you reduce that number even further by applying the availability of names to just slightly more than 10 million reachable consumers.

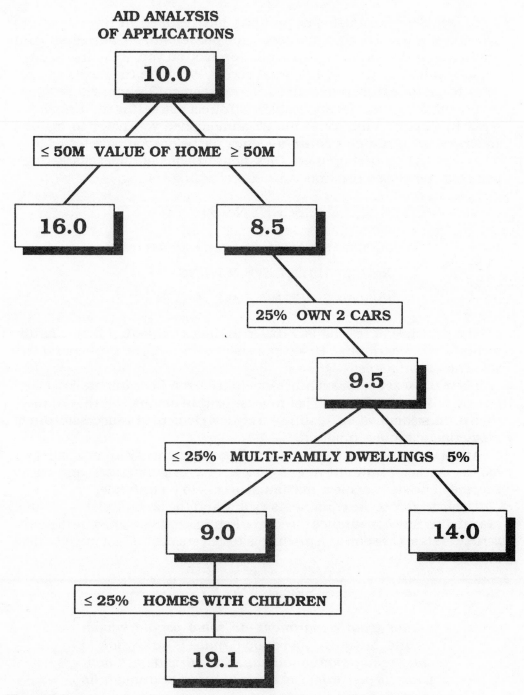

Figure 9-2: Automatic interactive detection analysis can help you determine your most profitable market segments.

Essentially, your customer profiling has resulted in helping you to determine *your working universe*, its *propensity to purchase* your product, and its *ability to pay* for the protection you are going to offer.

Next, you must deal with market access. What are the media you are going to use to capture your defined market segment? Now might be a good time to introduce a secret applicable to all direct marketing ventures. If you recall in Chapter VIII, Secret No. 22 admonished you never to mail an endorsing organization's entire customer file before you have tested it.

Expanding on that premise, Dick Benson—one of direct marketing's pioneers—developed two ironclad rules regarding testing:

SECRET No. 34

Dick Benson's rules for direct marketing testing:

Rule No. 1: TEST EVERYTHING.

Rule No. 2: SEE RULE NO. 1!

The principle of testing is so basic to direct marketing that it hardly seems worth mentioning. However, believe it or not, there are marketers who choose not to test.

There is no excuse for such an elementary error. The ultimate cost of not testing is business failure. That makes "testing money" worth a lot more than its immediate value. Testing is a critical element of a successful direct marketing insurance program.

And, as important as testing is to the development of your programs, so, too, is market communications. For a new broad-market venture to succeed, it needs to achieve maximum access to its universe.

The first part of the equation is media, and the second part is product availability. Since insurance direct marketing products must be filed in a variety of states as soon as a product is tested successfully, it must be filed everywhere.

SECRET No. 35

Your legal department—to some people known as the business prevention unit—is essential to successful program rollouts. Make that department your partner from the germ of an idea through its execution.

And make sure your "filing unit" knows how much money is at stake in each jurisdiction which they fail to successfully add to your state marketing mix.

The more states you are in, the more universe you can reach. The larger the universe you can reach, the greater chance your program has to succeed. This can be accomplished by using one or more direct marketing media.

Direct mail remains the workhorse of insurance broad marketing. However, the growth of telemarketing may—in the near future—alter this. The personalized direct-mail medium is the most powerful in the marketer's arsenal, especially today. In its classic form the direct-mail package contains five fundamental components: the outside envelope, a business-reply envelope, a selling letter, an application, and a brochure.

Computer versatility gives modern direct mail enormous clout. By blending known and inferential data with the one-to-one aspect of the medium, the marketer is able to tailor his message through the medium to the prospect.

Sheer power!

That's just a start. The medium has the advantage of the rifle vs. the shotgun. Computer-stored data helps isolate market segments. Merge/purge operations prevent duplicate mailings from arriving at the same household. Geodemographics, clustering, individual record-data, life-style analysis, and the soon-to-be-common nine-digit zip—all of these offer mouth-watering opportunities to aim the "rifle" directly at the marketer's target audience.

Most frequently, insurance direct-mail packages carry an *invitation to contract*. The application is live. And, when carefully developed, it is filled with information to add to your database.

Selecting lists is an art form, especially in insurance direct marketing. There are certain generalizations that can be made about lists:

SECRET No. 36

Direct-mail buyers almost always pull better than non-direct-mail buyers.

SECRET NO. 37

Hot-line names (purchases within the previous ninety days) almost always pull better than non-

Figure 9-3: Isolating a market segment focuses your efforts on the people most likely to purchase.

current names—those whose most recent purchase went back ninety days or more.

SECRET No. 38

Multiple buyers from the same list almost always outpull single-unit buyers.

SECRET No. 39

Enhanced files with actual date of birth appended almost always outpull files without DOB.

SECRET No. 40

Files that isolate life events—birth, death, household movement, serious illness, graduation, starting school, beginning a new job, etc.—almost always outpull lists that do not offer such data.

Please note the very selective "almost always." It is possible in direct marketing to generalize. But, and a big *but* it is, more than one marketer has fallen flat on his face by depending on conventional wisdom—without testing!

In the broad market, consumers are buffeted constantly by forces that are not necessarily present in endorsed markets.

Inflation, recession, sunshine or rain, happiness, depression, late or early mail delivery, unpredictable events, and a variety of predictable ones—all of these influence the momentary marginal propensity to consume.

The direct marketer has very little control over these events. Elections are a good example. For years, marketers could not figure out why, every four years, late third-quarter and early fourth-quarter-mailing response rates fell apart. Eventually, some bright marketer recognized that during a presidential election campaign the attention span of consumers squarely focused on the political race.

Basically, your direct-mail package is fighting for the consumer's attention. As a medium, direct mail delivers your message. The list you use and the offer you make are both very important.

SECRET No. 41

The proposition you make to your prospects—your

offer—almost always makes the difference between your insurance direct market program's success or failure.

Depending on the offer you make—even if considered ironclad, guaranteed, or whatever—differences in response of 25%, 50%, even 100% and more are common. *Structuring the offer is one the marketers toughest jobs!*

What should be considered? Here is the list:

1. *Price* What is the "right" price for your product? How competitive is it? Price sensitivity among consumers is very real. And the perceived value of your product is going to determine, in large measure, your success.

2. *Benefits* The companion of price. The price/benefits ratio that the consumer perceives is critically important. Consumers are not dumb. You may be able to convince them once, but consumers will not stand for a company who tries to "take them." If the perceived benefit is not there, the prospects unleash the ultimate retaliation...they do not purchase!

3. *Unit of Sale* Is it better to offer a single unit of GDB (graded death benefit), or GIDT (guaranteed issue decreasing term), or HIP (hospital indemnity protection) or whatever, if your objective is to acquire as many policyowners as possible? Or, is it better to offer a variety of units or options to increase average annual premium? Finally, is it better to offer a "Cadillac" or a "Ford"?

4. *Role of an Agent* Certainly, part of every successful mail-order insurance marketing offer is the phrase "no agent will call." Some companies actually eliminate the phrase from an offer in the amazingly mistaken belief that agents can sell the mail-order prospect some other product. Absolute nonsense. The markets are totally different. On the other hand—if your program requires the intervention of an agent—there is no good reason not to say so. It's probably better, however, to say something about "free, no-obligation information" will be delivered.

5. *Guarantees* These are critical. Guaranteed acceptance, guaranteed satisfaction, money-back guarantees—as many as can be fit into an offer is not too many.

6. *Time Limits* These refer to forcing response by requiring it before

a certain date. The "persuasion deadline" is fluid...you don't absolutely demand response by a certain date, you request it. The enrollment deadline is absolute, and subject to regulatory considerations. Blue Cross/Blue Shield runs "open enrollment" offers once a year. It works.

7. *Send-No-Money, or Cash with App* Depends a great deal on your strategy and your fulfillment system. Generally speaking, in insurance direct marketing it is always preferable to get cash with application. Yet the SNM (send-no-money) offer almost always doubles or triples responses. If you have a strong fulfillment package and an effective billing system, consider SNM. The non-takers provide a pool of names for subsequent offers. And they will almost always respond better than names that have never responded to you. Under the circumstances, it appears the balance favors the SNM method.

One more note here: Proprietary credit-card markets—J. C. Penney, Montgomery Ward, Sears Discover, Citibank Visa & Mastercard—are, in reality, cash-with-application offers. For the most part, insurance offers are made to these customer bases with only one means of payment—credit card.

8. *Payment Options* If you are not lucky enough to own a multi-million customer base, then—as a general rule—your offer should contain credit-card payment options. Do not let anyone convince you that this option is more expensive than direct bill. It is not true. *Consumers who pay premium automatically persist better than those who pay premium through direct billing.*

9. *Incentives* One of the most powerful words in direct marketing is FREE! *If you can weave an incentive into your offer, especially a FREE one, you will almost always increase your response.*

10. *Credibility* Always remember the consumer may not know your company at all. Using testimonials in establishing the solidity and dependability of your company will almost always help you.

11. *Ease of Responding to the Offer* Finally, but by no means least, application design is critical. More applications than you might imagine cannot be fulfilled because the application is incomplete, it is badly designed, or it is confusing. This area is too often abdicated to the corporate financial or legal area. Become involved in application design. Just as

order-form design is critical to *catalog marketers, so, too, is application design critical to insurance marketers.*

Building an offer that makes sense for what you're selling is, obviously, multi-variate. Expressing the offer is the job of your copywriter. This subject is covered thoroughly in Chapters XII and XIII. These are, however, the essential elements.

Having chosen your lists and formed your offer, you are faced with choosing a mailing date. Therefore:

SECRET No. 42

Response rates in the first quarter of the year (Jan, Feb, and Mar) are almost always 18% to 30% higher than response rates in the third quarter of the year.

SECRET No. 43

Average annual renewal premium is almost always 8% to 15% higher in the third quarter of the year (Jul, Aug, and Sep) than in the first quarter of the year.

SECRET No. 44

Insurance direct marketing program mailings in the second and fourth quarters of the year achieve response rates 10% to 25% lower than third-quarter mailings.

It may seem that insurance direct marketing is a six-months-a-year business. But these generalizations refer to new policyowner acquisition. You will have plenty to do in QII (second quarter) and QIV when you concentrate on talking to your own policyowners and your inquirers.

This brings us to the shotgun glamour of insurance direct marketing medium—television.

Who among us at one time or another has not dreamed of being a "producer"? Almost all direct marketers have grown up with the electronic media. Yet, it was only a handful of years ago that insurance direct marketing adopted the techniques, pioneered by Sy Levy and March

Advertising, Inc. in New York.

The source of television's power is its penetration of U.S. households. More than 90% of households in the United States have TV sets. The average viewer watches television (according to A.C. Nielsen) slightly more than seven hours a day. It has become the primary source of entertainment and information for the average American.

For the marketer involved in a television program, the psychic income is enormous. In the production environment there are the lights, the camera, and the "action." And, most frequently, on the other side of the camera is a "celebrity," who is going to pitch your product.

It is hard to match the excitement of having dinner with Eddie Albert to the non-event of having dinner with your list broker. Aside from the glamour, making television programs is hard work.

Based on a fundamental principle of direct marketing, qualified inquirers respond better than non-qualified ones. Insurance direct marketing programs which use television are two-step ventures. The first step is inquiry solicitation.

The architecture of an insurance direct marketing commercial is relatively simple: lead...pitch...tag. Figure 9-4 shows a script for a successful TV commercial. The lead is that portion of the commercial that attracts the attention of the viewer—the headline, so to speak. The pitch is the proposition or offer. The *tag*, usually occupying a minimum of twenty seconds, contains the instructions on how to learn more. It usually gives a toll-free number for free information.

The most successful commercials use a visual/oral mix. Principal points of the lead and the pitch appear as "supers" (in writing) at the bottom third of the screen as your story unfolds.

And, it takes some time to tell your story adequately. Television "time" is sold in 30-second increments. It's apparent that an insurance direct marketing commercial that needs a 20-second tag does not have quite enough time to tell its story in the remaining 10 seconds. That's true, as well, for a sixty-second commercial: 20 seconds for the tag, 40 seconds for the story...not quite enough time. Therefore:

SECRET No. 45

The most effective insurance direct marketing television commercial is 120 seconds long.

That gives 20 seconds for the lead...80 seconds for the pitch, and 20

141

Alan Bernhard Creative Enterprises, Inc.

655 Madison Avenue
New York, N.Y. 10021
(212) 752-7455

Continental American Life
GDB - Monty Hall
" Sandcastle "
:120 TV
5/30/86

VIDEO	AUDIO
	Monty Hall (VO, then on-camera):
OPEN ON 60ish woman walking on beach with dog. She passes deserted sandcastle and walks out of frame.	1. Ever think about how it feels to lose your husband or wife?
Dissolve to sandcastle as waves washes over it ... it crumbles. Superimpose long shot of woman against destroyed sandcastle &DSS.	2. It's like having a lifetime of love and security suddenly collapse and wash away.
Pull back from wrecked castle to see MONTY HALL. Super name and mandatory copy. Monty picks sand from castle up and sifts it through his fingers.	3. And once you're gone, how are the loved ones you leave gonna pick up the pieces ... not just emotionally, but financially as well?
Monty gets up from castle and slowly walks along beach .	4. Once you're gone, where will your loved ones get the needed cash to help pay bills and expenses without you?
DSS to Monty as he reaches rocks along beach coast. He sits on rocks and continues.	5. Well now, you can protect the loved ones you leave with guaranteed cash value life insurance from Continental American Life - the company that will not turn you down - regardless of your age, or your health, even if you've been turned down by other companies before.

Figure 9-4a: Created by Alan Berhard, this TV script graphically arrests attention supported by a voiceover opening by a recognizable spokesperson.

142

-2-

VIDEO	AUDIO
Appropriate supers throughout this section.	Permanent cash value protection for anyone 45 to 75 years old - And believe it or not - it costs only $ 6.95 a month !
Super 800 phone number	Make this toll-free call now for free information about this plan from Continental American Life - A company Americans have trusted for over 75 years. I trust them too. That's why I own the plan myself.
	Just think, only $ 6.95 a month guarantees you permanent cash value life insurance that can never be cancelled.
Monty leaves rocks and walks back along beach.	6.There's no medical exam ... not even a single health question to answer.* And because this policy builds cash value, you can even borrow against it for any financial emergency.
Dissolve to woman & pet returning along beach against sunset.	We all cherish the years we spend together. Still we must think of the day our loved ones will walk alone.

Figure 9-4b: Early use of the 800 number assures enough time for the viewer to write it down.

seconds for the tag. Now...that's the ideal.

But, in many cases, it's difficult to run a campaign buying back-to-back sixties. Stations make considerably more money on 30-second commercials, and therefore prefer to sell the shorter versions. They next prefer to sell sixties.

So, it makes sense to have a 60-second commercial in your inventory. *While it is true that your 120 will always outpull your 60,* it is equally true that there are more "avails" for sixties than for 120s in a television station's time bank.

Careful management of your program will result in a balance for lead-cost control. Thus, a mix of the two will yield the average cost-per-lead result which you are trying to achieve for your program.

And, the lower your cost per lead, the better off you are in your program. Fundamental to insurance direct marketing television programs is the fact that people watch television when they want to be entertained—or, when they are bored.

SECRET No. 46

Air your television commercials when people are bored!

It is unlikely that your prospects will interrupt an evening with a favorite sitcom or a first-run movie to gallop to their telephones to call you about an insurance offer.

It is much more likely that they will do so when their television set is on to "keep them company." Prime exposure periods for insurance direct marketing commercials are Saturday and Sunday afternoons, late evening to midnight, early morning, early fringe and prime time on independent stations—roughly, in that order.

Now this boredom issue is a two-edged sword. In looking at television response patterns, the best responding weeks in a thirteen-week schedule are, usually, weeks two through eight. So, too, is this generally true for converting inquiries to applications.

Therefore, in order to maintain response levels, it is a good idea to try to rotate commercials. To do that, you have to have more than one that is successful. And success is measured in terms of the net cost per lead that you are achieving.

Say, commercial "A" delivers a $5.00 lead, and commercial "B" delivers a $6.00 lead. If you can afford to spend $5.75 per lead, rotate the two to add longevity to your program.

Just as in all direct marketing programs, insurance direct marketing television requires management. And the only way you, as a marketer, can manage the program is to know what's going on. You need to know what's working and what's not—where it's working and where it isn't.

SECRET No. 47

To effectively manage a two-step insurance direct marketing lead-generating television program, set up a lead-management system that, on a weekly basis, delivers reports station by station and includes estimated cost per lead.

For a major program, setting up such a system is a lot of work! It requires your time buyers to know when your commercials are airing, where they are airing, and how they are doing, by coordinating the information with your answering services. Reports include responses per hour, responses per show, response per market, and more. Although it is unlikely that you will be buying specific shows (the cost is pretty high), it is likely that you will be buying particular day parts. At the least, you need to track the response-by-day part.

Don't avoid this critical step. Demand their reports. They deliver to you the maximum flexibility in successful TV lead management.

You will be able to add stations to a successful program, increase air time, decrease air time, cancel non-productive markets, and achieve your target cost per lead.

As well, in a successful program, you will be fighting for air time. Preemption rates in insurance direct marketing television are very high—frequently approaching the 50% vicinity. How do you get on the air and stay there? It's called "overbooking."

SECRET No. 48

Always book from 50% to 100% more air time than you think you will need at the start of a direct marketing TV program. It puts you "in control," and you can cancel the time you don't use.

You will seldom buy a "show" during which you air your TV commercial.

All your buys will be "run-of-station," which—loosely translated—means the station can drop your commercial into any time slot it chooses.

And, if an advertiser comes along who is willing to pay as much for a fraction of your two minutes as you have agreed to pay for the whole two minutes—guess who's out in the cold.

The amount of air time is as important as selecting the right market. Remember Secret No. 35? Insurance direct marketing television lead-generating programs work because you are reaching large numbers of people at an efficient cost. In order to get the number of leads needed, you must advertise in a sufficient number of markets. In reaching a decision as to the number, consider the probable decrease in leads resulting from overlapping coverage. In planning your program, aim it only at areas where you can fulfill the leads generated.

Keep your lawyers on their toes...and get into every state you can.

One of your many objectives in an insurance direct marketing TV solicitation is to generate the maximum number of valid leads that you can. You know how many commercials you see in the course of your own TV watching, and most folks see just as many.

How do you attract attention? People are most likely to decide to respond in the first few seconds of the *headline* portion of your commercial. And, people seem to respond better to a familiar face. It is a fact that:

SECRET No. 49

Celebrity-endorsed insurance direct marketing commercials generate response rates 15 to 25% higher than noncelebrity-endorsed commercials.

Under most circumstances the increased response rates more than make up for the $1.00 or $1.25 per lead that you pay the endorser. That's why you see folks like Betty White, Eddie Albert, Lorne Green, Harry Morgan, Monty Hall, Muhammad Ali, Dick Van Dyke, and Ed McMahon endorsing health and life insurance products. Note, however, that there are a few jurisdictions which prohibit celebrity endorsements or spokespeople. This prohibition is clearly challengeable in view of the television advertising aired by general advertisers. And, one day a company with courage will settle the matter. Nevertheless, the point here is: Using commercials featuring celebrity-endorsed products works.

This is not to say slice-of-life commercials don't work. They do. And, because you do not have an endorser to pay, the lower response rate can give you almost the same overall cost.

Here's the caution. Slice-of-life commercials sometimes do not convert to paid applications as well as celebrity-endorsed commercials. And, after all, conversion is what you're after.

In the process of TV advertising, you go through three steps: soliciting the inquiry, converting the inquiry to an application, collecting the first premium.

Inquiry—Conversion—Renewal

The conversion portion of the formula is most frequently a three-effort series of mailings. Basically, the sequence of events goes something like this: Air the commercial; answering service takes inquiries and delivers inquiry data by tape to a fulfillment house.

The fulfillment house processes the names and sends out a series of three mailings—labeled first, second, and third efforts. Mailings generate applications—either paid or send-no-money. Paid applications are fulfilled with certificates or policies. SNM applications are fulfilled the same way, but include the first billing notice and possibly generate subsequent billing notices.

On send-no-money offers, the application flow from each successive effort is roughly 50%/30%/20%. On cash-with-app offers, it differs slightly ...and it differs by product:

	Health	Life	
	Endorsed and		
Effort	Unendorsed	Endorsed	Unendorsed
1st	46%	42%	26%
2nd	40	42	56
3rd	14	16	18
	100%	100%	100%

Essentially, all this table is telling you is that 46% of the health applications you receive from a program is the result of your first effort. You generally will convert to a paid policy between 35 and 90 applications per one thousand inquiries mailed, depending on the program.

What happens to the people who do not convert?

They represent a treasure trove of premium, waiting for you to discover

147

them. Remember, in direct marketing terms, every lead you generate is classified as a qualified inquiry. And, testing has proven that qualified inquirers are worth a lot more than the name from a bought list. So:

SECRET No. 50

Re-solicitation of your TV-inquiry lead file produces response rates 25% to 30% higher than bought lists.

SECRET No. 51

Marketing cost, per application, on re-solicitations to the TV lead file is 20% to 25% less than solicitations to bought-list files.

SECRET No. 52

Average annual renewal premium on re-solicitations to the TV lead file are 7% to 10% higher than on solicitations to bought lists.

The result is that TV-generated lead files have a value which allows you to spend more on the front-end solicitation. You may be able to recover your acquisition cost through re-solicitation of the file—from the same product and products you crossload.

It is a concept very similar to lifetime policyowner value. And, for convenience, it might be labeled lifetime inquiry value. A series of mailings is made to the inquiry file on a cycled basis. Response declines with each cycle of mailings. Yet, response rates remain high enough to throw off solicitation profit. The accumulated solicitation profit helps in paying for the cost of original advertising.

Solicitation profit is simply the surplus marketing or acquisition allowance available after *breakeven* is reached on a program.

Understanding the nature of this value is essential to understanding the value of broad-market television solicitations. The truth is...it simply works. It is an adventurous financial concept, but one that has been proven in the crucible of testing.

Which leads to: How do you test TV commercials?

Unfortunate, but true, few television stations are capable of providing you with a perfect A-B split, and—what may be more important—are unwilling to do so.

There are three basic ways to test TV commercials: rotation testing, match-market testing, and—for want of a better name—QIII testing.

Rotation testing is the process by which you rotate two commercials on a given station on a weekly basis. You then measure the difference in cost per lead generated by the commercials. Since "time of exposure" must be roughly the same, it is the most difficult form of testing.

Match-market testing is somewhat better. Here, you simultaneously run your test commercial against control for a specific period in markets with the same general audience characteristics. You do this perhaps for one or two weeks, then measure the difference in cost per lead to determine the winner.

But, what if your program is new?

The best advice is to develop more than one commercial and test in QIII time periods. Run your spots for more than one week, and plan on a minimum of three to four weeks of testing. That is not to say testing in QI of the year is out of the question. But, since first quarter is the best responding quarter, your results may come in slightly skewed.

TV testing is an art unto itself. And, for the most part, insurance direct marketers work with media buyers and creative talent, who help them develop, execute, and evaluate the testing program.

And finally,

SECRET No. 53

Determine the number of leads you want your insurance direct marketing TV program to produce...and stick to the number!

Perhaps nothing is more tempting to the TV marketer than to continue a program that is going well. CPLs (single—cost per lead) are right on target; air time is available. Why not increase the investment? *Because, you will probably run out of fulfillment material, before you run out of leads to fulfill.*

Always keep in mind the lead time necessary to produce your fulfillment packages, and to arrange with your fulfillment operation the time necessary to get the material in the mail. Nothing will drive CPLs up faster than to have to factor the cost of unfulfillable leads into your program financials.

The tactical marketing plan you develop for a broad-market program echoes the essential outline you use for the endorsed, tactical marketing plan. It is probably longer, especially, if you include a section for media. You will be using a variety of lists for direct mail, and a variety of stations for TV. Each medium you use should be listed separately.

In TV marketing, the big question is segmentation. How do you segment the TV marketplace? The answer is relatively simple—you don't.

Broad-marketing *direct mail* targets an audience which you want to reach, and you talk specifically to that audience. Broad market *TV* targets, in a generic way, an audience you want to reach, and allows that audience to contact you.

And the audience does. As your TV program matures, you will discover a host of stations on which your CPLs are terrific. On the other side of the coin, you will discover another host of stations which do not do well at all. It doesn't take long, and you will build a core group of stations for your product that will deliver the lead costs you need.

The rifle and the shotgun. They both work. And so do several other media.

While the guts of broad-marketing insurance programs is direct mail, and the glory is television, these other methods can bring good results: telemarketing, space advertising, free-fall inserts, free-standing inserts, package enclosures, co-op mailings, billing inserts, supermarket take-ones, regional delivery vehicles, publication wrappers, door hangers, and even matchbooks. All of these have been used successfully.

Each medium should be evaluated relative to your objectives to determine if it has a place in your program.

Space advertising is the purchase of a blank page in a publication on which you place your proposition—either invitation to contract, or invitation to inquire—to generate response. There are some well-known space media in the direct marketing business that consistently deliver acceptable results.

Look at the "supermarket" publications—*National Enquirer, The Star, Weekly World News,* and others. Open almost any issue and you will find an amazing array of direct marketing offers from mail-order vitamins to bicycles to gold chains. And, yes, you will also find offers for graded death-benefit insurance, AARP membership, and small classified ads for whole life "burial" insurance. Several reasons are that these publications deliver a weekly audience in the range of 15 million people, they are relatively inexpensive, and they generate a lot of response.

That is also true about Sunday supplements to daily newspapers—*Parade,* for example, or the "Sunday" syndication. Your advertising will be read by a huge number of people. The delivered audience CPM (cost per thousand) is a little higher than television, but you have the advantage of an enormous amount of data on the medium's readers. Plus, the generally accepted advantage of the publication's credibility among its audience. This is an example of the concept of an *implied* endorsement.

Although a little old-fashioned, daily newspapers once provided enormous access to the mass market, and a lot of invitation-to-contract business was written from those pages.

Later, the free-fall insert provided the access. Appearing in Sunday newspapers, these six- or eight-page booklets were all the rage for invitation-to-contract offers. And, as the cost of television continues to rise, it may once again become economical to use this market access.

Today, *free-standing inserts*—the four-color booklets containing cents-off coupons—achieve distributions on Sundays and best-food days in excess of 25,000,000 weekly. Direct marketing offers of all types appear in them. Why not use for insurance invitation-to-inquire offers? It was successful once, and can be again.

Co-op mailings—like the Carol Wright or Donnelley programs—offer another mass market outlet, delivering to millions of households about ten to twelve times a year. Again, because of the ability to segment, invitation-to-inquire programs may work well. Figures 9-6 through 9-9 show how these programs generate leads that convert to applications.

Package enclosures are often overlooked as an effective medium. Simply, a non-personalized direct-mail kit is placed in a mail-order, product-fulfillment package. It is an economical access to the mail-order buyers market, and it works remarkably well. Best of all, you can choose the kinds of markets that work well for you, those with the characteristics that seem to pull best.

Billing inserts—offering information or, in some cases, an invitation to contract—have been used successfully, especially with credit-card billing.

In all, the point is that the broad market is *broad*. Any medium which delivers a mass market in the millions is a candidate for an insurance direct marketing program. The name of the game in this marketing technique is numbers. The larger your universe, the better your chances of making a program work, whether one step or two step.

Once you've made the program work and have your policyowners in the hundreds of thousands, you are about to enter direct marketing heaven.

For, here is the ultimate secret of insurance direct marketing, your policyowner. *If policyowner marketing is not the backbone of profitability for your company, it should be!* Let's look at some of the secrets of making it work.

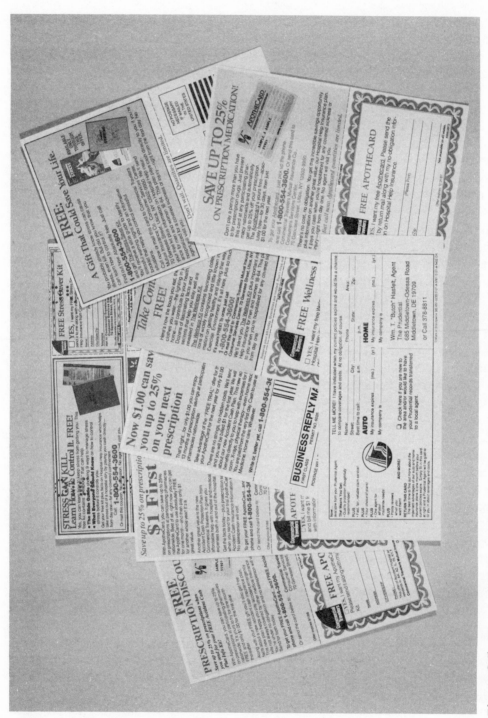

Figure 9-5: Co-op mailings and free-standing inserts generate qualified inquiries.

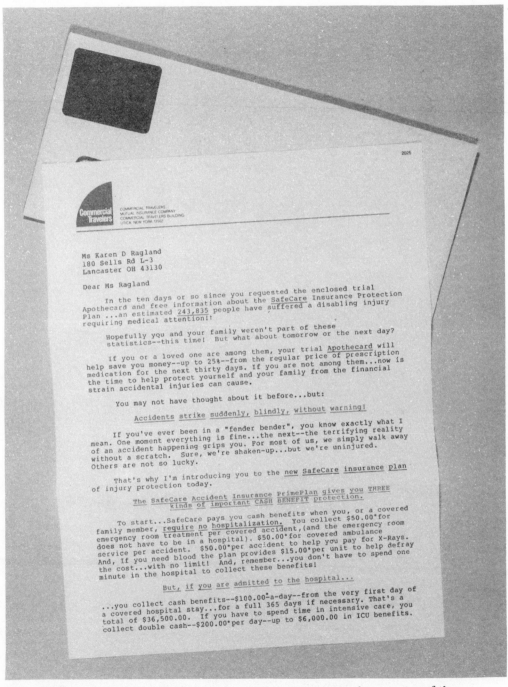

Figure 9-6: Twenty-four to 48-hour turnaround, that keeps the promise of the inquiry offer, generates high conversion.

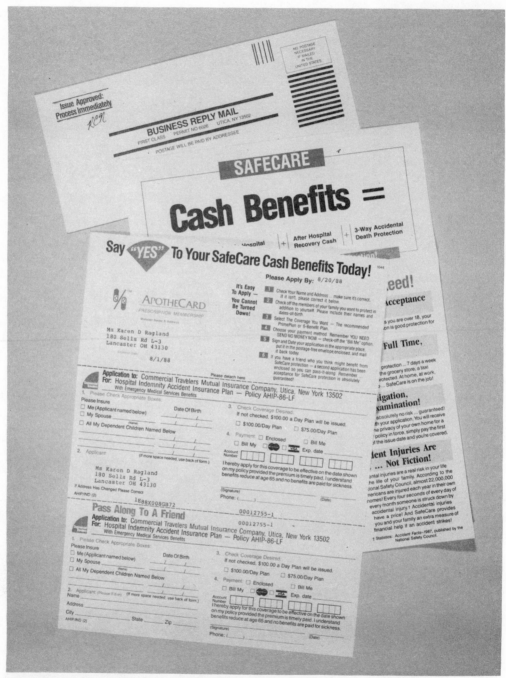

Figure 9-7: Simplified applications (especially for guaranteed-issue products) plus a detailed brochure and a pass-along application work in first-effort conversion material.

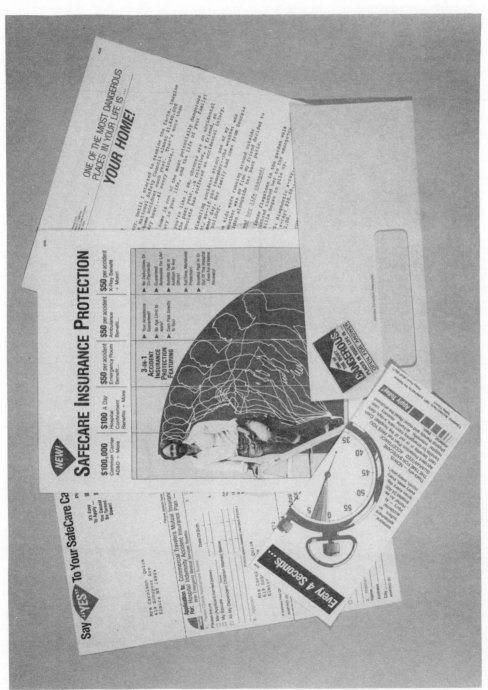

Figure 9-8: First-effort conversion is followed up by a second effort.

Figure 9-9: And finally a third effort. The system works for both print and TV-generated inquiries.

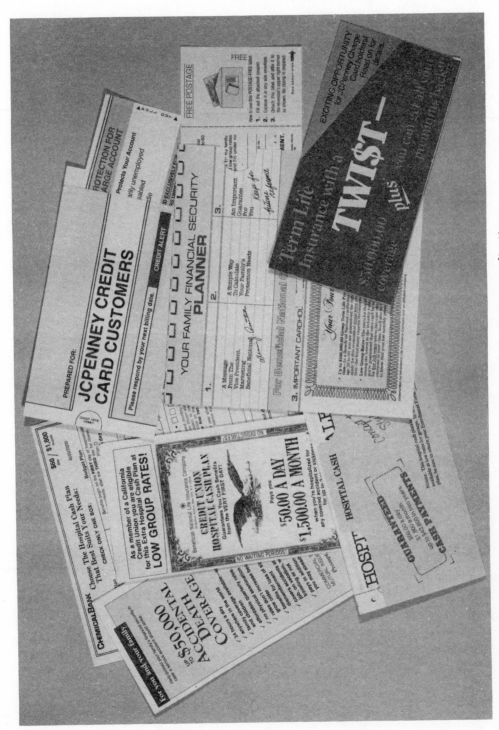

Figure 9-10: Billing and envelope inserts generate invitation-to-contract applications.

Figure 9-11: Newspaper free-falls remain a potential source of invitation-to-contract applications in the broad market.

The Secrets of
Internal Marketing

SECRET No. 54

The most effective marketing environment in which to work in insurance direct marketing is your own policyowner universe!

Policyowner marketing is essential to the development of the lifetime value concept. Here, through the use of relational marketing, is the proof that you can, indeed, spend more money on the acquisition of a policyowner than your initial, acquisition allowance indicates for product-solicitation marketing.

Historically, a *policyowner* has been defined as a consumer paying a premium for an in-force policy covering a specific risk.

While the definition is adequate, it is adequate only in the narrowest sense. Conceptually, policyowner marketing is much broader in scope.

Policyowner marketing is, in fact, internal marketing. It focuses on the events that transpire, *once you receive an application.* It really makes no difference whether the application is send no money or cash with app.

Internal marketing (Figure 10-1) concentrates on three critical elements of the insurance direct marketing process:

a. Fulfillment

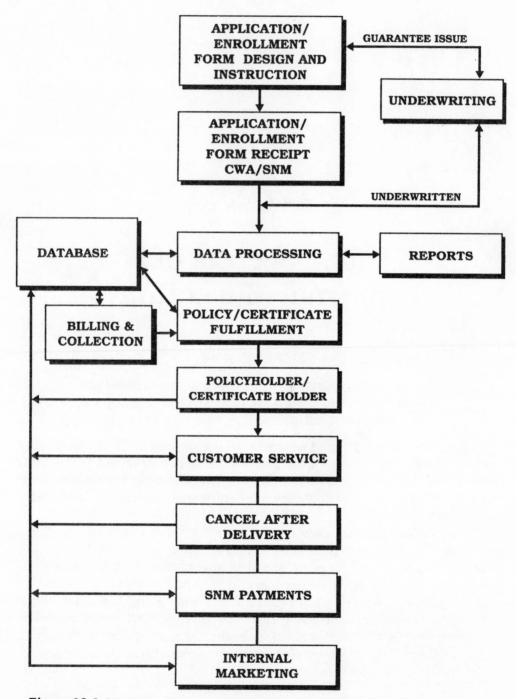

Figure 10-1: Internal marketing model. Note that every area is involved—from application form design to marketing riders and new coverages. It is database driven.

    b. Conservation

    c. Additional revenue centers

Here, a warning. For some inexplicable reason, some companies separate fulfillment and premium billing and collection from the mainstream marketing function. This is especially true of companies with an agency-distribution-system background. These functions are then assigned to a department known as "operations."

If the manager of the operations department is a direct marketer, no problems will develop. If the operations manager is not a direct marketer, conversion rates will suffer and lapse rates will shoot through the roof.

The reason is one of attitude. A non-marketer is more concerned about administrative considerations than marketing considerations. The truth is that *marketing* doesn't stop once you receive an application.

In fact, once you have received an application, your next step is to send along the applicant's insurance documentation. Some years ago, there was a vigorous movement among the insurance direct marketing fraternity to simplify policy language. Now, the basic rule of "keep it simple" applies.

The more understandable a policy is, the better your chance of collecting premium from the customer. Therefore, use plain English in writing a policy.

Your fulfillment material clearly reflects your opinion of your applicant. If you choose to send along an oversized envelope stuffed with preprinted material on shabby stock, your opinion of the person who has committed to paying you hundreds of dollars of premium each year is evident.

On the other hand, you should send along a highly personalized, well-organized, attractive, easily understood, "marketing"-oriented fulfillment package. Its quality will carry your message: Your customer is valued, you are glad to service him, and your promise to pay claims will be believed.

SECRET No. 55

Credibility is critical in fulfillment!

If you succeed in establishing credibility with your fulfillment material, your chances of collecting a premium payment is greatly enhanced. Now, what are the components of a fulfillment kit?

Basically, your fulfillment kit contains the policy, wrapped in an attractive policy jacket, a plastic identification card, a premium-billing notice, a business-reply envelope, some information on the company, how

161

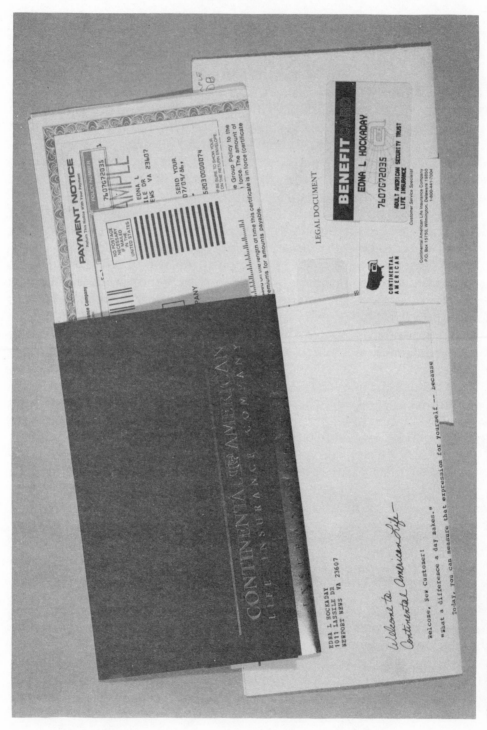

Figure 10-2: Your fulfillment reflects how you feel about your customer.

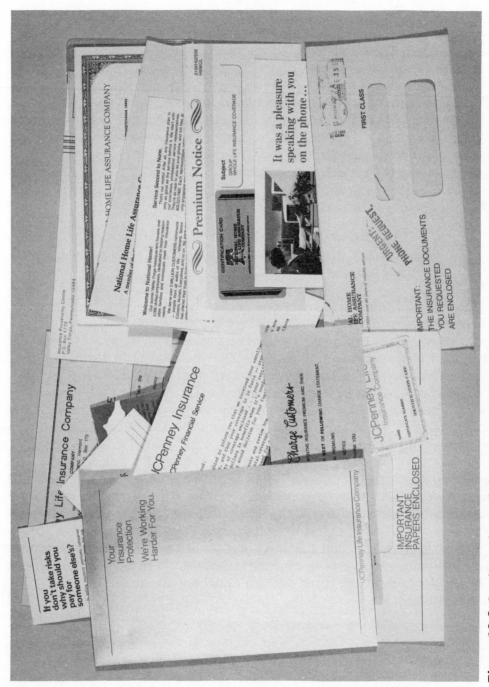

Figure 10-3: Leading relational, database marketing companies spend a lot of time reinforcing customer importance.

to file a claim, and—finally—a sales letter.

This sales letter is critical. It is your opportunity to confirm the consumer's decision to purchase. The fulfillment kit is called a *transmittal package* when you send it in response to a cash-with-app offer. Its objective is to collect the *next* premium payment.

For a send-no-money offer, your fulfillment kit is called a *conversion kit*. Its purpose is to collect the *first* premium payment.

These are lofty goals. It is absolutely critical that you apply the same tradecraft in creating your fulfillment material as you apply to creating front-end solicitation material.

And you must do it in a timely fashion.

SECRET No. 56

The faster you fulfill a direct marketing insurance application, the greater your chance of collecting the target premium payment.

As a rule of thumb, you are best served by turning around guaranteed-issue insurance products in 2.5 to 3 days. Underwritten products can take up to 5 days. In the event you are generating leads for agents, it is equally important to respond to the lead quickly—at least within three days of receipt. You can respond by telephone, setting up an appointment for later.

A great deal of testing has been carried on by the industry to determine the optimum time to fulfill. In general, your conversion will decline the longer you take to get material to the applicant. The same basic rule applies to inquiry conversion, as well.

If you wait until 10 days after receipt to fulfill guaranteed-issue products, your average conversion will drop 35%. If beyond 14 days, you will experience a 50% drop in conversion. Three weeks or more and your average conversion will drop by as much as 75%! The same proportionate decreases will be experienced in underwritten products, too.

Please understand that these are not traditional *working* days. These are days from receipt. It is extremely important to set up fulfillment schedules that meet the three-day (72-hour) maximum.

And, finally:

SECRET No. 57

Fulfillment kits work best when tied to the source endorser.

If you have generated an application from a solicitation endorsed by Texaco, tie the fulfillment material to Texaco. If your app has come in as the result of a Betty White TV commercial, then the fulfillment material should reference Betty White.

Impulse purchases are driven by endorser credibility. Therefore, it is logical that endorser communication will enhance conversion.

It is obvious that with strong fulfillment there is an equal need for effective *conservation*, since the key to successful insurance direct marketing is persistency.

For the concept of lifetime value to make any sense at all, business must be maintained.

That is the function of conservation. In our context, *conservation* may be defined as the process by which you *retain* premium-paying policy-owners for as long as possible, thus increasing persistency.

Some conservation strategies are obvious. Referring to Secret Nos. 12 and 13, the first strategy is to shift the emphasis of your business to the sale of life products from A&H products.

Following that, since group business persists better than individual business, a second strategy is to emphasize the development of third-party business to balance your broad-market business. It is simply a fact that broad-market business lapses at a higher rate than third-party generated business. This is especially true when comparing S&L-endorsed business to broad-market generated policies.

A third effective *conservation strategy* is to plan in detail your premium billing and collection system. Every successful insurance direct marketing product offers four modes of payments: monthly, annual, semiannual, and quarterly. Since annual business obviously persists better than any other type, the trick is to get as many as possible to pay annual premiums. And, that is a trick indeed.

Most direct marketing insurance-product premium is paid monthly. Depending on the product, it is not unusual to find 60% or more of the premium on any book of business paid at that frequency. In the case of high-premium products, like Medicare supplement, that distribution can shoot up to 75% or 80%.

So, perhaps it is best to think about premium billing and collection in some other way.

SECRET No. 58

The most effective way to collect premium for

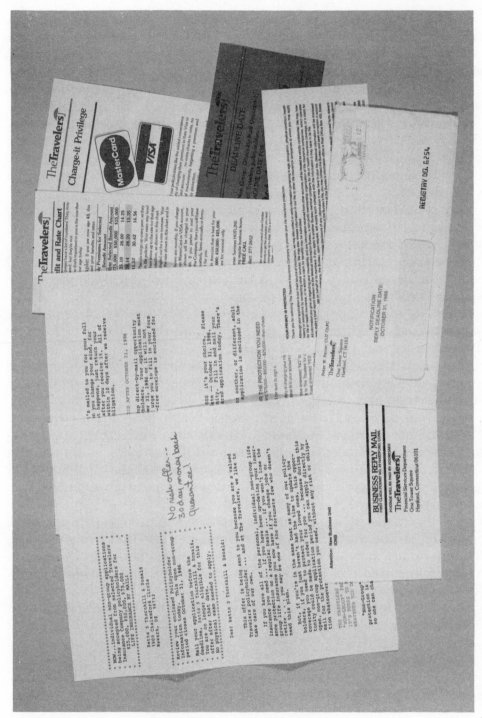

Figure 10-4: Old-line companies quickly learn that relational marketing works.

insurance direct marketing products is automatically!

There are two proven ways of collecting insurance direct marketing product premium automatically: credit-card payments and pre-authorized checking (check-o-matic).

You might start with direct bill. With each direct bill, you offer the option to charge to a credit card or to pre-authorized checking-account deduction. Anywhere from 20% to 35% of your premium-paying accounts will enter the automatic premium-paying system. On third-party, credit-card accounts, these percentage rates will be higher.

For the remaining 65% to 80% of your premium payers, you will have to have an extremely effective direct billing system. Every bill you send must reinforce the policyowner's original purchasing decision.

You have another option. It is called *book billing.* At some point in your billing cycle, perhaps after the third monthly billing notice, you deliver to your policyowner a booklet with twelve premium bills in it, along with twelve business-reply envelopes. A caution: Never attempt book billing until you have collected at least one renewal premium. You can, of course, test, but you will find book billing is most effective when your policyowner has made one or two premium payments.

What is the real secret to policyowner conservation?

SECRET No. 59

Policyowner conservation is a marketing function. It should be treated as such and be put into the hands of a qualified direct marketer.

Now, recollect...way back in Chapter III, a statement was made that policyowner marketing increases policyowner retention.

SECRET No. 60

Persistency is always higher among policyowners who hold more than one policy form, from the same company.

The conservation function is inextricably entwined with the development of additional revenue centers—the traditional definition of policyowner marketing.

Internal or policyowner marketing is divided into two parts. There are rider programs—selling add-ons to the originally issued policy. And, *crossloading*—selling different coverages to current policyowners: health to life, life to auto, auto to health, and so on.

Most companies will have four basic business markets for internal marketing: *active policyowners; lapsed policyowners; non-takers* (from send-no-money offers); and—perhaps—*inquirers*, although this market is frequently handled by the broad-marketing group.

Even though those names from the non-taker and inquirer files are not specifically policyowners, you own the names, and it is a function of internal marketing *to maximize the profit potential of every name that is acquired by your company.*

Your policyowner marketing program begins with your product mix, listed below are some classic life, accident & health product configurations from which to choose in preparing a program:

Riders	A&H Policies	Life Policies
Daily indemnity	Surgical care	Whole life
Surgical schedule	HIP	Term life
Convalescent care	ICU	Graded death
Outpatient care	Cancer	Decreasing term
Emergency room	Accident	Juvenile life
Major medical	Skilled nursing	
AD&D	Convalescent care	
Skilled nursing	Medicare supplement	
Long-term nursing	Hospital accident	
Home care		

Policyowner marketing is most effective when planned exactly like a front-end solicitation, complete with a tactical or program plan on a systematic basis.

In fact, once you've set up your product rotation, you should be in your policyowner's mailbox every month of the year. It is a procedure followed by most of the leading insurance direct marketing companies—and it works!

SECRET No. 61

Policyowner marketing works best when the program is automatic. This requires predetermined offers to appropriate market segments, based upon specific selection criteria.

What about selection criteria?

There are six functional areas to consider when establishing selection criteria. Because you may have hundreds of thousands of policyowners in a given segment—A&H actives, for example, it is unlikely that you can, or will want to, solicit every one of them every time you mail.

First, you will want to consider claims. You may decide to suppress names that have submitted claims within ninety days of the mailing date of your solicitation. You may decide on specific types of claims to suppress from additional mailings—heart attack or cancer claims, for example. *Claims file suppressions are essential to the profitability of your program.*

Second, you need to consider retention limits. Every company limits the amount of risk it is willing to accept. It is important not to exceed the defined limits, a maximum of $100 per day in daily hospital indemnity, or $100,000 per life for term-life coverage.

Third, consider state elimination. The content of direct-response solicitation is controlled by each state, and requirements vary widely. It simply may not be cost effective to mail a few thousand direct-mail kits into a given state.

Fourth, you isolate multiple policyowners. At some point you must determine how much insurance is *enough* insurance. There is a recognizable limit to the amount of money any consumer is willing to, or should, spend for supplementary insurance coverages. It is a function of the law of diminishing returns. At some point, when a consumer realizes how much he is spending, there is a propensity to lapse, if the cost exceeds the consumer's benefit perception level.

Fifth, you may have some policyowners as a result of third-party or joint-venture solicitations. These policyowners may or may not be solicited based on the kind of contractual arrangement you have with the third party.

Sixth and finally, think about age. Most direct marketing insurance products have issue-age limitations, with special provisions for renewals to a certain age. Your selection criteria needs to consider age eligibility for the product you are cycling.

Once you have created your suppression or selection file, you determine the market-segment size by line of business, and match the appropriate products to the file segment.

SECRET No. 62

Begin your rider and crossloading programs as soon

as possible after a new policyowner is on the
books—certainly within sixty days.

By so doing, *your response rates will be higher, you will achieve*
deeper file penetration, you will collect money faster, and you will reduce
lapse rates sooner.

You will, as well, enjoy higher profitability and return on investment. And, as a result of the enhancement of your lifetime value calculations, you will be able to afford to spend more money on front-end solicitations in an attempt to attract new policyowners. Thereby, you expand your policyowner base, which allows you to mail more riders and crossloads—thus making you more profit and a higher return on investment.

An aggressive policyowner marketing program creates a marketing loop, similar to the objective of broad marketing (Secret No. 30). And, that's exactly what you want to do.

In most cases, as well, policyowner marketing programs become fully developed faster than front-end solicitations. Usually, from start to finish, you can be in the mail in 6 to 8 weeks, compared to the 15 to 20 weeks front-end solicitations take. Premium flow begins sooner.

From the marketer's viewpoint, there cannot be too much emphasis on the speed of collecting premium. The faster premium flows, the more money your finance department can make by using it. It is important to remember, the finance department is one of your most important partners in the direct marketing system.

The more you contribute to their departmental objectives, in terms of strategic planning, the more they can do for you.

This is especially true in the area of providing funding for test programs. Since testing is the lifeblood of the direct marketing business, it is in the marketer's own best interest to foster, curry, and comb this critical relationship.

Assuming your policyowner and internal marketing programs are in place, there is one other generalized golden nugget that will help you.

SECRET No. 63

Follow-up mailings work in policyowner
marketing programs—specifically, rider and upgrade
mailings. Second efforts do not draw off response
from first efforts. And, third efforts work in 40% of the
cases.

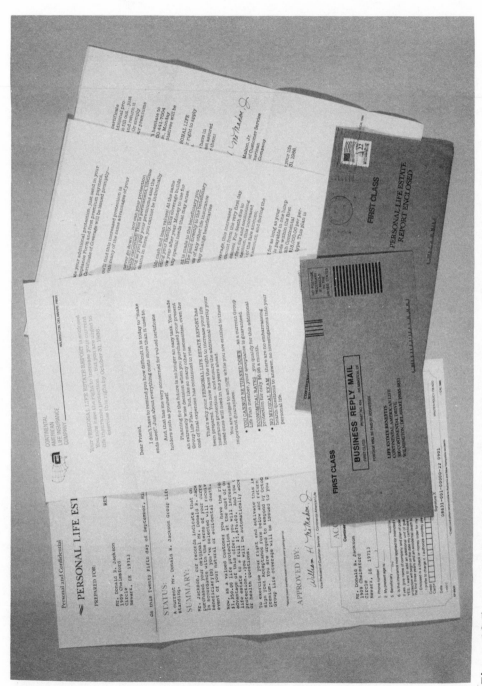

Figure 10-5: Formats for marketing riders come in many styles. Two-step solicitations frequently produce very high take rates.

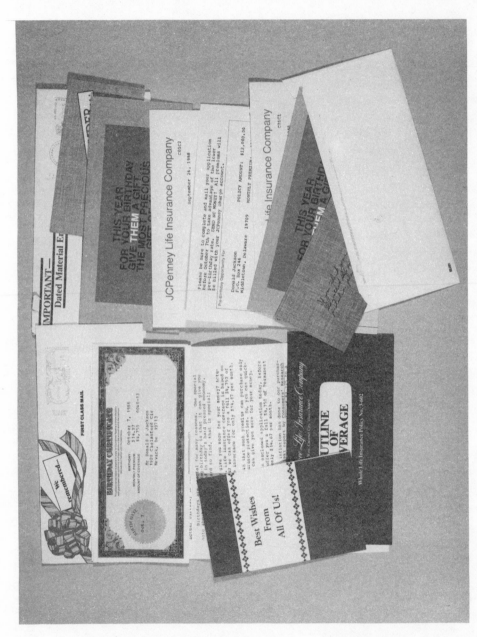

Figure 10-6: Every internal marketing system needs a "birthday" override. Take advantage of DOB information to generate additional sales.

Historically, follow-up mailings were a technique introduced in the sixties, and—for a while—worked well in front-end solicitations, especially to third-party groups, where an endorsement was used.

Rising mailing costs and increasing competition, however, invoked the law of diminishing returns—making the technique unprofitable. In your own case, *test.* Chances are, if your test is carefully constructed, you will be pleasantly surprised by the result.

Now, let's consider results.

One of the most difficult marketing tasks is projecting results. This is especially true for companies starting out in the business, or for the less sophisticated members of the insurance direct marketing community. It is quite difficult to predict results in front-end solicitations. The difficulty arises because so many external factors influence response rates...from rain, snow, and sun to elections—and personal life events.

Policyowner marketing is somewhat more predictable. Some generalizations have been developed over the years, which have essentially survived the test of time.

To start:

SECRET No. 64

The most effective average annual renewal premium for a rider is $60 to $84.

Policyholders appear to respond well to average annual renewal premiums in the $5 to $7 a month range. There's more:

SECRET No. 65

Broad-market policyowners respond to rider offers 20% better than third-party endorsed policyowners.

And, because you don't have to pay commissions on broad-market business, profitability can increase 25% to 50%.

SECRET No. 66

Riders and upgrades outpull front-end solicitations by 300% to 400%.

SECRET No. 67

Crossloads outpull front-end response by 100% to 200%.

Chapter X

SECRET No. 68

Therefore, riders and upgrades outpull crossloads by 100% to 200%.

Keep in mind these percentages apply to *active policyowners*. What about NTO (non-takers) and lapse files?

SECRET No. 69

A&H lapse and NTO files pull 100% to 150% better than front-end solicitations.

SECRET NO. 70

Life lapse and NTO files pull 150% to 200% better than front-end solicitations.

Be careful with these files. While the response rates are mouth watering, there is a good chance that the axiom—once a lapse always a lapse—is applicable. The marketer must carefully track lapse rates on both these files to ensure that excessive lapse is not harming profitability.

There are some other response guidelines you may find helpful. For example, guaranteed-term upgrades respond between 22% and 33%. Graded death benefit (or guaranteed benefit life) upgrades respond at 14% to 20%.

HIP daily-benefit upgrades and scheduled surgical-benefit riders pull between 10% and 20%, but a convalescent care rider delivers about one-half of that. Birthday life programs offered to active policyowners deliver 5 to 10 apps per thousand. The latter offer life protection, usually whole life, to an individual just before his birthday at his age then. If the individual should wait beyond his birthday, his rate would be higher because of having attained a higher age. But, birthday life programs *to lapses and NTOs* deliver about 3 to 8 apps per thousand. Now, it's important to recognize these generalizations for what they are.

Consider these as guidelines. Your own programs, as they mature, may equal or exceed these results. And, in some cases, they may not equal them. If that happens, it is worth taking a hard look at your program to ensure you are exercising every effort in your tactical planning.

Many potentially successful programs have gone down the drain in insurance direct marketing because tests have been misread, tactical planning was shoddy, or some detail—at the time—appearing insignificant, was not adequately evaluated.

It is *absolutely inexcusable* for any insurance company involved in the direct marketing system to avoid the internal marketing function!

Pioneered by companies like National Liberty, Physicians Mutual, Old American, Union Fidelity, and Montgomery Ward Life, these systems have proven themselves over and over again. And, in good times or bad, they have produced profit and return on investment that clearly exceeded even minimum standards established by our friends in finance.

As a marketer...there is a way. Your challenge is to find it.

One tool that can be used to help you find your way is the DATABASE. Database marketing is a critical factor in the success, or lack thereof, of most insurance programs. Don't rely on what you think or feel—only on what you know.

A *database* is a comprehensive collection of integrated data, serving multiple applications, and allowing timely and accurate retrieval or manipulation of the information included therein.

A database is different from a file, which is typically a single collection of records of the same type. A real database is made up of many files. All the files can be linked together, on a demand basis, easily and cheaply.

Your database will have two sources of information—internal and external.

Internal information includes customer information, transaction information, product/media-promotion information, and some geo-demographic information. Each record is linked to a component in another record.

For example, the address from the customer record is linked to the geodemographic record. The customer ID is linked to the order—or transaction—record. And so on and on.

External databases that are most interesting to the insurance direct marketers are the compiled databases. Information from multiple sources is overlayed onto the customer files.

What is important to understand is that database marketing supports all phases of the direct marketing system. Each direct marketing effort has two effects:

First, it produces sales, inquiries, leads, or some other measurable response.

Second, it enhances the information in the database. The information has real quantifiable value. Therefore:

SECRET No. 71

Your database has three critical functions: planning and analysis, execution of marketing efforts, and precise measurements.

More specifically, in planning and analysis, your customer database allows you to develop financial models that accurately reflect likely customer behavior. Your database also provides information on how customers have behaved in the past. This provides a basis for behavior modeling. You also use the database for a series of *what-if* scenarios—comparing, for example, a business-as-usual strategy versus an expansion strategy.

As well, new business proposals can be evaluated by defining customer segments, sizing segment potential, and locating target segments.

Database-driven marketing efforts use the extensive information contained in the database for the development of multivariate statistical models, which predict customer response to programs. The same techniques can target circulation to profitable groups of potential customers.

Sophisticated segmentation analysis precisely isolates the most effective offers to each customer. And, depending on the detail you choose, this can be done individually.

Perhaps what is most important is the long-term view. It is critical in a database marketing system to make marketing decisions *both* to achieve sales targets *and* improve the usefulness of the database.

Database-generated measurements and analysis are greatly enhanced over the traditional direct marketing measurements. Analysis of response by customer group, lists, medium, offer, product and product variation, persistency and claims experience, as well as geodemographic factors, supply the marketer with far more detail on which to base future marketing decisions.

In fact, it is the information flow which can help the marketer. This removes some of the intellectual speculation that dominated the marketing system just a short decade ago.

Complex measurements to support modern direct marketing are frequently needed. The impact of direct marketing can be measured when there is an ongoing stream of marketing efforts. In TV inquiry-file re-solicitations, for example, the frequency of offer and type of contract are critical to profitability.

This is critical in co-ordinating multiple distribution channels and in analyzing relative impact. Distribution-channel interaction can be viewed in relationship to overall profitability, as well as being broken down into individual element profitability. The techniques are particularly useful when an agency distribution system coexists with the direct marketing distribution system within the same company.

Finally, the database measurement system can examine the relational value of timing issues in relation to seasonality, customer ordering intervals, competitive moves, inquiry/prospect ordering, lapse marketing effectiveness, and claims interval impact.

Generally, database marketing represents a body of thinking, as well as the elegance of analysis. Since the database is the foundation for planning, executing, and measuring marketing efforts, it is obvious that all marketing efforts are linked together.

Current marketing efforts make use of accumulated information from the past. Current marketing efforts contribute to the body of information which will be available in the future. Therefore, it is possible for a marketer to view every marketing effort in its overall, long-term impact and effect on that line of business.

SECRET No. 72

The fundamental principle of database marketing is that marketing efforts are designed, executed, and measured on the basis of the long-term impact on a business.

Expediency is no longer acceptable. Certainly, the classical approach to insurance direct marketing included the analysis of profit and loss per offer or effort. It was product- or media-driven, maintained basic customer records, and used rudimentary, offer-based segmentation.

Today the modern database marketing approach analyzes profit and loss *plus* business development per offer or effort.

Whether it is customer- or market-driven, substantial information is stored in an "ad hoc" retrievable database. And, advanced multivariate statistical models optimize long-term results.

Today, the majority of insurance companies don't understand clearly the sophistication of database marketing. Part of the reason is that most senior officers of these companies developed in earlier distribution systems.

Measurable response remains a mystery—and not a little intimidating. Accountability is a new concept. The new generation of direct marketers eventually will change these attitudes.

Converting from classical to modern insurance direct marketing is the key to future profitability! The relational nature of the information in your database, plus the mental commitment to long-term profitability, yields enormous marketing impact.

There are seven steps in the process of creating a database. Stated as briefly as possible:

1. Specify data to be retained
2. Specify outputs, reports, and methods for accessing data
3. Collect, insert, and update database information
4. Analyze database information
5. Plan marketing efforts
6. Execute marketing efforts
7. Measure results

Keep in mind that each step in the procedure requires an extraordinary amount of detail and brainstorming. It is most important for the novice organization to seek, accept, and heed the advice and counsel of a database professional!

Two hints:

SECRET No. 73

The basic element of your database will be most effective if it is transactional, using the individual record as the source.

SECRET No. 74

Library extracts must include every element that impacts profitability.

In other words, every transaction that occurs within the masterfile is updated on an occurrence basis. As a transaction happens, it is recorded. From the acceptance of an offer to the payment of a direct bill, or the entry of a credit-card charge.

Within the architecture of your database, all transaction information flows from relational data kept in all departments. These data are extracted from data libraries. In insurance direct marketing companies, the basic libraries most frequently developed are:

Active policyholders	Active claims
Lapsed policyholders	Completed claims
Inquiry files	Campaign results
Not-taken files	Campaign costs

Most file definitions are obvious. The *not-taken* file contains the accumulated records from rejected offers mailed to inquirers.

These libraries of information are then parsed into datasets by line of business: health insurance, life insurance, auto insurance, and home-owners or casualty coverages.

By assigning a value—from -1 to +1—to each transactional individual record, a view of preferred customers can be established, and formed into a subset of another dataset.

In selecting information to be included in your database at setup, you first move into the basic elements of your masterfile: name, address, city, state, and zip.

Then add: gender, entry codes, product codes, marketing number, line of business, and payment form. Next, you add insurance: type, policy ID, number of units, value of units, tarp, and payment form.

Still more: split ID, media ID, issue date, birth date, issue age, billing mode, number of dependents, relation of dependents, and dependent data.

Then, lapse date, activity status, total number of claims, total dollar amount of claims, and claims data. Then, date, type of policyowner marketing effort, and policyowner marketing product.

And, if there is any value in so doing, all of these can be broken down even further.

While creating your database may seem complicated—and it is—the net effect on your overall business as you learn to manipulate the database is astounding.

The basic objective of statistical analysis is to find useful summaries of database information that are concise, clear, complete, and accurate. You will most likely deal with two types of statistical analyses.

Predictive Which attempts to find ways of predicting customer and potential customer behavior, based on known information.

Descriptive Which attempts to describe groups of customers or prospects. These could include either simple descriptions, like customer cell counts, or more complex analyses which produce generalized descriptions, such as characteristic clusters.

Basic statistical analysis is either univariate—examining only one variable at a time, or multivariate—examining many variables together.

Variables may be scalar or categorical.

Relationships among variables may be causal: One particular variable is a *cause* of another variable's value.

Or, the other correlative: The values of two variables may tend to be related because both have a common/causal relationship with a third variable. You understand relationships between two variables by using correlation matricies, scattergrams, breakdowns, or cross-tabulations.

Normally, the marketing manager will pose a specific information target necessary to run a marketing program. A specialist then produces the analysis that delivers the target information.

It is most important to understand that the objective of database marketing is linking knowledge to action. Analysis alone does not lead to profitability improvements. The analytic results must be tied to financial benefits.

Such results lead to creative ideas for products, media, copy platforms, and more. Short-term financial benefits are calculated by working through a P&L statement. Long-term financial benefits are estimated through financial modeling.

Financial modeling is a precise, quantitative description of the financial structure of your business. Financial models are built by specifying the characteristics of individual business components, and then specifying the interactions among the components.

It is clear, by now, that a database is essential to the development of your company's lifetime-value calculations. By examining every transaction in the past, the lifetime-value model can be developed and updated *on a current basis* to constantly test its credibility. As Chapter VI pointed out, lifetime value is so fundamental to modern direct marketing techniques that your operation's profitability depends on it.

The secrets of policyowner marketing... internal marketing, actually... are as intriguing to the novice as to the expert in insurance direct marketing. Here is the very fabric of what you seek to accomplish when you develop your own insurance direct marketing system!

For a business reaching maturity, policyowner marketing fosters continued expansion. In hard times, it provides survival income streams. In good times, it enhances profitability geometrically.

A new approach in the internal marketing program has taken the mass aspect of normal direct marketing techniques and converted these techniques to the highest degree of personalization: CONVERSATION.

The technique is electronic intervention—telemarketing. It is a highly personalized medium that allows the mail-order marketer to compete with the insurance agent on a one-to-one basis with a customer or prospect. It is a harbinger of the future...when conversations with prospects will be interactive communications generated by mass-media exposures.

Telemarketing is a bright light in insurance direct marketing, opening challenging opportunities for traditional-product sales, as well as new-product sales. Let's explore its secrets.

The Secrets of
Insurance Telemarketing

It's fascinating.

Almost no one can do without it today...the ultimate consumer service...communications. When you hear the bell or buzzer, your hand—almost irresistibly—reaches out to lift the receiver.

The telephone is a lifeline. A window on the world from the comfort of your own home. When most folks answer the phone, there is an instant of vulnerability, a moment of curiosity about the message, only seconds away from delivery.

The voice on the other end can deliver glad news, or sad news, or no news—from uplifting messages, to IRS collection calls. When the phone rings, people answer. In the privacy of their own homes, it stands to reason the call is for them.

But, a host of folks will answer a ringing public telephone—even when they know the call could not possibly be for them.

Combine the elements of curiosity and momentary vulnerability with the sure knowledge that there is a person on the other end of the phone, and you begin to perceive the power of telemarketing.

For a little more than two decades, telephone marketing has been developing as a discipline and a medium in the arsenal of heads-up direct marketing insurance organizations.

It is successful. One major insurance direct marketing company handles

7 million phone contacts a year, generating in excess of $25,000,000 in TARP. A second company has generated $150,000,000 in sales.

Telemarketing growth has been dynamic, and remains so today. It began in the late 60s. Major insurance direct marketers began to experiment with telephone conservation programs. In the early 70s the call-collect customer service system was inaugurated—giving way, a few years later, to the inbound 800 system.

The second half of the 70s saw glimmers of outbound testing, maturing in the latter part of the decade and, by the early 80s, moving into a solid outbound sales effort.

Telemarketing has spent the first half of the 80s proving just how powerful a medium it really is.

What is that power?

SECRET No. 75

The telephone is personal. *No other direct marketing medium gives you the ability to establish such a one-on-one dialogue with your customer or prospect, in a personal service atmosphere—human-to-human contact.*

Telemarketing is the closest our industry will ever come to the agency distribution channel. And, remember how successful it was...and remains today!

Truly effective telemarketing happens when a trained and prepared individual telecommunicates a sales message to a selected prospect. In the process of the telephone conversation, a personal relationship is established between seller and buyer. There is no more powerful sales device!

Now, that's just a start.

There are three more secrets to prove telemarketing is the power medium of the eighties, nineties...and beyond.

SECRET No. 76

The telephone is immediate. *When you call someone, that person can't put the phone call aside to focus on it later.*

SECRET No. 77

When your customer calls you, he expects to receive

the instant gratification that only a telephone call can provide.

SECRET No. 78

The telephone is flexible. *You tailor your pre-sentation to an individual person—as opposed to broad-stroke demographic, geographic, or psychographic considerations used in direct mail. In fact, while you're speaking to your prospect, you can change your presentation to fit the circumstances of the conversation!*

And,

SECRET No. 79

The telephone is controllable *and* accountable. *Unlike a field force, your "sales force" is sitting right in front of you. You maintain solid management control, as well as controlling the information generated by the call.*

You get a double benefit. You know the results of your call immediately. You also know what your customer is saying to you. *This gives you free market research, frequently overlooked by field sales representatives, as well as by company management.*

Additionally, telemarketing has developed acceptable financial formats to track program cost effectiveness and efficiency. Cost per hour or cost per call measures success.

Finally, telemarketing substantially eliminates marketing risk. It allows the marketer to stop an unsuccessful program, modify a weak script, or quickly continue to a rollout, after a successful test. *Such flexibility as this is not available in any other insurance direct marketing medium.*

In mail, television, or other lead-generating programs, your marketing investment is considerable—and up front. Not so with telemarketing. Up-front marketing investment is relatively modest. You cannot recall a mailing if it's not working. But, you can surely stop short a telemarketing program that, in some instances, is an obvious failure.

Now, how can you use this medium?

To start, there are two categories of telemarketing for the insurance direct marketer: inbound and outbound.

Inbound telemarketing is divided into two general areas—customer service and inquiry data capture. Inquiry data capture is normally associated with broad-market television or print inquiry-generation programs. And, most frequently, such programs are handled by external service bureau resources specializing in this type of operation. Inquiry generation creates "call bursts"—large numbers of calls in response to a broadcast spot, received in a very short period of time.

The service bureau takes your inquiry calls and records the basic data necessary to fulfill your TV offer—usually, in an efficient data processing environment. This basic data includes, for heaven sake, date of birth—*not age*! This data is then transmitted electronically (when you are running a volume program) to your fulfillment house, where the direct mail conversion procedure goes on. In this kind of environment there is a critical need for speed. The sooner data transmission takes place, the faster the first fulfillment effort can be mailed.

It is essential to follow up telemarketing leads within one to two days of receiving the call. *The speed with which you follow up your leads will have a signifcant impact on your conversion percentages.*

Customer service, however, is usually in-house. Its function is to support the entire spectrum of your direct marketing efforts. Customer service representatives handle queries about current marketing programs, providing prospective customers with information that will help them make a buying decision.

These representatives provide the same service to policyowners. Customer service reps handle questions about coverage and claims status and generally act as "comforters" for customers.

Since your policyowners cannot reach out and touch an agent, the customer service function is a critical part of the marketing mix in your insurance direct marketing operation. It is equally sensitive to the needs of broad-market and endorsed-market customers.

However, it is absolutely critical for endorsed-marketing programs—from two viewpoints: the policyowner's and the endorser's. Most successful insurance direct marketing companies in the third-party business sell *service* as a benefit for signing up with an endorser. Endorsers, rightfully, worry about their credibility with their own customers. It is a very good idea to have an inbound 800 number prominently displayed on your solicitation and fulfillment material. Nothing can replace the comfort level of human contact in satisfying the needs of both endorser and policyowner.

Chapter XI

SECRET No. 80

Separating customer service and outbound sales telemarketing is the key to the success of the unit.

The simple fact is that—no matter how good your customer service representatives are, or how well trained they are—there are fundamental differences between the service and sales functions.

Customer service representatives ask basically *closed-end* questions—those that generate data, on which the service representative will act to satisfy the customer in a positive, time-efficient way.

But, consider this: A customer is most vulnerable either when his problem has been solved or when he is satisfied. At the conclusion of a successful customer service episode, several things have happened. First, the caller is feeling good about the company. Second, a personal relationship has been established with the service representative. Therefore, what better time to offer the caller a new buying opportunity?

This situation can instantly convert a cost center into a profit center. There are two procedures to recommend.

First, in an automated environment the customer service representative, using a random access lookup procedure, determines that the caller is eligible to receive an offer. That done, the customer service representative asks the caller if he is interested in learning about a new purchasing opportunity—perhaps, a rider to his existing policy.

If the representative receives a positive reply, the call is turned over to one of the outbound sales reps to give the sales pitch.

A more benign procedure is for the customer service representative to query the caller about his interest in receiving free information on a new policy or rider. If the answer is positive, the rep orders that direct-mail solicitation material be mailed to the customer.

In neither case is the customer service rep selling. The representative is making efficient use of the established contact to convert a satisfied customer into a prospect for additional business.

Significant income is generated by companies following one of these "tel-comm" procedures, thereby earning income that would be lost without such a program.

The essential difference between inbound 800 telemarketing and outbound sales is the difference between "passive" telemarketing and "active" telemarketing. Inbound 800 is basically passive. Outbound selling is fundamentally active.

Figure 11-1: Automated telemarketing environments increase productivity. Photo courtesy of Bill Miklas, Idelman Telemarketing, Inc., Omaha.

An outbound telephone sales representative needs to be "up" constantly to sell effectively. It is virtually impossible for a customer service representative to be "up" after handling several complaint calls or policyowner problems in a row.

Technically, telephone sales representatives ask open-ended questions to help close a sale. Such questions require positive answers from the prospect, which allow the rep to eliminate sales objections...all the while keeping a smile in the voice.

So, the task of the outbound telemarketing representative is to get the prospect to buy an insurance product.

The task is a clear sales function—one that produces profit through the use of extraordinary efficiency. It is used in the three principal areas of income production: broad marketing, endorsed marketing, and policy-owner marketing.

Amazingly, outbound telemarketing is extraordinarily ineffective... when you don't have a telephone number to call. Therefore:

SECRET No. 81

On every lead generated, on every application, in every program...ask for the prospect's telephone number.

Years ago, direct marketers asked for the telephone number as a credit-checking device. Today, the customer's or prospect's telephone number opens the door *to sales and profits which you could miss out on*, without a telemarketing operation.

There are services that append telephone numbers to data records. The process costs about $40/M. But, *if you don't have the phone number*, these services are definitely worth exploring. A good appending service may be able to provide phone numbers for 60% to 90% of your list.

It is particularly necessary to obtain telephone numbers for your existing in-house names—for policyowners, inquirers, lapses, and non-takers. The more records you have with telephone numbers, the more chances you have to make additional sales.

Selling is the name of the game! There are nine general outbound telemarketing applications that can help the insurance direct marketer to sell:

1. Conservation—Calling behind your billing series to encourage

payment of renewal premiums.

2. Upgrades—Calling in front of issues in send-no-money programs to upgrade coverages.

3. Add-ons—Calling in support of direct-mail offers, or independently in support of rider offers.

4. Conversions—Calling prospects who have requested information or applied for insurance on a trial basis:

    a. *Direct mail*—Calling two to three weeks after a fulfillment kit has been sent to a respondent.

    b. *TV 800-number inquiries*—During the conversion process, calling about one week behind a follow-up conversion kit.

    c. *Renewals*—Calling respondents who have enrolled in one of your programs for a trial period, which was offered free or at nominal cost, to convert them to fully paid.

5. Exdating—Calling to lists to find out when present coverages expire, then following up with solicitation material. Most frequently associated with P&C coverages.

6. Direct mail follow-up—Known as a "chase-the-mail" program. You call *behind* a major mailing to alert prospects that the material is coming, convince them to review your solicitation, and encourage them to sign and return the application. This is most often used in support of endorsed-marketing efforts.

7. Cross-selling—There are two applications. First, offering different insurance products to current policyowners. Second, offering different insurance products to inquirers—life insurance to Medicare supplement inquirers, for example.

8. Research/surveys—Calling present insureds or members of organizations, groups, or associations to develop customer profiles that enable your company to more effectively target the market and define new product needs.

9. Underwriting—Using qualified personnel, perhaps a registered

nurse, calling behind an underwritten application to obtain missing information, to stimulate the submission of an attending physician's statement, and to obtain electronic signatures on insurance applications.

In fact, in more sophisticated product environments you can use telemarketing to convert policy surrenders to policy loans or policy conversions, to generate term-life replacement sales, and to stimulate the purchase of SPDAs, single-premium deferred annuities.

When you employ these applications, you can expect solid results, like:

SECRET No. 82

Conservation programs can increase payments between 15% and 30% as compared with response rates generated by the billing system alone.

SECRET No. 83

Add-on or upgrading programs directed at new policyowners can sell increased amounts of insurance at a success rate of 50% or higher.

SECRET NO. 84

Conversion on send-no-money policies can be improved overall between 20% and 30% with a follow-up phone call.

What about inquirers? In terms of priority of prospects, people who identify themselves as interested enough to "take a look" at a policy are going to convert better than those who have not indicated any interest. Setting up a telemarketing follow-up program in support of your direct-mail conversion efforts results in improved efficiency. This type of program helps overcome the natural inertia of the prospect . . . and may move him to action.

In TV-inquiry programs, you can increase conversions as much as 40%. In direct mail, between 10% and 25%. And, in a renewal program, conversions are generally enhanced between 10% and 15%.

A telemarketing follow-up program works with cash-with-application offers, especially for TV-generated inquiries, increasing paid response in the 10% to 15% range.

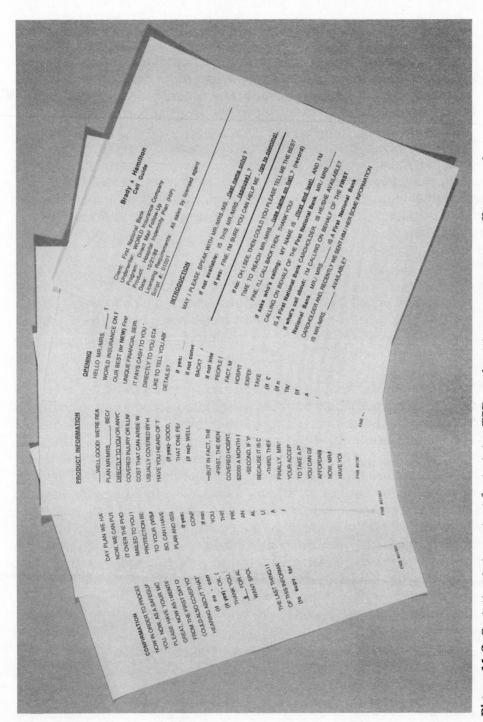

Figure 11-2: Scripting is important for training TSRs and getting your programs off to a good start. But, list quality and TSR training are keys. (Script, courtesy of Jon Hamilton, Brady & Hamilton.)

SECRET No. 85

Calling endorsed-marketing customers as a follow-up to a third-party, direct-mail insurance solicitation can produce sales, when billed to a credit card, of 45 to 65 applications per thousand.

Telephone follow-ups to "invitation-to-contract," direct-mail solicitations, in many cases, can double the mail-only response rates. As a general rule, non-insurance programs experience take-rate increases of 3 to 7 *times* the mail-only response. Because of the nature of direct-mail insurance products—compared to hard goods, for example—the improvement is somewhat lower.

SECRET No. 86

A "herald" call—a call prior to mailing a solicitation to a third-party list—increases response to the solicitation effort, decreases mailing costs, and yields overall increased cost efficiency.

This technique works most effectively in conjunction with an "event" in a prospect's life...perhaps a birthday, purchase of a new home, birth of a child, and so on. The customer contact determines the degree of interest and screens out unqualified or uninterested prospects. By so doing, you need not prepare a full-circulation mailing. You target your audience, and the higher degree of interest results in far higher response rates. This may increase these rates by 25% to 50%, as compared with a full-list mailing.

The existing body of evidence overwhelmingly indicates that insurance telemarketing operations are very successful. But, in establishing an operation, you have to take into consideration a number of factors.

The first one is how to plan an operation. As a guideline, you may start out by looking at MC : TARP ratios of some standard programs:

Conservation	1 : 3.00-4.50
Conversions	1 : 1.50-2.25
Upgrades	1 : 1.60-5.00
Add-ons	1 : 1.25-5.00
Cross-sales	1 : 1.15-2.50

Then, compare the numbers above to the numbers developed from your regular programs. The difference is an *incremental increase* in response, AARP, or TARP, which you can expect from the addition of telemarketing to your marketing mix.

Eventually, you will test your assumptions against the results of actual programs.

SECRET No. 87

When you set up a telemarketing operation, establish your testing to measure incremental differences with/without telephone intervention.

This procedure helps to convince your general management that telemarketing is an effective medium. But, to measure the incremental difference, you must have a way of calculating expenses.

The cost-per-hour concept seems to be a good way to do that, initially. Cost per hour is composed of four specific cost factors: representative charges per hour (including fringe benefits and bonus plans if any), telephone charges per hour, overhead expenses (light, heat, rent, and so on), and administrative hourly charges. Depending on the way you set up your telemarketing unit, these charges will come out to between $20 and $30 per hour.

Again, depending on the type of program you are running, you may have to add a cost for fulfillment in order to derive a marketing-cost number.

Now, a financial-planning model looks something like this:

Leads	1,000
% Callable	75%
Callable	750
% Contact	80%
Contacts	600
% Sales	30%
Sales	180
AARP	$60
TARP	$10,800
% Renew	50%
Renewal TARP	$5,400
Hours	75
CPH	$25
Fulfillment	$180
Total Marketing Cost	$2,055
T/MC	$2.62

(See explanations beyond.)

Simply moving down the chart, the number of leads coming into the operation is 1,000, of which 750 have phone numbers. Therefore they can be contacted. Of the 750, the outbound-sales representative is able to contact 600, resulting in 180 people saying "sure, send me the information." AARP on this mythical product is $60; TARP is $10,800. Half the respondents decide to take the product and they pay the first premium. Then the renewal TARP is $5,400.

At 10 calls per hour, 75 calling hours were used in selling the program. At $25 per hour the cost is $1,875. Next, add a generous $1 for each of the fulfillment kits sent out to the respondents, bringing the total marketing cost to $2,055. T/MC is $2.62.

In addition to the cost per hour for expense, calculations can also be made to indicate cost per call or cost per sale. Initially, however, the CPH measure gives you a solid control figure for expenses.

Of course, the financial considerations and the methods displayed are the foundation considerations for your telemarketing program.

But—during your telemarketing planning—inevitably, you will be faced with deciding what kind of facility to create. You have three basic choices: in-house, outside service bureau, or a facility-management arrangement.

If you are just testing the medium, it is unlikely that you'd opt for an in-house group. Inside telemarketing facilities are expensive to create. You would have a large set-up expense, and you must hire qualified management and supervisory personnel to run the operation.

On the other hand, you will have total management control of the facility. And, chances are very good that your cost-per-hour expense would be lower than for either of the other two options.

Yet, if your testing does not prove out, you will have the additional expense of dismantling the facility. Creating an in-house telemarketing facility is the most adventurous choice you can make.

It probably makes more sense to use an outside service organization, if your intent is to put a "toe in the water." While your expenses will be higher, you can base the ultimate creation of an in-house facility on the results achieved by the service bureau. This approach is possibly the most conservative. But, you must carefully analyze the degree of risk you are willing to take.

Finally, you might consider the *facilities-management* approach. Here, *you* create the facility—investing in the physical space, the design, and the phone lines. An outside firm provides the personnel—management, supervisory, telemarketing representatives—at a fixed hourly fee. There are three advantages to this arrangement.

First, expenses are completely controllable, because they are fixed. As well, you can specify the target number of calling hours you seek to achieve during the year.

Second, you can set up the facility quickly. You can be on the phones, so to speak, in a very short period of time. Telemarketing personnel have access to company personnel on a day-to-day basis. Problem solving is facilitated, and it allows hands-on management by the responsible corporate manager.

Third, among company personnel, the telemarketing learning curve accelerates rapidly. This enables the company to take over operation of the facility at some later time.

Facilities management is a middle ground between in-house and an outside service bureau. It takes some confidence that the technique will work, and it depends on the facilities manager to properly operate the telemarketing group during start-up. Since, assumptively, the facilities manager has considerably more expertise and experience than company personnel, this option can be the most cost-effective in the long run.

When considering this option, you should consider three criteria by which to judge the facilities-management group with which you want to do business.

The formula is: experience, training, and success.

Experience: To start with experience is absolutely critical to the success of a facilities-management operation. Experience needs to be in-market and practical. The group you are considering should display management and supervisory depth. They must clearly demonstrate that they have the know-how to create, implement, and administer the programs you are contemplating. And, if the company you are hiring already has facilities-management experience, that is to your advantage.

Training: Training skills are absolutely essential. The stronger the facilities-management company is in the area of training telemarketing representatives, the more successful your program will be. Training is the key, critical difference between failure and success.

Success: The company you are considering should have a record of successful programs. Make no mistake about it; telemarketing companies are springing up like weeds after a heavy rain. It is essential that you check the track record of the management group, especially regarding in-marketing program success. *That means programs must produce profit.*

Ultimately, once your facility has been established, your objective should be to move into automation.

SECRET No. 88

Automation of a telemarketing facility can increase productivity 20% to 30%.

Quick access to detailed information, as well as auto-dialing efficiency, dramatically increases each representative's ability to sell or to handle customers. Ideally, your facility should be tied into your computer system on a random-access basis. To the customer service representative, this means few—if any—call backs, and a higher customer-satisfaction ratio.

To the outbound sales representative, this tie-in allows direct policy issue to telemarketing respondents, as well as detailed analysis and tracking of programs.

OK, now you have a telemarketing facility, a strategic plan, and a group of tactical marketing plans to execute programs.

What is the real and absolute secret governing the success of your telemarketing program?

SECRET No. 89

To maintain an effective, efficient, and profitable telemarketing operation, you must provide lead flow every month of the year. However, because of telemarketing's ability to penetrate lists far deeper than mail solicitations, lead volumes need not be gargantuan!

The great majority of insurance direct marketing companies concentrate their efforts on the acquisition of new business in the first and third quarters of the calendar year.

Since most telemarketing operations feed from lead and policyowner flow which is generated during those two periods, other programs must be available for the second and fourth quarters of each year. This is for the purpose of making efficient use of the facilities.

On the outbound side, a large number of your representatives will be *licensed insurance agents.* Assume you determine that you want a core of 25 permanent licensed representatives. Consider what they will do during the 26 weeks of downtime each year. Good representatives are enormously hard to find, expensive to train, and difficult to keep. Thus, the situation requires a substantial amount of planning ahead, along this line.

In fact, personnel turnover is one of the big problems every direct marketer faces on this score. What might it take to keep your core group of 25 sales representatives busy 12 months a year? *About 11,000 leads a week*, assuming a 25-hour work week.

By feeding these leads—about 286,000 a year during downtime—into the telemarketing unit, you will always have a solid group of sales representatives available for programs all year long. Not, of course, to mention the income they produce.

In a new operation, there is a reluctance on the part of product or program managers—even marketing directors—to co-operate with the telemarketing unit as fully as they should.

Normally, such co-operation is initially dictated by general management. Ultimately, once the marketers experience the enhancement which telemarketing provides, the penetration in depth of lists, and the high T/MC ratios produced, objections diminish and disappear in favor of sales and profits.

In simple fact, the more leads delivered to the telemarketing unit, the more money the company makes.

You should anticipate that, in the initial stages of developing your telemarketing operations, there is going to be resistance from almost every department in the company! *Setting up the system for this intensive medium is intrusive.*

But, thankfully, there are some things that can help you overcome the tacit and active objections. If your administrative people are like most, they have a problem with incomplete applications. So:

SECRET No. 90

Calling those persons whose new applications are incomplete, obtaining the necessary information, and issuing the policy on a cash-with-application or send-no-money basis increases the number of policyowners who pay the first premium or pay renewal premiums on the coverage by 17% to 32%!

That kind of help will cause your administrators to warm quickly to the idea of telemarketing. Since the normal way to obtain missing information is through a slow series of form letters, this kind of incremental assistance can mean big dollars flowing through the system. And, it works on any product—guaranteed issue or underwritten.

There is one remaining source of telemarketing revenue that is very important to every insurance direct marketing organization. For one company leading in this type of business, it represents 12.8% of total telemarketing annual revenues.

SECRET No. 91

Unsolicited referrals, contacted by telephone follow-up, result in policy issues in excess of 100 per thousand.

MC/TARP ratios are frequently in the $3.20 to $5.00 range. Yet many companies pay little attention to "call-ins" and "write-ins." The consumers represent pre-sold prospects. And, with response rates of 10% or more, they should not, cannot, and—at smart marketing companies—will not be ignored!

These smart companies will not ignore the enormous benefits of effective telemarketing either. This brings about the personal communication that the direct marketing industry has sought from the beginning. Its emotional content is enormous. It compels, it motivates, and it performs—at exceedingly high efficiency ratios!

Proper training, proper scripting, and adherence to professional ethics—all three are critical elements in the development of your own phone facility.

The growth of the business is exploding. It represents, today, the leading edge of the technological revolution. And, until we add *phonevision*—which may not be so far in the future—it will remain the power medium of this decade...and perhaps for decades to come!

That fact does not diminish the power of each of the media available in the direct marketing mix. Just as an outbound telemarketing representative needs a script to perform his or her job, so too does an actor when filming a direct marketing TV commercial. Consumer contact begins in insurance direct marketing in the creative group.

Internal and external resources—writers and art directors—come together to perform the creative ritual. The amazing process by which concepts blend with words to develop clear and convincing arguments compel consumers to complete applications, generate inquiries, and say "yes" to selling propositions.

Now, let's take a closer look at the secrets of the insurance direct marketing creative process...and how you can unlock its mysteries.

The Secrets of Creativity

SECRET No. 92

Effective, persuasive communication is the
foundation of direct marketing creativity!

Since Neanderthal man roamed the inhospitable environs of the last glacial period, the drive to communicate might be considered the sixth human sense.

Humans, it seems, are incapable of silence. The mute vacuum of that distant time has given way to almost ubiquitous babble of the modern age.

The signs, symbols, icons, gestures, and proxemics—the utilization of time, space, and body position to communicate—of today are the heirs of more than ten thousand years of development.

"Communication . . . ," according to I.A. Richards, "takes place when one mind so acts upon its environment that another mind is influenced, and in that other mind an experience occurs which is like the experience in the first mind, and is caused in part by that experience." This IS the art of persuasion.

The communicators of insurance direct marketing are led by copywriters—wordsmiths charged with the responsibility of consumer contact.

For all of us, consumer contact is the *moment of truth.*

Months of work, including hundreds of hours of thinking and planning by every member of your direct marketing team, focuses on this instant in time.

In fact, all the work in the world cannot change this secret of insurance direct marketing creativity:

SECRET No. 93

You have less than 20 seconds to capture the attention of your prospect!

To get your prospect to open an envelope, read a headline, or pay attention to a television commercial—for this you have 20 seconds, maybe less! That's why it is so important to understand the creative process in insurance direct marketing.

Since most insurance direct marketers have a skimpy sense of the creative person's art, an exploration of the process is essential to an understanding of how to get the most from your creative resources.

Copy is basically persuasive communication in print or on electronic media. A copywriter is no more, nor less, than a salesperson. The writer has developed craftsmanship, inventiveness, intuition, discipline, style, and perception.

He employs insight, inspiration, knowledge, and instinct—in more or less equal parts—to shape a sales position for your product. Then the writer concentrates on that position and conceives a compelling presentation to interest the prospect, entice him to read or listen, and—what is most important—to act!

The direct marketing copywriter creates the lyrics; his partner, the art director, adds the music. The integration of the two produces a symphony that prospects cannot resist.

They cannot resist it, at least in theory. The sad truth is that prospects resist the "music" just about eight out of ten tries.

It's true. Out of every ten creative tests you execute, you will create a *winner*—that is, will increase the efficiency of your program by at least 25%—in just 2.5 tests.

In theory, that 25% increase in response or efficiency, makes up for the other 7.5 failures. But, the failures may not be completely that. Some testing will do as well as your *control positions*, some will be dismal failures, while others will improve results, but less than 25%.

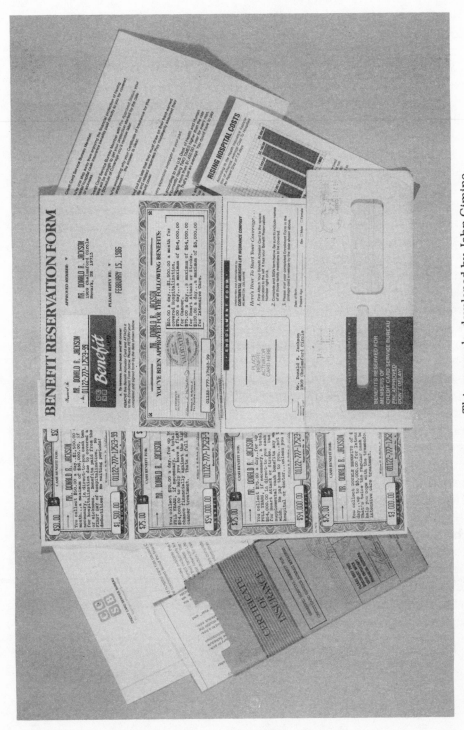

Figure 12-1: Inventive creative inspires response. This example, developed by John Cimino, Hockessin, DE, displays style and perception.

To the marketer, however, the only result to target is the 25% increase in efficiency. In the real world, there are creative tests that have increased efficiency by 50%, 75%, 100%, even 200% or 300%. But these breakthroughs are few and far between.

Since they do occur, how do they happen? The first step is the *idea*.

Every writer has a different technique for producing power ideas. Generally, however, each technique will include four parts. Initially, the writer will immerse his mind in the product, the competition, and the audience—cold facts. He will draw liberally from his reservoir of general information, personal life experiences, and previous bodies of work. He will keep at this *research* phase of concept production until he has obtained a jumble of facts and figures—bits and pieces of thoughts—some related, some unrelated. Included will be words randomly selected, snatches of rhythms, and elusive illuminations flickering in his brain.

Next, the data is mentally massaged. The writer looks for new relationships between facts and unique combinations. Many are discarded—some retained. His mind molds the research clay into shapes and formats—some tried and true, others never chanced at all. Words and phrases spill in colorful patterns and lists of "don't forgets."

Then, most frequently, the writer will stop seeking for a while. His search is not ended; he has simply sown seeds. Now it's time for the subconscious to take over. It is a period of germination, where—locked in the abundance of information—is the "idea." Breakthrough ideas and breakthrough copy, like fine wines, need aging. They cannot be rushed. But, finally, the *idea* is birthed.

James Webb, author of *A Technique For Producing Ideas*, adds a fifth step to the process...shaping and developing the idea for practical usefulness. For the most part, the direct marketing writer seldom loses sight of the fact that his idea must be *producible.* After the concept is born, the writer organizes the elements of the idea into practical formats. In a sense, the writer is trying to see with his audience's eyes...attempting to blend words with eye-catching formats that will persuasively communicate the value of the product.

To help the writer in this arduous journey of producing power ideas, the marketer and the internal staff can provide the elements of what will ultimately become the creative strategy.

SECRET No. 94

You geometrically increase your chance of break-

through creative execution when you base your program on a solid creative strategy!

The creative strategy is part information, part financial calculation, and part tactical plan. *It is all written!* It supports the overall marketing strategy and the specific program plan which it represents. It has seven parts.

1. *Product* Everything that has a close relationship to the product. Start with benefits and rates; then, exclusions; limitations; and reductions. Consider every group and non-group—in every state in which it can be marketed—as to renewability or conversion. Make sure your creative resource has a copy of the contract. Include average annual premium and previous experience with the product. Reveal prior and current conversion or renewal problems and collected premium experience. Comment on claims experience. Have there been complaints? Has there been praise? Are testimonials available? Be detailed.

2. *Competitive products* Compare your product with the competition. Work out a product-comparison chart that covers media, policy numbers, enrollment deadlines, specific benefits, elimination periods, benefit periods, pre-existing conditions, special provisions such as reductions at age 65, additional benefits, rates, issue ages, basis of rates, policy fees or absence thereof, and any special considerations. Include samples of other packages or creative work the competition has used. Try to keep records on how many times you've seen the same commercial, the same direct-mail package, or the same ad. Only successful creative efforts are repeated.

3. *The market* List everything you know about your audience: demographics and distribution of your existing book by state, gender, and age. Also list premiums and modal distribution, results of research—qualitative or quantitative. Have available the complete tactical marketing plan...articles, old files, history, hopes, and prognostication. Remember, the creative strategy searches for the clues available to unlock a breakthrough. Nothing is trivial!

4. *Media* Reveal the total book on media. If you sell the product through more than one medium, record how it works in each. Break media down; reveal results of past media tests, including the top-ten lists, TV stations, or other media. Also, reveal the bottom ten. Tell where you hope to take the program once it has been successfully tested.

5. *Budget* Here reveal how much money you intend to spend. Express your budgets in cost per thousand for direct mail, cost per lead for television, cost per application for space or alternative media. The point here is to overlay a financial rationale to the creative process. *It makes no sense to create a wonderful direct-mail package that is so expensive it has no chance to succeed.*

6. *Objectives* What is the objective of the creative project you are working on? It's too simplistic to merely say you want to increase response. Every insurance direct marketing program should have multiple objectives. The creative team needs to understand what the priorities are—from number one to number ten. Then you define your creative objectives.

7. *Execution* The final step in the process and in the creative-strategy document is to outline how you're going to meet your objectives: How your product is going to be positioned. What the offer will be and how you will apply the twenty seconds you have to capture the audience's attention. What the copy theme will be. How your creative effort fits into the system. And what will be the overall tactical plan. What benefits to promote, and what features to emphasize.

The creative strategy is the blueprint for your copywriter/art director team. It contains parts of all the work you've done to this point. And, it requires some sound thinking. The tighter your thinking, the more you will achieve, using your creative resources.

The creative strategy is in hand, the mental juices are flowing, the writer gets his big idea. Part of this technique is understanding human motivation.

Recall Chapter V on product development. Andi Emerson identified the eight basic human needs used to motivate a consumer direct marketing purchase:

- Making and saving money
- Winning praise
- Helping children and/or family
- Self-improvement
- Having fun
- Saving time and effort

○ Impressing others

○ Avoiding loss

The writer translates the motivations into emotional appeals. Themes are built carefully on these emotions. Consider these appeals:

Fear Frequently the fear of loss is an overpowering motivation in insurance direct marketing. It is sometimes more powerful than the positive motivations listed above. The fear of loss plays an important role in hospital indemnity and P&C coverages. Fear, alone, plays a role in guaranteed life products—especially if the respondent has recently been turned down for life insurance.

Guilt In terms of human emotion, guilt drives many people. If your creative position uses this motivator, it needs to be accompanied by a description of the dilemma...and the offer of salvation.

Greed To many people, insurance is a lottery. Where possible, the *living benefit* of a product should be emphasized. Things such as daily hospital indemnity, cash values, or return of premium make an impression on the consumer, because he has a benefit in the here and now.

Responsibility The sense of responsibility among consumers in your audience needs to be well established. It's a particularly effective theme for term life insurance sales.

Love Is there a more powerful human emotion? So many impulse actions are based on love. Since most supplementary insurance products are impulse purchases, it makes sense to invoke the emotion where appropriate.

Satisfaction Such things as intelligent decisions and selfless actions evoke satisfaction among people. And, in a sense, satisfaction leads to peace of mind.

This idea of *peace of mind* is important, but somewhat overused in the world of insurance direct marketing. Life is not a "cher of bowlies." It's hard for anyone to achieve a continuing sense of well-being and peace of mind. To most of the audiences we service, life is a struggle. Emphasizing the momentary advantage of achieving peace of mind...now, by acting today, remains a workable motivator.

Any others? As many as there are human emotions—for example: joy, happiness, anger, embarrassment, and need. Powerful ideas these, in their own right. As you weave the copy themes for your product, these power ideas and power words—to an extent—are worth weaving in.

There are two other words you need to consider: SAVE and FREE!

What can your product "save" the consumer: money? time? effort? worry? Focus on this word *save*. It is one of the most powerful direct marketing connotative words in the English language!

And, bless *free*—free information, free medical emergency card, or free membership. Anything free is likely to generate instant interest. A number of the most effective accident-product offers are likely to feature free protection for one, two, or three months. It's a wonderful list builder, generating qualified leads that will produce power response for two to three years.

Obviously, word concepts that motivate consumers to respond are very desirable. Frequently, the most successful are compound concepts. They use two or more ideas to express your offer or your product benefits.

Once your writer has isolated the buyer motivations around which the creative work revolves, the next task is formidable, indeed.

SECRET No. 95

Benefits must persuasively outweigh price in the mind of the consumer in order to cause him to assign irresistible value to your product, and to stimulate the action you seek!

Benefits divided by price equals value. Consumers in the late eighties are not the consumers of decades ago. The growth of direct marketing— and insurance direct marketing, specifically—has left a body of public knowledge about the products you sell.

Comparison, once urged as a credibility device, is a marketing reality today. Consumer buying decisions are made when the buyer considers how valuable the product is that you are selling. According to Bob Stone, this process is completely subjective...and very subconscious. In communication theory, the process can be described as *selective perception*. If the potential buyer perceives your product is sufficiently valuable, chances are good he will purchase it.

Obviously, if the potential buyer perceives the product does not have value—if the benefits do not overwhelmingly outweigh the price you are charging—he/she will refrain from buying.

That's why it is so important to express price properly:

SECRET No. 96

Never express the price of your product on the basis

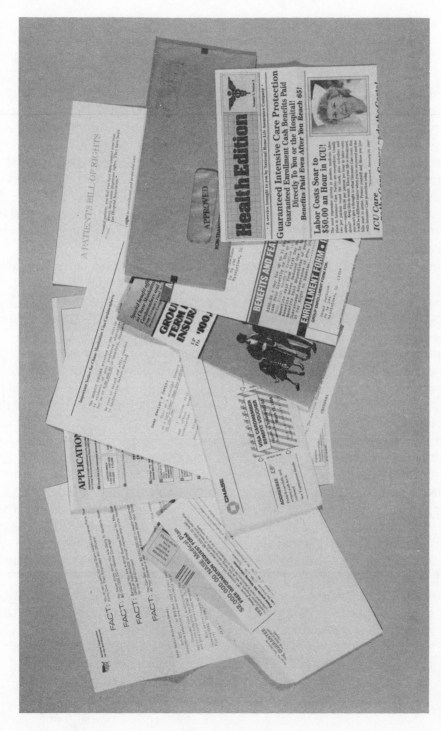

Figure 12-2: Free offers and free looks, stressing benefits, help produce the response you're looking for.

of annual, semianuual, or quarterly premium.
Always express your price in the smallest available
unit—usually monthly!

Remember the idea of conquest rates? The more benefits delivered for the lowest possible price drives the consumer to assign a high *value* to the product. Today, the expression of conquest rate is usually a monthly premium—which can be further broken down into weekly or daily cost.

Moreover, the idea of a deviated premium—a quarter or a dollar for the first month of coverage—is not dead. And, as has been noted, it is used quite successfully by a number of companies.

The fact is that price sensitivity does exist in insurance direct marketing. It is one of the principal factors in conversion and retention of policyowners.

Which leads to this: Do not confuse product *features* with product *benefits!*

The primary question every copywriter needs to ask is: *How will the product I'm writing about personally benefit the consumer?* This phase of copy development is essential and critical.

What does $50 a day in-hospital benefit mean to the consumer? How does an additional $50,000 of life insurance coverage benefit your policyowner? Of what earthly benefit to the policyholder is a $100,000 AD&D policy? What are the product's features and how do they become the product's benefits?

It is this process of translation that separates poor copy from good copy—from breakthrough copy. And this process of translation loops back to the motivations discussed previously. Basically, traditional insurance benefits do not translate, necessarily, to consumer benefits They are, in fact, a product feature. The $50-a-day in-hospital benefit makes the consumer benefit possible. Probably, the consumer can eliminate the worry of paying his bills, if he's hospitalized for a long period! Renewability is a feature, as is group vs. individual coverages, cancellation clauses, grace periods, or money-back guarantees—and free-look periods.

Blending these features, and the dozens more you can think of, into overwhelming benefits—psychological consumer perceptions—breaks the failure chain in testing and leads to sweet victory!

SECRET No. 97

The 40-40-20 rule is as applicable to insurance
direct marketing as it is to the industry in general.

Freeman F. Gosden, Jr. in his book *Direct Marketing Success* shares this rule, developed by Ed Mayer, who was long considered the dean of direct marketing.

The rule simply states that the success or failure of your program depends: 40% on the audience, 40% on you, your product, and your offer, and 20% on creative and format.

Turning these obvious thoughts around, *you will succeed in insurance direct marketing if you effectively communicate the right product with the right offer to the right audience!*

Consider this. You will never sell a Medicare-supplement product to an audience of 18 to 49 year olds. It is equally unlikely that you will sell a term-life product that issues up to age 59 to anyone in the retired market. So much for the importance of audience. *Writers need to know their audience.*

Your writer is justified in assuming that the product you have asked him to work with is the "right product." On the other hand, any writer worth his salt will tell you when your product is wrong.

That leaves the writer with the *right offer* to *effectively communicate* to the *right audience.*

SECRET No. 98

Creating the right insurance direct marketing offer increases your chance of success by 100%.

What is an offer? The offer is your deal. What you are going to give the consumer in return for something. It is the dream of every copywriter to come up with an absolutely irresistible offer. The one *offer* that no prospect can refuse.

In the early days of deviated premiums, offers were relatively easy to make—and almost always were "trial" offers: $1.00 for the first month's coverage!

Today, you still find that offer in the marketplace. But there are others:

○ *Guaranteed life insurance for folks over 50...$1.00 a week!*

○ *$50,000 of term life insurance...less than $10.00 a month for a man age 35!*

○ *$60 a day...$420 a week...$1,800 a month, when you are hospitalized for any covered accident or illness—your acceptance is GUARANTEED!*

○ *Free information on how you can save 10%, 20%—as much as*

209

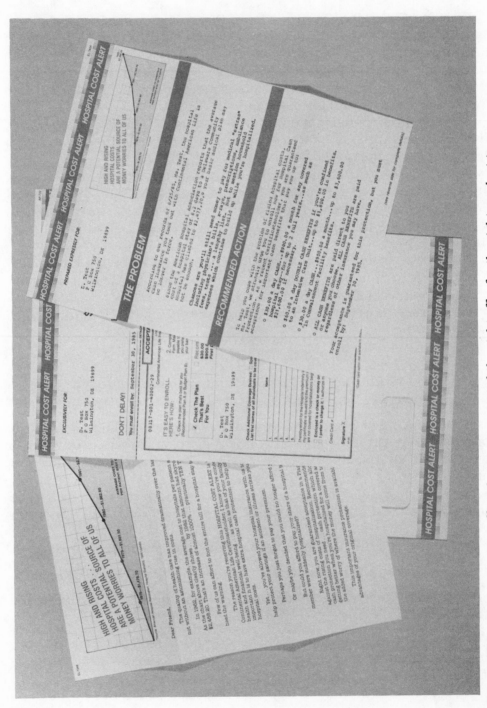

Figure 12-3: Another Cimino effort that communicated the right offer for the right product to the right audience.

40% on your automobile insurance!

Testing has shown that offers of this kind are the ones that work. The question is: Are they the only type of offers that will work?

Every adventurous writer will attempt to alter tried and true offers to create new ones. New offers seek to achieve three objectives. First, your offer seeks to attract your prospect's attention. Second, it seeks to capture your prospect's imagination. Third, it seeks to drive your prospect to the action you desire—by compelling him to believe it is in his best interest to act. And, almost every offer is a compound of many elements.

There are roughly 42 proven insurance direct marketing offers. Many of them are similar, but a little analysis will show that similarity is not duplication:

Right price
Money-back guarantee
Send no money
Automatic checking
  account deduction
Free gift for trial order
Mystery gift
Free booklet
Free survey of your needs
Cash discount (for annual
  premium payment)
Early bird discount
Nominal charge sample
  (deviated premium)
Enrollment periods
Limited enrollment
  (benefit reserve concept—
  you are going to limit
  sales to $20 million
  of life insurance)
Multiple guarantees
  (the more, the better)
Guaranteed return of
  premium
Good-better-best offer
Positive option
Free trial

Cash with order
Charge-card privilege
Free gift for inquiry
Free gift for enrolling
Free information
Free fact kit
Free cost estimate
Short-term introductory
  offer (first 3 months
  free)
Free sample
Limited-time offers
  (persuasion deadline)
Charter membership offer
  (new product)
Extended guarantees
Guaranteed acceptance
Deluxe offers
Write your own benefit
  offer
Blank-check offer
Yes/no option
Policyowner-get-a
  policyowner offer
Establish-the-value
  offers
30-day free look

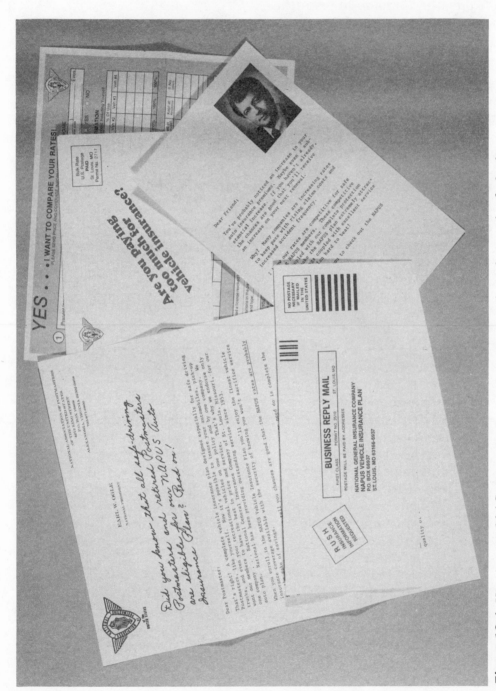

Figure 12-4: How irresistible! Saving money on auto insurance. A good example of a lead-generating piece with a strong, simple offer.

Third-party referral offer	Delayed-billing offers
Reduced down-payment offer	Stripped-down product offer

With a little imagination, you probably can add many more. You may want to consult Jim Kob's book *Profitable Direct Marketing*, in which he has developed the industry's comprehensive list of 99 Direct Marketing Offers. But, you will undoubtedly recognize that the offers you use today are made up of two or more from the above list.

As the offer is being shaped, keep in mind that you must not dilute the power of your offer by trying to achieve several non-complementary objectives! Generating a sale and an agent inquiry simultaneously, for example—or, trying to sell two dissimilar products in the same medium.

Remember that your deal needs to be a *good deal,* if you are going to generate acceptable response levels. Expressing your deal—using persuasive communication—is the guts of your creative effort. And that is, to a large degree, a matter of style.

Remember that style is the glue that holds together your creative efforts. Good grammar plays a marginal role in copywriting. Clarity and brevity are the keys that unlock persuasive communication. But, clearly, direct marketing copywriting marches to the proverbial beat of a different drummer.

In fact, copywriting may be the largest cottage industry in the direct marketing business. Consequently, writing style is as varied as a botanical garden. Nonetheless, there are some standards of style you can bet on.

SECRET No. 99

Use more you *than* I *or* we *in writing copy.*

Readers are more interested in what's in it for them than what you think about your products. Second person, present tense makes power copy.

SECRET No. 100

Avoid the tyranny of generalization.

Stay specific when presenting your benefits. Ensure that your copy is honed sharper than a machete!

SECRET No. 101

Short paragraphs, simple style, and impact *sentences lead to reader involvement.*

And, the more your readers are involved, the more you'll end up selling.

SECRET No. 102

Use emotional words—not intellectual words.

Demise is *death*, harm is *hurt*, exhibit is *show*, ill is *sick*, and omit is *leave out.* Do you get the idea?

SECRET No. 103

Copycat copy seldom succeeds like the original.

Good writers attempt to allow their grasp to exceed their reach. Analyze copy to find out what made it work. Then use these "success elements" to form a new platform or direction. In this way, *diamonds* are pressed from copycat carbon.

SECRET No. 104

Headlines prepare the reader for the feast to come.

Letters, brochures, space ads, inserts, or free-falls—the headline combines *curiosity* with *self-interest. What's good for starters? Announcing, new, how, how to, now, at last, reduced price, feature price, special offer, free, which, why, who else, wanted, advice,* or *audience call-outs.*

SECRET No. 105

Write with sizzle, hype, and psych!

Copy written in the white-hot heat of enthusiasm can be tamed. *Nothing can breath life into dead copy.*

SECRET No. 106

*Redundancy—repetition of major points—allows
the reader's mind to grasp what it tends to avoid
seeing.*

A basic principle in persuasive communication modeling is: Creative redundancy drives home the principal selling arguments, makes offers understandable, and propels purchases.

SECRET No. 107

*Conditional stoppers—"would," "could," and
"should"—are the* antithesis *of the assumed sale.*

Those auxiliary verbs seldom enhance effective copy. *Would* corresponds to *will*, in the subjunctive mood. It is undesirable, for our purposes, with *I* or *we*, since it expresses condition, doubt, or possibility—something that happens from time to time. *Should* with *I* or *we* makes the statement conditional, expressing only a *possible* future event. *Could* is the subjunctive mood of *can* and expresses a condition, a possibility, TO SELL, your attitude needs to be *positive*—not passive or conditional. These words are STOPPERS. To not use them requires craftsmanship and skill.

SECRET No. 108

*Parallel sentences and paragraphs inexorably
pull the reader through your writing, propelling him
to a moment of decision and compelling him to act!*

The most important sentence in an ad or direct-mail letter is the first one! If it fails to induce the reader to proceed to the second sentence, your sales effort fails at the start. And, if the second sentence fails to propel your reader to the third, it's equally dead. And so on and on.

Your lead paragraph works most effectively by revealing an interrupting idea, smashing the reader's *boredom barrier*. Then, each sentence that follows definitely tugs the reader onward, hooks him, and entices him to go on.

Here, your technique is dominant. As you write each concept, each idea becomes a pearl, strung together in an easy rhythm, similar to human speech. Subheads are *rungs* on your *ladder of logic*...simple...powerful. All evoke an ascending crescendo of benefits, culminating in:

SECRET No. 109

*Urging the reader to action is your goal. Simply
put, direct marketing copy always*, always asks for
the order!

To do anything else is a fool's trip—and an expensive one at that. But, "the order" might equally be either an application or an inquiry. *The order* in direct marketing is that action which you want your reader to take. And, what is most important, you want your reader to take it *now*!

SECRET No. 110

Avoid helping competitors!

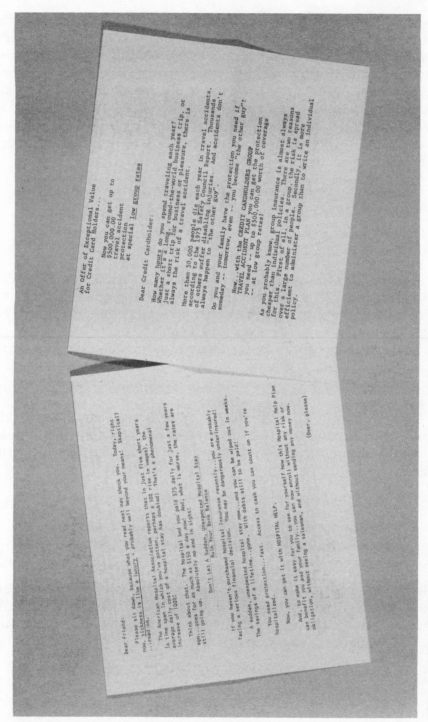

Figure 12-5: Strong, short opening paragraphs that lead the reader sentence by sentence to the next. Parallel construction works.

The job you want your copy to do is to sell *your* product, pointing out the benefits of your offer, your price, and your features. Convincing consumers that the generic category of product is good is wasting your time and your money. Don't just convince people they need life insurance. Convince them they need *your* life insurance!

SECRET No. 111

Believe in the power of the postscript.

The *P.S.* is the second most noticed part of a direct-mail letter. Reserve it as a "clincher"—a principal benefit, an idea, a thought that ties together and emphasizes the essence of what you are selling. Keep in mind that a *P.P.S.* dilutes the power and, in some cases, makes its imperative role totally neutral. That is not a very good idea.

SECRET No. 112

The more you tell, the more you sell!

This is perhaps the most tested axiom in direct marketing—the long copy vs. the short copy argument. Long copy, however, does not mean loose verbiage. It is not the function of copy to fill white space. It is the function of copy to propel readers to the decision to purchase.

Copy is relevant to the product. The attempt is to touch people on points of human contact. Long copy demands natural showmanship, human interest, and personality. The copy needs to be so entertaining that the prospect is induced to read it, and it needs to emphasize "buying points"— from your audience's point of view. A *buying point* is the converse of a "selling point." Remember *reader benefits?*

SECRET No. 113

Subscribe to Robert Louis Stevenson's observation:
"It takes hard writing to make easy reading."

Successful copy does not pop—ready to publish—from the word processor or the typewriter in first draft. Write, rewrite, and rewrite again! Craft your copy by using a vigorous, non-static style that suggests action. March the reader in the direction you want him to go! Use short sentences that are as clear as mountain streams and crystal words that tinkle in the mind's eye.

Style! It is the glue that holds together the creative effort. Apparent in these generalizations is the fact that insurance direct marketing copywriting has its own diction and rituals. Tested formulas exist for developing direct mail, as well as space and television copy. There is no great mystery to the technique, *but there is a mystique.*

The marketer's grumble about an unsuccessful test most frequently focuses on the failure of language. Yet language, per se, is responsible for no more than 20% of a successful mailing effort (Secret No. 97). Writers with an instinctive sense of rhetoric frequently cringe at the compliance phase of copy approval. *Test failures are more directly attributable to compliance specialists than to any other element in the direct marketing system!*

These paralegals—or, in some cases, attorneys—are known within the marketing environment as the "business prevention unit."

That is not to say that compliance people are not trying to be helpful. They are. It is their attitude that is the problem. Insurance direct marketing is highly regulated. In many cases, it is regulated by political appointees or elected officials who have no more sense of the direct marketing system than they have of insurance.

These bureaucrats believe their mission is to protect consumers from themselves. They insult the intelligence of the American consumer by prohibiting—as unbelievable as it sounds—the use of specific words in solicitation copy.

There is absolutely nothing wrong with the demand that advertising must not be misleading. There is a great deal wrong with an administrative devotion to the principle that the consumer cannot tell the difference between puffery and fact.

Consumers have been successfully doing that for years. It's simple, really: Consumers vote with their pocketbooks. You may be able to fool a consumer once, but it's unlikely that a company will become successful by consistently misleading consumers.

The argument that consumers are dumb about insurance matters, and need to be protected, doesn't hold much water in this day and age. You simply cannot underestimate your audience.

Against this background, the compliance folks begin to interpret the various state regulations and NAIC guidelines. The result is a veto power over copy distinctly out of proportion to the contribution by the compliance people to the business.

Business decisions are, rightly, left in the hands of a company's management group. Depending on the system and size of the operation, these decisions are made from the marketing director's level on up to the CEO.

Compliance is essentially a staff function, as opposed to a line function.

Since lawyers do not deliver profit, it seems reasonable that compliance should remain in an advisory role. The way corporate compliance policy is handled is obviously critical to success.

SECRET No. 114

In an advisory capacity, the compliance department of a direct marketing insurance organization is responsible for informing the business decision makers of the risks involved in executing a program. Compliance personnel should hold no veto power over creative material.

With the compliance function being considered advisory, you have a greater chance to create successful tests. This is not to say that the marketing decision maker can ignore the advice of the compliance people. Let's face it, insurance regulators carry a pretty big stick. The big stick is not the possible fines.

Repeated offenses, however, can cause an insurance company to lose its license to do business in a given state. From the marketer's point of view, that's losing a market. Winning a copy argument is not worth the cost of losing a market. So, it makes sense to balance the needs of marketing with the reality of regulation.

Despite the above, it is clear that the compliance unit is another partner in the marketing process. If the desire to reach the profit goal is mutual, ways and words can be found to achieve it. The plea here is for reason, not blind compliance. Working together, the writer and the compliance specialist can achieve the necessary balance—without destroying the selling power of the creative execution.

A friend once observed that the creative person needs to possess the wisdom of Solomon and the patience of Job. Writers always find themselves walking on a tightrope of some kind.

Marketer vs. creative director, CD vs. compliance, writer vs. marketer, and so on. If you allow your writers to maintain creative integrity in their work, you enhance your chances of developing, on some consistent basis, the *winners* you need to succeed.

SECRET No. 115

Breakthrough creative is built on a foundation of testing!

219

Chapter XII

Creative testing is different from media testing. Since 60% of the success of your creative effort depends on relating the product, offer, copy and format, it deserves a close look. So, let's examine the secrets of creative testing.

Figure 12-6: New format testing sometimes produces terrific results. Snap-paks are a good example.

XIII

The Secrets of
Creative Testing

Recall Secret No. 34!

Dick Benson's ultimate secret of creative testing: Rule No. 1: Test everything; Rule No. 2: See Rule No. 1.

Testing everything is a pretty tall order. But developing breakthrough creativity requires a kinetic approach to your creative material.

The first step is to take a look at your present material, the *control position review*. The objective of the review is to ask some serious questions about your current control position. A position that has accomplished the creative objectives you've set in your creative strategy document.

You need to ask four essential questions:

1. *Can production costs of the material be reduced?*

Reduction of costs leads to improved T/MC ratios.

2. *What changes and corrections must be made to the material?*

Are the required alterations significant? Do they change the basic thrust of the promotion? Do the changes of compliance relate to either elegance or improvements? Are they simple, complicated, and/or necessary?

3. *Has the target audience changed since the material appeared?*

As a result of the program, new information about your audience may have been, or could be, developed. New marketing data may have become obvious. The market itself may have undergone a transformation. For example, Medicare supplement products have changed dramatically, since the passage of catastrophic legislation.

4. *What lessons have been learned since the material last appeared?*

Nothing ever remains the same. Laser printing may be less expensive than impact. Markets, production techniques, and offer developments are all dynamic. In the direct marketing environment, change fosters new evidence. New facts require action.

It has been postulated that a direct marketing promotion is at its best when first conceived, and it's downhill from that point on. If this is true, improvement is always possible, and it's a delight when such a control position review results in a return to former glory.

There are two objectives to the review process.

First, you try to discern what minor alterations to the material will result in cost reduction, response improvement, and/or increased efficiency.

Second, you stimulate your gray matter to view the material multi-dimensionally, seeking radical alterations that can be made to test into a new control position. Let there be no mistake about it:

SECRET No. 116

Minor alteration to control packages can be made with impunity. Response and efficiency will, in almost every case, not be affected significantly!

That *does not include* changing the shape or size of an OSE, dropping in an untested offer, or adding a new sales letter. These are all examples of significant changes. It *does mean* maintaining the offer and sales appeal in a letter, but *tightening* the copy and adding a toll-free number is OK.

Always review your creative material after a successful test, or when a significant deviation in response occurs. Direct marketing *creative material seldom ages gracefully.* Acceptable performance can "metamorphosize" into disaster virtually overnight.

In many cases the *disaster* is the result of external factors. A new compliance review, a changing market, a production error, even a mis-

223

understanding of the original test results. Any of these, in addition to many others, can wreak havoc.

That's why you test! Then confirm your test results before designating new material as "control."

If minor alterations to your creative material improve results incrementally—from 5% to 15%—you're in good shape. But, remember, a breakthrough needs to be designed to improve results a minimum of 25%.

And, improving results means an increase in *efficiency*, as discussed in Chapter XII.

Offer testing has been explored in Chapter XII. Copy testing is different. Offers are part of your overall marketing strategy. Copy involves new sales ideas designed to make significant improvement in the performance of your creative effort.

Copy testing delivers an opportunity for you to take a chance with a reasonable expectation of success.

SECRET No. 117

Insignificant testing wastes your money, your time, and your effort!

This fits hand in glove with the minor alteration concept. You are taking a relatively insignificant risk when you include minor copy alterations in a rollout package. If response remains the same, you have hurt nothing. If it increases 1/10 of a percentage point, you're ahead of the game. *It is highly unlikely that your response will decrease—as long as you do not touch your sales idea.* Why, then, test your original control against a revised control with minor changes? *Reserve your energy for testing BIG DIFFERENCES!*

SECRET No. 118

Breakthrough creative is the result of animated, explosive, vibrant NEWNESS!

New offers, new formats, new sales positions, new graphics, new copy, direct-mail kits, television commercials, and media ads that are dramatically different from the current control position—all of these can come up winners.

Case in point: Shell Alpert, a veteran direct marketer, shared with the industry—in an article published in ZIP Magazine, 1979—the amazing story of one of the biggest direct-mail creative breakthroughs in insurance direct marketing history.

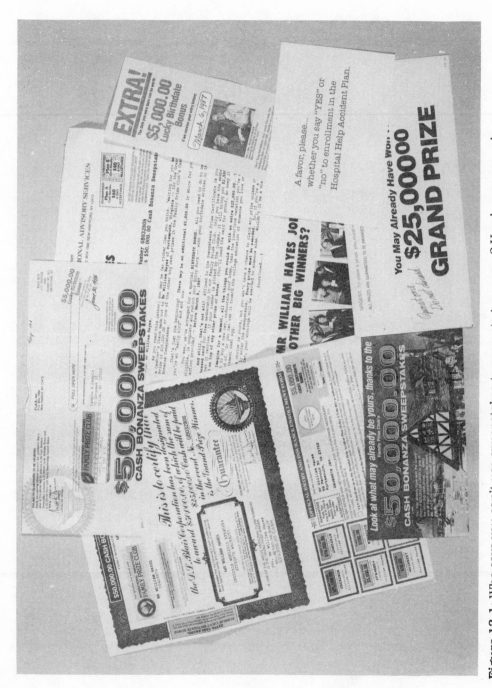

Figure 13-1: Who says you can't use sweepstakes to promote insurance? Here's one example of how to do it.

Figure 13-2: The Unit-set...a new format, with strong copy and graphics (another Cimino idea) blew away the control.

Union Fidelity Life Insurance Company, in the persons of Tom Garvey and Mike Wert—now principals in Dimark, Inc.—tested a dramatically new direct-mail package. Their old control—targeted to the Medicare supplement market—consisted of a No. 10 whitewove *OSE* with a teaser, plus conventional direct-mail kit components.

The test kit was "fancy-bordered, heavily computerized, show-windowed in a brown kraft 9"-by-12" jumbo—with a *shiny gold seal* so bedazzling it made me reach for my sunglasses ... " according to Alpert.

This now-famous UFLIC kit—modified for use today—outpulled the No. 10 control by 368%!

This was accomplished at a cost: The control kit in 1977 went into the mail for $150 per thousand. The test kit cost $400 per thousand. They increased cost by 167%, but increased response by 368%!

The point is made. Creative breakthroughs are, indeed, the result of big differences!

The success of this test points up another shibboleth worth examining: It is indisputably correct that, if you change more than one thing in a test, you will not know which "thing" is really responsible for the success or failure of the test. Yet, over and over, it has been proven that multi-element tests result in breakthroughs more frequently than single-element tests.

New sales ideas demand new shapes, designs, images, and treatments. Creating a new sales letter compels a compatible application, brochure, and OSE. A new celebrity endorser stimulates a new television script, scenario, and situation.

SECRET No. 119

Creative material that focuses on a breakthrough in testing philosophy is more apt to achieve a breakthrough result.

Minor control-kit modification achieves modest improvement. Multi-element testing (major changes)—newness—achieves breakthroughs.

Is there an in-between? Of course. Significant improvement in creative efficiency is most frequently accomplished by revision. Testing provides you with the chance to rearrange your proven sales ideas to display new facets. It is the building-block technique of copy testing.

Modifications, although not slight, do not represent a major overhaul. You attempt to keep what's good—what's been proven—and expand on it, by adding additional selling points, benefits, or new techniques.

Consider the plastic card. Package modifications built around the plastic card—a known response-producing device—are the most frequently

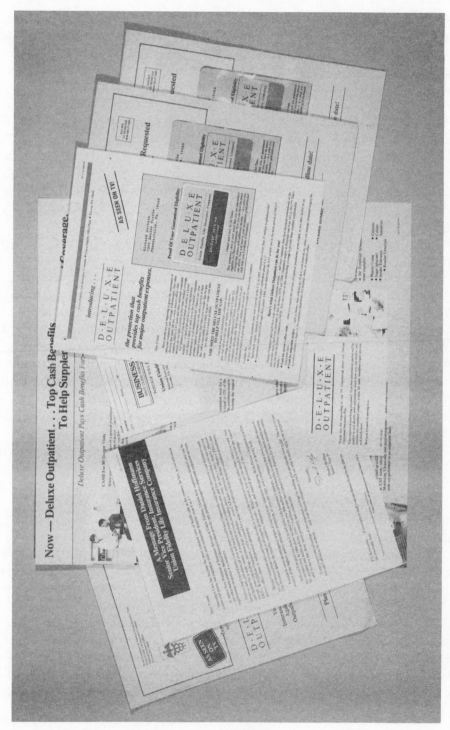

Figure 13-3: TV inquiry "Jumbo" fulfillment packages, without the gold seal remain part of UFLIC's creative strategy.

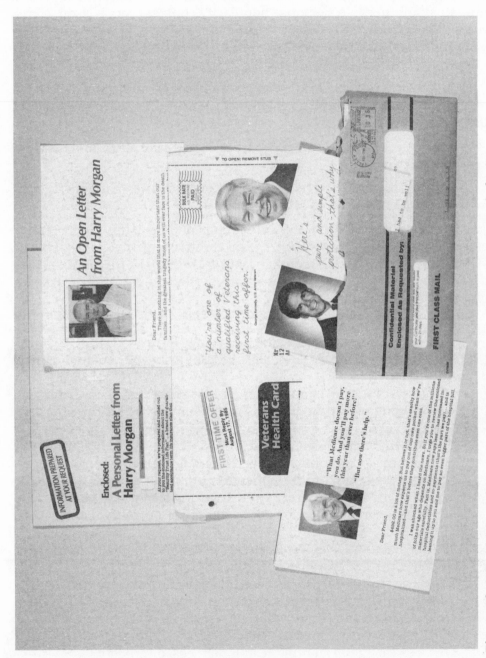

Figure 13-4: Remember, if you use a celebrity endorser, show your endorser's face on fulfillment material.

tested packages in insurance direct mail. Celebrity TV endorsers are pitted one against another in a response popularity contest every season. A rule given earlier in regard to creative testing applies here as well: Rule No. 1: Test everything. Rule No. 2: See Rule No. 1.

Three options for creative material:

1. *Modify your material* Make adjustments, additions, deletions, and maintain your sales ideas. Then roll. No need to test insignificant differences.

2. *Revise your material* Keep what's good, add more, and test into a new control position.

3. *The Blockbuster* In multi-element testing, concentrate on newness which could lead to breakthroughs.

Chances are pretty good that modifying and revising your creative material will be a function of the internal creative staff.

Going for the Gold—blockbuster testing—will most frequently fall to outside creative resources. The question is: How do you, as a marketer, evaluate new creative material?

You might consider silently asking these questions:

1. Is there a strong, irresistible copy platform?
2. Is the material dramatically different from your current control position?
3. Do graphics or visuals support and enhance the copy platform?
4. Will consumers be driven to open the envelope or to pay attention to the television set?
5. Do headlines persuade and pop?
6. Do copy and graphics deliver a forceful, impact-laden direction?
7. Does the benefit to the consumer jump out at you?
8. Is the material different from anything else you've seen?
9. Does the material reach out to you, grab you, pull you out of your chair?
10. Does the material use language in a colorful, imaginative way?
11. Does the material have enough YOU in it?
12. Is the material fresh, or does it look timeworn and tired?
13. If you use a plastic card, what meaning does it have?
14. Is NEED established?
15. Is GREED developed lustfully?
16. Does the material build fear, loneliness, or anxiety?
17. Is GUILT developed aggressively?

18. Does the material make you want to buy?

19. Does the material tell you what's in it for *you?*

20. Do dollars pop?

21. Are you moved through the material quickly?

22. Are arguments logical? Do they make sense?

23. Do arguments build to a frenzy level so the reader has no choice but to act...now?

24. Does copy get to the point fast?

25. Is the architecture of the material appropriate? Is the time right? Are there enough components in the kit?

26. Are you driven to the application, the form, the telephone?

27. Can you find the application easily?

28. Is the application easy to fill out? Are your prospects told HOW TO DO IT?

29. Is the approach suitable for the target audience?

30. Is it too highbrow? Too lowbrow?

31. Does the material make the most of the tools of the trade as to: format, personalization, full-color photos, testimonials, toll-free numbers, company history, crawls, supers, sets, cast?

32. Does the copy tell a story?

33. If it does, are you in the story?

34. Is the material believable?

35. Does the material support the marketing objective?

36. Can the material be produced?

37. Is the material too expensive?

38. Does the material work for you?

As a direct marketing professional, it's always dangerous to place yourself in the position of your customers. Evaluating new creative material is part historical perspective—knowing what has worked before—and part passion!

When you select material for an attempt at a blockbuster, creative breakthrough, you must be passionately behind your creative material 100%!

Now, let's examine some specific techniques for the three primary media: direct mail, television, and space advertising. And then take a peek at rules for inquiry generation.

The classic *invitation-to-contract* direct-mail package configuration starts in a No. 10 or 6x9 outside envelope. It includes a sales letter, brochure, application, "lift letter" or a hot sheet, and a business-reply envelope.

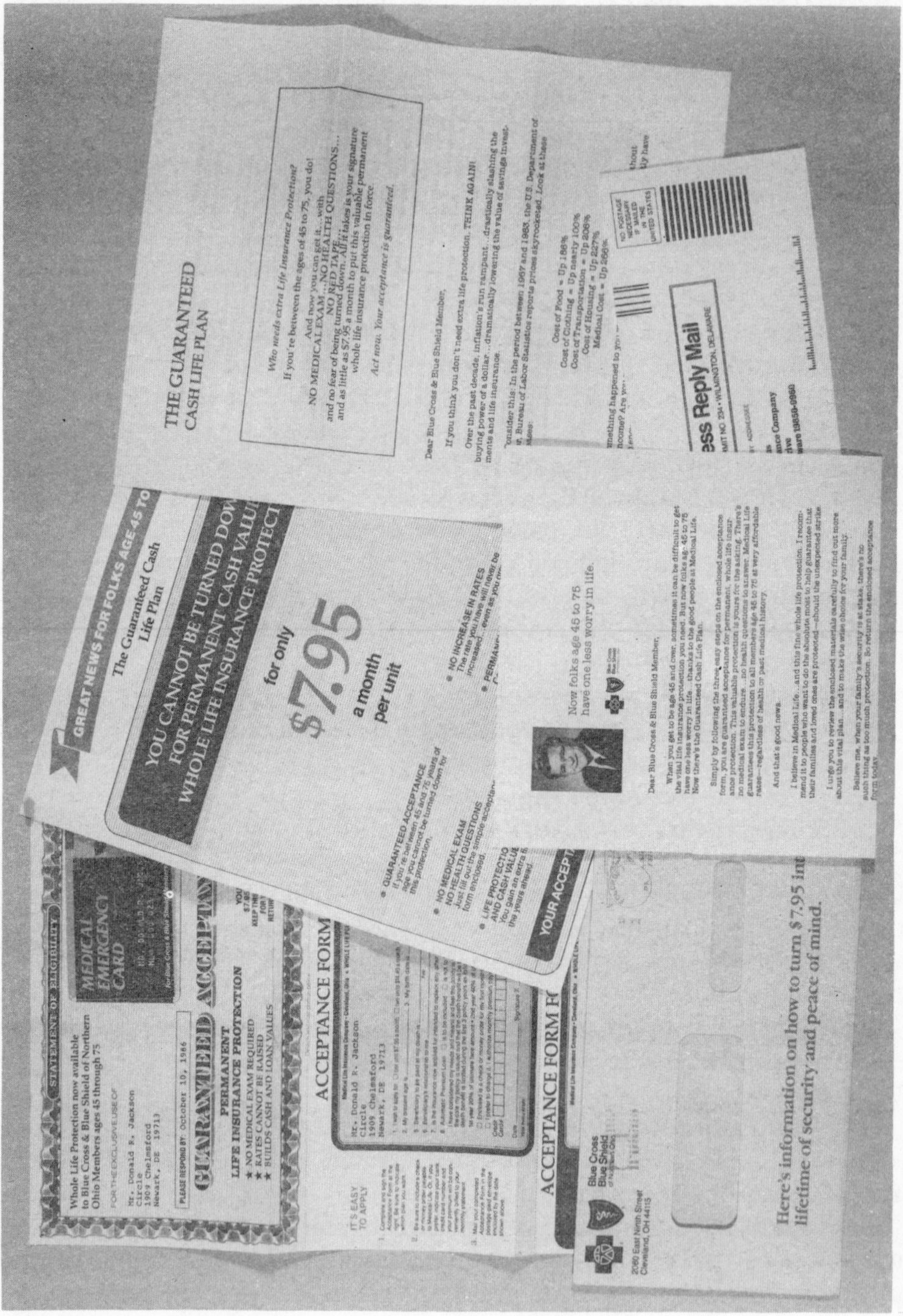

Figure 13-5: The classic direct-mail package

Each of these elements plays a critical and compatible role in selling your insurance product. The sales letter essentially substitutes for the agent. It provides the consumer-benefit leverage for the kit, communicates the offer, and propels the reader toward purchasing.

The brochure provides the detail. Explains features, illustrates guarantees, answers questions, carries testimonials, tells about the company, and—in general—supports the sales letter.

The application is the action device. It bounces back with or without cash and provides the underwriter with all the information necessary to issue the policy or certificate of insurance.

The business-reply envelope provides the prospect with a "no-cost" way to respond to your offer.

The lift letter acts as an endorser for your offer. It comes from a third-party in an endorsed-marketing effort, or perhaps from the president of your company in a broad-market offer. The hot sheet provides an attention-getting, power communication, emphasizing some special information about your offer…a real hot potato.

Finally, all the elements are placed in an outside envelope. The OSE in a direct-mail package is your door-opener! It is—arguably—the most critical element in the material. If your prospect does not open the OSE, the sale is lost forever.

It is the purpose of direct-mail testing to beat control positions. For the most part, the simple objective is to increase response in the blockbuster or breakthrough environment. You have to admit that a 368% increase is rather fantastic.

While the fundamental architecture of the direct-mail package will almost always remain the same, formats play a unique role.

SECRET No. 120

Major direct-mail breakthroughs are most frequently the result of unique formats, combined with compelling offers, rich information, and vivid copy.

All of the following are examples of the march of technology: The Union Fidelity jumbo, snap-paks, unit-sets, internal and external blow-on stickers, metallic impressions, computerized booklets, and ink-jet and laser personalization. The *march* also includes breakthrough format enhancements that result in blockbuster creative packaging.

Nowhere is the impact of format more crucial than in endorsed marketing.

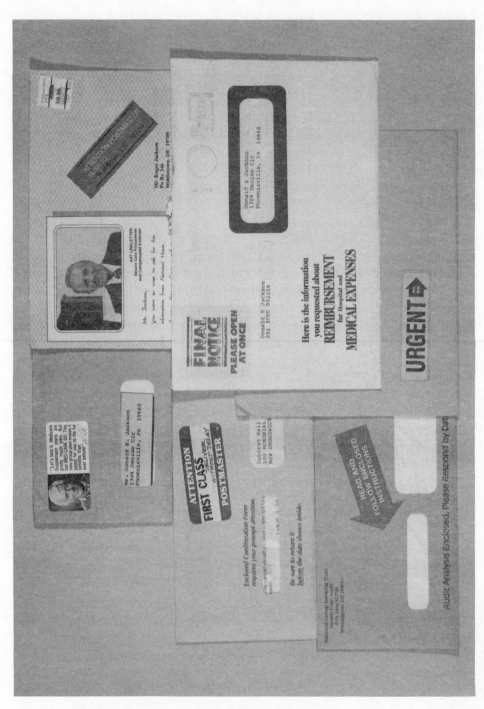

Figure 13-6: Blow-on stickers help get your envelopes opened.

SECRET No. 121

*In order to achieve maximum market penetration
for the same product, package rotation is a bare
necessity in endorsed-marketing environments.*

That means you need two control positions for each product you market to a third-party list. The reason is *boredom*. The same package repeatedly mailed to the same list experiences declining response rates. This is especially true when the third-party list is more or less static.

Your prospect may think he knows what's in the envelope. And, if the envelope doesn't get opened, your sale is lost. One national insurance direct marketer, who held a principal position in the small to medium S&L market, lost his position because he could not solve the problem of declining response rates. *The company had mailed the same control package more than ten times to the same lists!*

The place to begin developing a breakthrough direct-mail kit is the format, and the OSE.

The format determines the outside envelope. And, OSEs come in two kinds—solicitational and personal. Here are some stimulators that will help you and your people get started.

Elements of Solicitational OSEs:

Polybag	Jumbo
Coated stock	Giant windows
Multiple windows	Tear strips
Different colors	Full-color photos
Illustration	Ad-teaser copy
Legends	Copyrights showing
Labels/stamps	Plastic card showing through
Handwriting	Big type
Packaging innovations—	Blow-on stickers
wrappers	Personalization
Odd-shaped dies	Unusual stocks
Foil	Offer displayed
Unusual entrances—side,	Self-mailers
bottom, perforations	Aggressive graphics—
Third-class indicia	arrows, screens,
Company corner card	trap lines

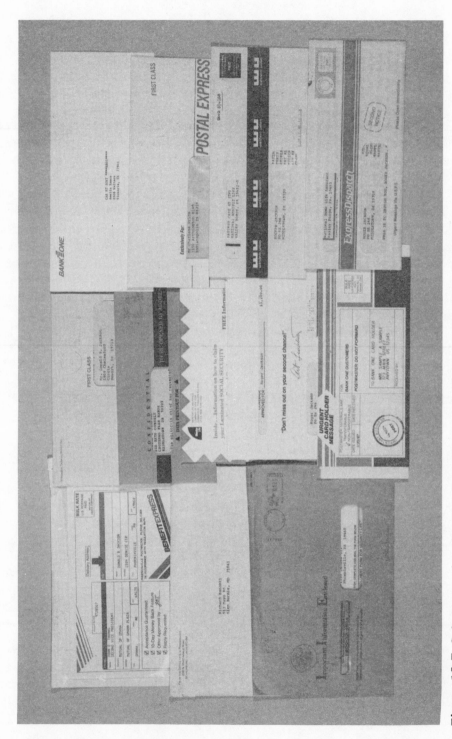

Figure 13-7: Solicitational or deceptively personal—spend time developing your OSE.

Elements of Personal OSEs:

Handwritten name/address	Closed-face envelopes
Small-card size	Plain white/buff
Live stamp	Personal name/return address
Typewritten name/address	Single window
Name of third party/address	Special delivery
Governmental/official	Quality stocks
Business size	No card showing through
Personal stationery	Script fonts
Metering	"Official" screens
Par Avion	Frosted glacene
Monarch size	Broken type, errors in
Watermarked stock	typewriter look
Embossed corner card	Foil lining
Banker's tint	

These are only a beginning. Your analysis of successful competitive packages will stimulate more thoughts. The things that are most important: keeping in touch with suppliers and vendors, ordering sample portfolios, and staying on top of the technology.

Next, comes the sales letter. After getting your prospect to open your envelope, the most important element of a direct-mail package is the sales letter.

Some thoughts for you to consider:

○ Letter headlines pay off envelope promises! If you use an envelope headline, it must co-ordinate with your letter headline. In short, when you make a promise on the envelope, show it the first thing in your letter.

○ Negative headlines work less well than positive headlines!

○ Trap long headlines in a "Johnson Box"! A *Johnson Box* is a graphic device, which *traps* your words in a box at the top of your letter.

○ Preprinted booklet letters (4 pages) outpull preprinted two-page letters in invitation-to-contract kits!

○ The more personalization, the better you'll pull—as long as the personalization is relevant.

○ There's absolutely nothing wrong with four separated pages in a sales letter.

○ The length of your letter is governed by the product you're selling.

○ Keep pace with technological innovation. Use ink-jet, laser printing, holograms.

○ Design your letter so it's easy to read—typewriter-size type for the under-65 market, 12-point type for the over-65 market.

○ Personal letters should look personal—not printed! Use a typewriter or printer to prepare.

There are many formulas for writing sales letters—from AIDA (attention-interest-desire-action) to more complicated breakdowns. Regardless of how your letters are written, in whatever architecture, *style* plays the key role. This subject is covered in Chapter XII.

Sales letters must not be dull. They need to be interesting, easy to read, easy to understand, and compelling. They must also be believable! In fact, the more credible your copy, the better your chance of developing a creative breakthrough.

If you use personalization, seek uniqueness. Using the name/address record as a guide, build tables that supply relevant information in the body copy of your letter:

○ The number of accidents in the prospect's state

○ The state capital or the governor's name

○ The cost of a hospital stay in the state

○ The cost of a nursing home stay

○ The average cost of health care in the state

○ The average number of life insurance policies issued in the state during a year

○ The average cost of auto repairs, homeowners insurance, the miles of roads, the state flower

○ Something unique about the neighborhood in which the prospect lives

The closer you come to relating the product you're selling to the needs of the prospect, the more you will sell. And, if you have DOB (date of birth), develop a birthday program.

SECRET No. 122

Birthday programs are most successful when you create a direct-mail package that is mailed first class—1 oz. or under!

This is tough to do. You bet! But it works.

Capture DOB data and you can create material that cites the signs of the zodiac, or relates to the number of people in the state of the same age, for example: Did you know that, of the 567,000 people in Nebraska turning 40 in 1988, less than half have enough life insurance? Are you among them, Mr. Jones? Also, you could show the amount of premium payments for a selected period.

The richer your relevant information, the better job personalization can do! But, you and your creative resources have to think. You have to use all the tools available, including all the mental power you possess, to come up with a breakthrough.

Now, a word about plastic cards.

You can show them or conceal them. When you mail them with the sales letter, they can be embossed or unembossed. If you use an unembossed plastic card, with the idea that the prospect must return it with his application, tell the prospect specifically what you want him to do with it!

If you use a concealed, embossed plastic card, let the prospect know it's in the package. Cover the area with a screen on the OSE. Don't let the prospect guess what you want him to do.

That's especially true for an application or enrollment form. In addition to all the things a filed app must have on it, you can add both detailed and clear instructions on how to fill in the form. Say it in the sales letter. Say it again on the application—*in more detail.*

Use arrows, numbered steps, handwritten instructions, screens. Incomplete apps are troublesome to most insurance direct marketing programs. But, it is remarkable how many incomplete apps are received, primarily because the prospect isn't at all sure what to do.

And, always show on the application form, your company name and address, as well as a toll-free telephone number. Always include with the letter a return envelope. You might be surprised at how many apps show up in plain, white, hand-addressed envelopes.

Consider including more than one application—for a spouse or friend— in every package. "Pass alongs" can be treasure troves for additional sales.

Finally, fill in every line you can on an application. The idea is to get the prospect to sign the thing and send it back. The easier it is, and the less your prospect has to do, the better off you are.

Brochures support the action elements of your kit. In order for you to be successful, your prospect has to open the envelope, read the letter, and send back the application—all are actions.

To get the finer points concerning the details of the product, your

Figure 13-8: Plastic cards remain tough to beat. Note the Social Security card—it was used for 13 years in a lead-generation program as a free gift. The trick? Make your card relevant.

prospect needs to turn to the information-heavy brochure. *The brochure is no less a selling effort than the letter.* However, its architecture is to inform, as well as sell.

Numbers should *pop* in brochures and express benefit amounts in "cents." ($25,000.00 vs. $25,000.) Fill your brochures with facts, details, benefits, features, guarantees, and testimonials.

In all, remember: The more you tell, the more you sell!

Finally, the lift note and the hot sheet. In direct-mail packages, the lift note does one or more of the following: 1) Draws the prospect's attention to the enclosed material. 2) Tells the prospect what he will lose if he does not act immediately. 3) Tells the prospect what he will gain if he acts immediately. 4) All of the above!

Hot sheets, frequently small-sized messages on colored stock, isolate and dramatize a unique feature, fact, or opportunity contained in your mailing. They may refer to a free gift...a deadline...a new feature...the offer...new information (current, of course)...a special chance...an item lost or gained. Hot sheets are strong, energetic, intense, incisive, and spirited. They represent the pop-art "pow" in your package. Keep in mind that they have two sides. Use them both.

The search for a breakthrough direct-mail kit is elusive, formidable, and expensive—but *it always pays dividends.*

The fact is, testing is not nearly as expensive as not testing! You must think as clearly and creatively as your writers, who keenly express your sales proposition.

Use your imagination! Challenge your mind! Refuse to accept "it cannot be done." Seek new truths, new rules, new axioms. Blaze creative trails! *In short, animate your creative, direct-mail testing.* Guaranteed: It adds zest to your professional life, and it lines the pockets of your company—and yours, as well.

The zest that direct-mail breakthroughs add to your professional life is matched by the thrill of a breakthrough television spot.

Television production, while glamorous, is darn hard work. While the result of these mini-movies looks easy, you haven't lived until you've worked on the twentieth take of a particular scene which is crucial to the success of your spot. A shot of a hand, inserting a key into a lock to open a door, for example.

The thing to remember about television creative testing is that you must attract the attention of an audience to your offer and product—and fast. That makes television commercials tricky little devils. So, most writers depend on invoking acute emotion in the first twenty seconds

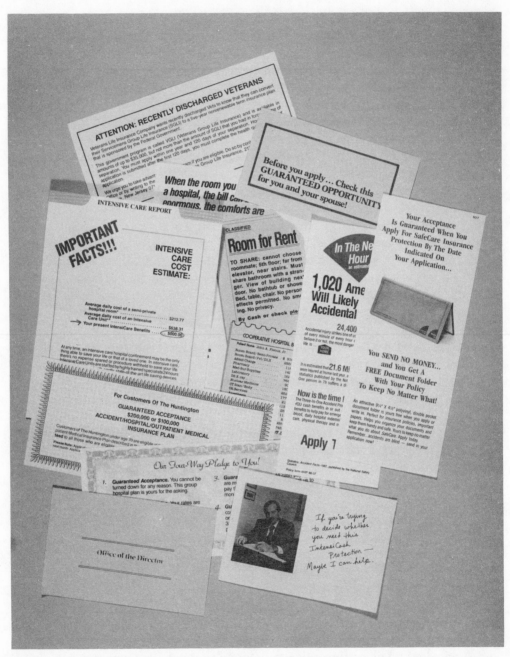

Figure 13-9: Hot sheets work to focus attention on a single element of your mailing.

of the commercial.

If you remember, from Chapter IX, the architecture of the most successful insurance direct marketing television commercials is divided into three parts—the 20-80-20 sequence.

    a. The first 20 seconds captures attention.

    b. The next 80 seconds is the pitch.

    c. The last 20 seconds is the end-tag.

Generically, there are four effective commercial formats:

1) The celebrity endorser
2) The spokesperson (usually a non-celebrity)
3) A slice-of-life
4) The parallel structure technique—showing a situation with the product and without

Whichever format you choose, there is one secret that must always be in the front of your mind:

SECRET No. 123

The key to a breakthrough insurance direct marketing television spot is product demonstration!

Demonstrating an insurance product on television is, at best, a serious challenge. Regulations forbid making a product look to the consumer as if he could unduly benefit from it. You cannot imply, for example, that the consumer might make a "profit" from your insurance coverage.

But, keep in mind the essential difference between an invitation *to contract* and an invitation *to inquire*. Television is invitation-to-inquire advertising and, as such, offers considerably more creative latitude than a direct-mail invitation to contract.

Your first job is to clearly identify the audience you are seeking to attract. The number of ways of doing so are infinite. You might choose the *announcement* technique. For example: Attention: If you are an honorably discharged veteran between the ages of 18 and 64, please stand by for an important announcement from (name of spokesperson or organization).

You use the visual technique, perhaps, of scrolling the words on the screen, and the audio technique of reproducing them as voice-over.

In a straight spokesperson spot, you might have your speaker talk directly into the camera, with a "super" at the bottom third of the screen displaying the basic elements of the audience "call-out"—veterans, ages 18-64.

Television is a relational medium.

The traditional techniques of audience call-outs can be modified by using identifiable visual images, coupled with high-impact scripting. Obvious senior citizens playing bridge and discussing the high cost of hospitalization, for example, should be effective. Or, a group of middle-aged men who, while playing cards, are talking about a friend who recently passed away, from a heart attack.

The idea is: You want the first twenty seconds of your commercial to be an attention getter as much as possible. It is your "envelope," and this segment of your spot is designed to get it "opened." At the same time, you establish the rationale of your commercial, hinting at the product you're going to be selling. Sensitivity and emotion are key concepts at the start of your spot.

Try to make a distinction between invitation-to-contract direct mail and invitation-to-inquire television. Most successful insurance direct-mail control positions are *offer/benefit* heavy. Most successful television insurance spots are *emotion* heavy—with the offer and benefits to follow.

In any event, once you have your audience's attention, the next job is to hold it. This is done with your offer and benefits. Use visual impact to help you do it.

Regardless of the format you've chosen, make your sets interesting. Relate them to your audience. For the marketer, this creates an unusual financial problem.

The question is, of course, how much you want to invest in a television commercial. A large production-dollar investment in a successful commercial dwindles to pennies per lead as the spot runs over and over in many markets. Conversely, the same dollar investment becomes financially intimidating if the spot does not work. You might consider two elements.

First, the spot you want to test needs to be as different as possible from your control position. If your control position is a celebrity spokesperson in an interior set, you're going to have to invest money—perhaps in a slice-of-life or parallel-structure challenge. Your budget, therefore, is dictated by your control position.

Second, make prudence your companion. Construct your test spot to achieve the marketing objective you've set for your program. Remember, your measure of success is not only cost per lead, but cost per conversion, as well.

Scripting is extremely important in this middle section of your spot. Make your copy here as compelling as possible. To the greatest extent possible, demonstrate the benefits of your product. *Product benefits answer human needs.*

Somehow you must make the inquirer understand that your product is going to make him feel better, answer a personal need, fulfill a desire, or reduce or eliminate a problem.

Attract attention with a dramatic opening; create and maintain interest with sharp visual and verbal structure. And, of course, ask for the order.

Now, we move to the end-tag. Spend the last twenty seconds of your spot telling people how to get the free information you've promised in your commercial. End-tags contain the 1-800 number for response, your name and address for those folks who prefer to write in, disclaimers if you need them, plan identification, and reinforcement of your audience call-out.

SECRET No. 124

Television commercial creative testing is "keyed" through 800 numbers.

Each creative test you run needs to have *its own 800 telephone number.* You then accumulate leads generated against each inbound telephone number. In this manner you can measure your cost per lead to determine the success of your spot testing.

Depending on how many tests are run, you may need a dozen or more inbound 800 numbers. The procedure is familiar to most inbound telemarketing services. As you search for such organizations to service your business, it's best to find one with experience that matches the kind of program you are running.

SECRET No. 125

The longer your 1-800 inbound number is on the screen, the greater the response you generate.

Displaying your 1-800 number is an important part of the architecture of your spot. Testing has shown that, in addition to displaying the inbound number for the full length of the end-tag, it will be most effective when displayed on the screen during the interior portion of the commercial. This is normally accomplished by "supering" the number at some logical point in your scripting.

In fact, keep in mind, *supers* are an integral part of your spot. Supers are used to emphasize principal selling points during your commercial. Supers can "crawl" along the bottom third of the screen, providing emphasis to the spoken word. A *crawl* displays words moving horizontally. A *super* appears on the screen, is held for a few seconds, then dissolves. A *scroll* moves words vertically from the bottom of the screen to some point halfway up the screen, where the words dissolve.

Supers, crawls, scrolls, sets, and people all help to hold the interest of the viewer during your spot. The insurance direct marketer uses all these devices to build intensity. And the person who helps the marketer achieve the best mix of audio and visual devices is the director.

Do not play *director*. Although the temptation is overwhelming to the experienced TV marketer, it is much smarter for the marketer to fill the role of *client-side producer*. Ensure that the spot meets the objectives of the program, displays the offer properly, has the appropriate disclaimers included and the right inbound 800 numbers displayed.

It is up to the director to co-ordinate and shoot the commercial. There's no substitute for experience in this regard. And there's no substitute for the post-production experience which a qualified television director brings to a program.

Editing a TV spot is a complicated business. It is necessary to maintain continuity, match scenes, use cuts and dissolves correctly. Keep in mind that your TV director supervises a team of highly qualified technicians.

The results are often startling. Gleamingly polished TV spots that are professionally developed, produced, and directed will enable you to achieve your targeted cost per lead.

In inquiry-generating programs, cost per lead and its companion—cost per conversion—are the name of the game. The glamour of television obscures, to a certain degree, the fact that other media also participate in inquiry-generating programs.

Space and direct mail generate leads at perfectly acceptable cost-per-lead ratios. The most important thing to understand about lead-generating programs—regardless of media—is that you are not asking for the sale, a commitment of money at that time.

What you are trying to do is get a qualified lead. An honest indication of interest among responders. Again, regardless of media, there are some common principles direct marketers use to achieve acceptable lead generation.

SECRET No. 126

KISS—Keep it short and simple *is critical in inquiry generation.*

Long copy is generally accepted as the key to closing a sale in an invitation-to-contract environment. But, for lead generation, short copy usually works best. The idea is to *telegraph* to readers that you have something vitally interesting to them and that they need to call or send for it now!

SECRET No. 127

Specific, attractive offers generate responses.

Many people send away for offers that are helpful, provide useful information, or provide something that can make their lives easier. But not for something that is vague and ill-defined.

SECRET No. 128

Never bury your offer.

Make your offer the hero of your inquiry-generating technique—whether for television, space, or direct mail. Once you have an attractive offer, feature it. Don't allow it to get lost.

SECRET No. 129

"Free gifts" usually hype response.

As long as the *free gift* is relevant to your foundation offer, it can significantly boost response. The foundation offer is the product you are selling. Free gifts, over the last ten decades, have been used to generate leads for a sales force, a direct marketing offer, and almost every kind of insurance product offered to the public.

SECRET No. 130

News attracts readers.

If you have news to report, feature it. News interests people and attracts them to consider your offer. A TV commercial that begins "The news from Medicare is not good...and that worries me" leads to a powerful sales pitch for the latest information on Medicare increases.

SECRET No. 131

*Target the specific interests of your audience.
Remember that the markets you are seeking are
different.*

There is no such thing as a "mass" market in insurance direct

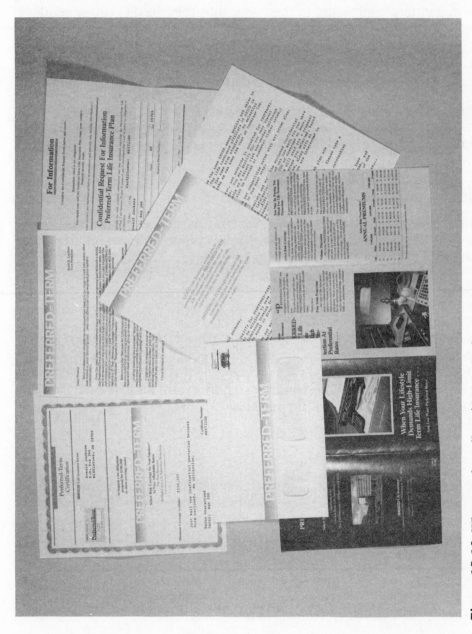

Figure 13-10: When you're selling $100,000 of term life, you give a little more information to generate the inquiry. This high-class effort teased throughout the copy.

marketing. Several types of people may be prospects for your product. *It pays to address each group differently.*

One more note: If you are using direct marketing lead-generating techniques to develop leads for your sales force, make your agents or brokers your partners in the effort. Agents—salesmen—hate to give credit for a sale to a direct-response lead. If they make the sale, it is their salesmanship that did it. If they don't, the lead was no good. It's best to get them to "buy into" the program right from the start.

Lead-generating programs are placed in newspaper and magazine space, "take ones," free-standing newspaper inserts (like Valassis), package enclosures, co-op mailings (like Carol Wright), Advo, and, yes—even on matchbook covers. They all work, especially when you pay attention to the basic principles above.

From direct-mail invitation-to-contract programs, to the variety of invitation-to-inquire programs, creative testing is critical. Space advertising for invitation-to-contract programs can still work, and creative testing is an essential ingredient. Consider newspaper advertising.

In the sixties and early 70s, newspaper advertising was a mainstay of insurance mail-order advertising. Full-page ads for HIP products appeared in almost every newspaper in the United States on a regular basis.

The architecture of the ads was common. There was a quick product identification in the headline, followed by big dollar benefits—spelled out in graphic details.

The copy was terse, filled with impact words. Subheads guided the reader from the first paragraph to the application. Side-bar boxes spelled out specific information. Frequently, graphs were used to support sales arguments.

Graphically, the advertising followed the format of the newspaper—four, five, or six columns. Photographs were used because testing showed they pulled better than illustrations. And response rolled in.

Eventually, full on-page advertising gave way to the free-fall insert. The FFI was organized in a similar way to the full-page newspaper ad. However, these booklets appeared mostly on Sundays and best shopping days. And, what is very important, the offer appeared on both the front and back covers of the FFI. Regardless of the way the insert fell out of the newspaper, the first thing a reader saw was the offer.

FFIs provided the testing grounds for celebrity endorsements. For the first time, Art Linkletter, even Roy Rogers and Dale Evans, promoted the sale of insurance products.

First came newspaper advertising. Then, free-fall inserts. Both provided

TEST DESIGN MATRIX

TEST: _____

PROJECT: _____   TARGET DATE: _____   PERSUASION DATE: _____

DESCRIPTION: _____

Description	Circ.	Apps.	Apps. /M	Issues	Issues /M	AARP	TARP	MC Test	R/O	TMC Test	R/O	CPM Test	R/O

COMMENTS: _____

CONFIDENCE LEVEL: _____   SIGNATURE: _____

Figure 13-11: Clear objectives lead to well-defined tests. . . as long as the numbers work.

the creative testing ground for the ultimate move into television.

The question, of course, is: Can newspapers and free-fall inserts still produce *invitation-to-contract* applications? The answer is...possibly.

To find out for sure, you've got to test. Can newspapers and free-fall inserts produce *invitation-to-inquire* response? The answer is...yes! It is being done successfully right now.

Part of the success of creative testing is clearly defining your objectives. To do that, as part of the tactical planning process, you set up a test-design matrix. See Figure 13-11. The matrix identifies the details of what you are testing—invitation to contract or invitation to inquire. The matrix helps define and clarify objectives. And, it provides detailed information on which you, the marketer, can make an intelligent judgment about the value of the proposed test.

To the insurance direct marketer, the process of creative testing is akin to the process of breathing. If you are to succeed—regardless of your assignment—you have to test. Obviously, if you want to live, it's a good idea to breathe.

Thinking up a new test is a tough job. To stimulate your thinking, you might consider these key copy and graphics points—and then add to them:

Guaranteed acceptance	You're chosen
Low group rates	Exclusively for
Red	Eligibility
Yellow	Guaranteed eligibility
Money green	Johnson box
Certificate borders	Graphs
Exclamation points	Charts
Qs and As	Arrows
Preferred	Hand graphics
Select	Scissors graphics
Pre-approved	Detach here
Entitlement	Here's how
Toll-free telephone number	Here's why
Photo of building	You cannot be turned down
Number of years in business	No matter what
Pays you	No questions asked
Add $XX.00	Absolutely
Cash, cash, cash	You're approved already
Testimonials	All you do is
Pix with testimonials	It's as easy as
Signatures in color	For the cost of a _____
Over please (handwritten)	Pennies a day
Handwritten message	Pennies a week

Check graphics	1, 2, 3
Accident *and* illness	A day, a week, a month
Important	In all
Valuable	No medical exam
Remarkable	No health questions
Revolutionary	No long forms
Designed for you	Permanent protection
Please reply by	You can never be cancelled
Rushed to you	Only you can cancel
Immediately	Don't delay
Right now	Act now!
Extra	Why wait?
Big-dollar	Do it now!
Additional	Take a minute
Just for you	Do yourself a favor
Direct to you	Think of them
Direct to the consumer	Do it for them
Notice	Your loved ones
Notification	Your family
Announcement	Those you love
Bulletin	Those who love you
Verification	Computer fill-in
Revision	Sell letters with no letterhead
Acceptance	Cartoon graphics
Big type	Easy to read
What can be easier?	Full-color photos
You'll never regret it	Families
It's a smart move	Hospital-room photo
Four plans to choose from	Big benefits
Take your pick	Acceptance form
Optional coverage	Guaranteed-acceptance form
At no extra cost	Urgent
30 days to decide	Cash values
No risk	Gaps
No obligation	Fill the gaps
In the privacy of	The rest is up to you
No pressure	The rest is up to them
No salesman will call	How will you pay?
Show it to a trusted friend	Think again
Yours to keep	Your estate
Keep it in a safe place	Your security
Official	Peace of mind
Costs are rising	You'll rest easier
Costs are skyrocketing	They'll be protected
Can you afford	They'll love you for it

Ask yourself this question	Don't forget
One for you, one for your spouse	You can trust (company)
Supplemental	Everyday expenses
Two coverages in one	Cost of living
80/20	But what about _____
Yours to spend as you see fit	Take the first step
You decide for yourself	Sign here
I urge you	Only your signature is required
I advise you	Enclose your check
Take a look	We'll do the rest
You get all these benefits	Expressly
For only	Express
For just	Stickers
Activate	Sweepstakes
Put your coverage in force	Open enrollment
Borders	Voucher
Stamps	Report
Rates do not increase as you get older	Retain for your records
Hotline	Postage-free
Call us anytime	Postage-paid
Guarantees	No postage necessary
What's more	FREE
Discount	Your money is refunded
00% off	Money-back offer
You can't lose	Cash-back
Friendly specialists	100% back
On standby	Backed by
Fast claims payment	Our pledge to you
Plus	Features
We're in the business of paying claims	Personal
	P.S.
Convenient payment options	Handwritten P.S.
Fast	Numbers on pages
Easy	Prompt
Convenient	On the money
You get	Increase in benefits
Handwritten margin notes	Carbon spot
Compare	Action device
Outstanding	Transfer device
Portfolio	Enclosed
Good news	Included
Respond/reply	For your convenience
Summary	Details inside
Plan	Look inside
	Check here

Live stamp
Charge it
5-way pledge
Closed-face OSE
Odd-shaped windows
Cards showing through
Nothing showing through
Pull this off
Put your thumb here
Here's how to enroll
Prepared for
Update
Policyowner
Policyholder
Valued
You have the right
Whomever you choose
Your attention
Signature "X"
Mail today
Mail immediately
Questions
Low
Affordable
Round-the-clock
24-hour
Proven track record
Paid in _____ days
Foil seals
Snap-paks
Risk free
Make it bigger
Gifts that last
Certificates
Bank draft
Registered

Your personal rate
Your rate quote
Cover the entire family
One low monthly payment
Short words
Startle
Impact
Customers
Cardholder
Automatically
Or, you can
It's up to you
Complete and sign this form
Month/day/year
Mail now
Mail right away
Group
Modest
Economical
Around the world
Recommended
$$$$ in claims paid
First-rate service
Foil embossing
Unit sets
Your chance/opportunity
Make it smaller
You earned the best
Checks
Coupon
Certified
Premium
Attention, postmaster
Bonus
Detach here

The list is probably incomplete. Use it as a beginning to generate your own testing ideas.

By now it's apparent that concept is the coin of insurance direct marketing. And, hopefully, the point has been made that insurance direct marketing is a "team" effort.

There is an area of the business that deserves further consideration. It is administration. Without the administrative function, all the great marketing, terrific creative work, and successful testing end up in the garbage.

Let's find out why, and reveal some of administration's fundamental secrets.

The Secrets of
Administration

It is impossible to separate administrative functions in the insurance direct marketing system from internal marketing procedures. Period!

And, it is important for the marketer to understand some of the more basic functions of administration in order to appreciate the problems that administrators face in program execution.

To begin:

SECRET No. 132

Administration is an integrated part of the entire insurance direct marketing system.

Administration concerns itself with seven areas of the direct marketing system:

1. Data processing
2. Underwriting
3. Fulfillment
4. Premium billing and collecting
5. Customer service
6. Claims

7. Mail processing

As you have already seen, Chapter X (Secret No. 55 through No. 58) isolates the critical factors in fulfillment, premium billing, and collecting.

And, while these factors are critical (credibility, speed in fulfillment, endorsement source, and automatic premium collection), you can add one more to the list. Perhaps an even more basic factor.

SECRET No. 133

Insurance direct marketing is a market-driven system! It is not a system driven by administrative considerations, claims considerations, data processing considerations, or anything else.

Administration exists to support the marketing effort. Too frequently, companies getting into insurance direct marketing attempt to force the elements of the distribution technique into a pre-existing administrative system—one that was created, for example, to handle agent-generated business. *It doesn't work!*

If you recall, policies (or certificates) requiring underwriting must be turned around in the direct-response configuration—sent back to the consumer—within three to five days. Now, companies who turn around their policies within that time frame achieve *paid* rates in the 65% to 75% bracket. Companies who take ten, twenty, even thirty days to issue an underwritten policy achieve *paid* rates of less than half—in the vicinity of 15% to 35%.

No direct-response marketing program can be successful with policy-paid rates that low! It's a small example, but it demonstrates how critical the back-room operations are to the front-end, direct-response marketing-program success.

It all revolves around money! The administrative department processes the applications and collects the premium that your marketing programs generate. Without the premium, nobody collects a paycheck, because there isn't any money coming in. It's simple, isn't it?

Administrative personnel must be as devoted to and fired by the system as the marketers. They need to be totally responsive to the requirements of the marketing program. And, it doesn't matter what type of marketing program you're thinking about.

Agent lead generation requires administration that is different from direct-response insurance. TV-inquiry fulfillment is different from a cash-with-app direct-mail program. The key is efficiency.

Efficiency is needed in moving product to consumer. The more efficient your operations are, the lower your administrative processing costs. The lower your administrative processing costs, the greater the impact on your financial condition. Administrative efficiency can help to lower product prices, increase marketing allowances, or a combination of both.

There is, really, nothing sadder than seeing an operations department eating up 18% to 30%, or more, of first-year premium simply to get a paid policy on the books.

Hopefully, the point is made. In insurance direct marketing...everyone is a "marketer."

OK, that leads to:

SECRET No. 134

The absolute secret to administrative efficiency is
processing in large volume.

The reason for this is easy to understand. The lower the policy or certificate unit cost for processing, the higher the efficiency of the operation. And, make no mistake about it—the measure is *unit cost.* It is simply more efficient to process 100,000 new policies a year than 10,000 new policies in the same time.

It is essential for you to know the *administrative unit cost to process an application.* Without knowing the cost, there is virtually no way for you to run profitability analysis on your programs.

In any event, computers are set up to handle large volumes of business. It is a dragon that requires constant nourishment. As a marketer, you must feed the administrative dragon constantly.

Since a large portion of insurance direct-response marketing business is written in the first and third quarters of each year, the operations folks face a very real problem of peaks and valleys that needs your attention.

For the most part, insurance direct marketing is thought of as a twelve-month-a-year business. That is to a large extent true. In marketing terms, the insurance needs of a prospect don't disappear every April and every October. Yet, because of seasonal variation, you experience better response rates in first and third quarters than in the second and fourth. How do you, the marketer, assist your administrative brethren in ironing out the peaks and valleys? It is a function of planning an effective tactical marketing strategy.

SECRET No. 135

Run broad-marketing programs in quarters one

and three.

SECRET No. 136

*Run third-party programs ten months a year
...probably eliminating June and November.*

SECRET No. 137

*Run internal-marketing programs twelve months
a year.*

SECRET No. 138

*Run telemarketing programs twelve months a
year.*

By running your marketing programs this way, you will be constantly feeding certificates, policies, and riders into your new-business processing system. While some peaks and valleys will still exist, the operations personnel can plan for them and control expenses more efficiently.

To help them do that, you must provide them with response projections—*real* response projections. For the most part, you've already done exactly that when you created your tactical plans which support your overall strategic plan. What remains is to deftly update your projections on at least a quarterly, if not a monthly, basis in order to reflect changes in your various marketing-response patterns.

Now, at the heart of the insurance direct marketing fulfillment system is new-business processing. At the outset, you and your administrative partners need to make a decision as to *what point in time you will begin to process new business internally.*

It doesn't matter which of the three selling methods you are using: mail-order, agency or brokerage, or direct.

SECRET No. 139

*Internal new-business processing is most effective
when you initialize the system by handling
applications or enrollment forms.*

In a sense, this takes your operations people out of the inquiry/fulfillment business. In volume, inquiries generated from television or print campaigns are better handled outside your normal new-business processing system. In mail-order insurance sales, these inquiries enter an automated three-to-five-effort fulfillment system. Quantities are generally so large that it is difficult, at best, to create an internal administrative staff to handle them. This is true, especially when, in fact, there are external organizations that specialize in the process.

As with most "rules" in insurance direct marketing, there are exceptions. Low-volume lead-generating programs can be successfully handled internally. If you are generating leads for a captive sales force, it is likely you are best served handling them internally for tracking, as well as for security, reasons.

But, remember, in direct-response insurance marketing, every application has a value—an average annual renewal premium, and a lifetime value. As well, every application contains information to input to your database. In systems development this is the logical jumping-off point.

Now, in a macro way, let's look at the basic requirements for your data-processing system. The first thing to realize is that data processing is divided into two parts. In simple terms, Part A is the marketing area, and Part B is the accounting and finance area.

In general, there are two or three architectural concepts that need to be integrated into your data-processing system. The first requirement in the database system is the *policyowner master data* file.

In general, this file accumulates name and address, personal statistics, policy ownership (including status by plan—in process, declined, not taken, in force, reinstatements, lapsed, and cancellation). All of these items form a basic library of data. Chapter X covered this in detail. Next, this library interacts with other datasets or libraries: *policyowner administrative data*—consisting of policy change audit trail and correspondence history; *policyowner marketing history*—including offers made, and status (accepted, declined, or ignored); *policyowner paid data*—including billing detail, payment detail, period summaries, credit-card numbers, and checking account numbers; and *policyowner claims data*—including open claims, claims history, and status (paid or declined).

The second architectural concept is the *product master data* file. Its purpose is to extract and accumulate data relating to each of the products in your mail-order marketing portfolio. This file contains plan identifications and detailed descriptions.

Then, that file interacts with the *underwriting* file, which contains acceptance criteria, underwriting rules, and data requirements. Then comes a *telemarketing script* file, which contains script texts associated with specific projects. The *claims rule* file follows. This holds coverage risks, coverage levels, adjudication rules, and waiting periods. Lastly, there is the *marketing data* file, which is a pivotal library of information regarding the tactical elements of a marketing effort.

Most companies have some sort of ALERT document that allows administrators to set up for a specific program. This form contains all the information needed to achieve proper fulfillment for a program. It begins by identifying the product to be sold and its parameters—health, life, accident, auto, homeowners...whatever. Then comes guaranteed issue or under-written, how it's to be sold—through trusts, third party, telemarketing, or internal marketing. The ALERT document covers a control number (identifying the project), split codes for testing, media codes, drop or appearance dates, circulation, estimated issues, persuasion or enrollment deadlines—as well as classifying as to group or individual configurations.

ALERT continues by defining the payment options to be offered—direct bill, credit card, automatic checking account deduction, or combinations. It lets the administrators know if an agent or broker is involved and commission arrangements with the third party. It specifically outlines the states in which the program will appear. It specifies the fulfillment configuration—plastic card type, policy or certificate jacket, letters to be sent, add-on offers to be made with the fulfillment, and other fulfillment inserts.

This same document also contains all the estimated costs and revenues associated with the program. All these data end up in the marketing data file, which is the first of three "swing" files in your system. A *swing file* is one which acts as a bridge from the marketing-data-processing area to the accounting-data-processing area.

Two other files interact, as well, with the product master data file: The *actuarial basis* file contains data on mortality and morbidity as-sumptions, as well as claims assumptions for casualty products. This file also holds the expense formulas and reserve-basis requirements. The *costs/revenues* file extracts actual premiums, marketing costs, claims costs, and other costs associated with every product and every program, as they enter the system through accounting input.

All these data libraries interconnect with your company's accounting system—usually designated the general ledger system. Taken together, they form the basis for the data-processing requirements in insurance direct marketing.

There is one other bucket in the system that you may need, if your company is in the third-party (or endorsed) marketing business. The *third-party master data* file contains a host of data specifically for this marketing technique—including the name and address of the endorser, contacts, affinity definition, current status, group size, key demographics, limitations on solicitation, and so on. This file interacts with the marketing data file and extracts and sends some of the file data (described above) to a *special commission data file*. The latter file extracts the commission basis for compensating the third party and the appropriate internal sales people, or external agents or brokers. As well, it tracks the applicable campaigns conducted to the group and creates a commission-paid history for the endorsing group.

Finally, three other datasets are created to assist in the administrative process. Two concern the customer service function: First, the *correspondence text* file allows you to create "personalized" texts to help answer the multitude of questions generated by the business. This file establishes paragraph selection criteria in regard to extracting data from applications, claims administration, policy change data, lapses, cancellations, and so on, from the various libraries in the system. As well, it defines paragraph insert requirements, supplies paragraph texts, and accumulates usage statistics.

The *service referral data* file allows your customer service people to handle large volumes of information requests. Input data identifies the service requestor by name and address, telephone number, and policy number. The service requested is identified, the date requested, the disposition of the request—including to whom referred, action taken, action date, and follow-up.

In the most sophisticated operations, there will be a *credit billing transfer data* file. This extracts policy data, billing amount, credit-card type, and expiration date and account number. Also, it creates control totals. This allows electronic debit procedures through tape-to-tape transfer with a credit-card clearing house, and basically eliminates the need for a manual process.

Obviously, this is only *one* architectural design for an insurance direct marketing data-processing system. But, it covers all the bases. Each library of data interacts with others to allow efficient handling of most requirements. Most essential is the database described in Chapter X.

Next, consider how parts of this system work for you. To begin with, let's examine the new-business processing part of the system.

Now, there are two distinct mail-order insurance new-business processing systems: cash with application and send no money.

The difference between the two is that the cash-with-application system (including credit card) issues a live policy with a *live* effective date (effective date = issue date). While, in contrast, the send-no-money system issues a live policy with—in most cases—an *advanced* effective date (effective date = issue date + 10 to 20 days).

Cash-with-application issues drop directly into the normal premium-billing and collection system. Send-no-money issues drop into a special premium-billing and collection system. The two billing systems are distinctly different, for they seek to achieve different objectives:

Cash-with-application fulfillment material seeks to conserve the policyowner by collecting the next premium installment.

Send-no-money fulfillment material seeks to convert the consumer to a policyowner by collecting the first premium installment.

Review, for a moment, the contents of the fulfillment kit. The policy (or certificate of insurance, in the case of a group product) is wrapped in an attractive jacket or holder. A plastic identification card serves the purpose of establishing *affinity*—in a sense, the idea of membership. A business-reply envelope, company information, and claim-filing information are also included. Next, there is the appropriate premium notice (for first or next premium) and a sales letter (or welcome letter). Finally, included is a brochure covering the various options the policyowner has to 1) save money on premiums and 2) authorize automatic premium payment.

The key to the effectiveness of this fulfillment material is personalization. Output from the new-business processing system generates three pieces of material: First, there is the *schedule* page of the policy or certificate. This includes all the information about the policyowner and the coverage purchased. This page is then folded into the preprinted policy-information material and tucked carefully away inside the policy jacket. Next, an output tape is created for embossing the plastic cards. The embossed plastic card is fitted into a card carrier and inserted into the package.

Finally, a computer form is created that includes the welcome letter (or sales letter) and the premium notice...a portion of which is to be returned with payment.

Make sure that the part that is to be returned fits easily into the business-reply envelope. That will make it convenient for your premium-billing and collection staff to handle. Now, how to collect the premium?

If your policyowner already has authorized credit-card billing, you have no problem collecting the premium. If the policyowner has sent cash with application, you can safely assume chances are good that, in a direct-bill environment, the majority of policyowners will pay the next premium.

The problem is with the send-no-money applicants. In most cases, only 50% to 60% of these folks will pay their first premium.

SECRET No. 140

Policy paid rates *increase in direct proportion to the amount of personalization contained in the billing material.*

Consider this: Even when you have a paid policyowner, there is a nagging doubt in the back of that individual's mind that, when and if the time comes, perhaps "the company" won't pay "the" claim.

Constant reinforcement of the individual's initial purchasing decision, under these circumstances, seems logical. Therefore, reminding the individual, on a regular basis, why he or she purchased your product reinforces that decision.

And, it is in your best interest to constantly provide the policyowner with the opportunity to shift his payment to one of the automatic-payment options previously discussed.

Some companies charge their policyowners 50 cents per billing in the direct-bill mode. Obviously, if the policyowner shifts to credit-card billing, he saves money. Other companies offer a 10% discount when the policyowner authorizes payment on his credit card.

Getting your policyowners into an automatic-payment system, regardless of the conversion device you use, will impact mightily on your bottom line. The trouble is worth the doing.

Return for a moment to the idea of personalization. Premium-billing and collection material need to be treated with the same skill as the original solicitation material. Don't limit personalization to a constant and boring "Mr. Jones, Mr. Jones, Mr. Jones." By the time you are billing premium, you have a wealth of information on Mr. Jones.

Use some of this information to tie together the whole package. Reach back to specific statistics from your solicitation material. Refer to Mr. Jones' wife, his children, his hometown...and so on. Make your material sincere. Make your material "real." Make it aggressive. And, please...ask for the order. In this case, "the order" is asking your policyowner to pay the premium! Do not stop asking your policyowner to pay his premium with your first effort.

To maximize send-no-money conversion efforts, you must ask over and over again. That requires some thought. There are no hard and fast rules about how to sequence a premium direct-bill collection system. For the most part, each company's system is built on its own testing. To start with, however, you are looking at four efforts to collect a conversion premium.

The first effort is sent with the fulfillment material. The second one, called a reminder notice, is mailed first class—from ten to nineteen days after the effective date of the coverage. The third effort, perhaps labeled the "lapse notice," is mailed first class—from 25 to 35 days after the effective date. The final effort, called the "reinstatement notice," is mailed first class—from 39 to 45 days after the effective date.

All of these efforts are mini-solicitation kits. The rule that most frequently applies to these send-no-money billing efforts is the same that applies to the general direct marketing business. *You continue to attempt to collect money until your efforts no longer pay for themselves.*

Testing helps you determine what the point of diminishing return is—three efforts, four, five, six or seven efforts.

Policyowners who ultimately pay their first premium fall into your normal policyowner population. Those who do not pay the conversion premium fall into a "not-taken" file—available to you for resolicitation and crossloading.

Sequencing your premium direct-bill collection efforts to the normal policyowner population is done in a slightly different way. Each paid policy is assigned a "paid-to" date. This date becomes the key date for your billing cycles.

First billing in this general cycle is mailed 15 to 25 days in advance of the *paid-to* date. A reminder billing is mailed 5 to 15 days after the paid-to date. A lapse notice is mailed 15 to 25 days after the paid-to date. And, the reinstatement notice is mailed 30 to 39 days after the paid-to date.

Technically, you are cycling through the "grace" period for your policy form—normally 30 days for most direct marketing insurance products. If the policyowner does not pay the premium due after these four efforts, the name drops out of the policyowner file and into the lapse file.

A word of caution: There is a great temptation among internal marketers to solicit the lapse file with the same or other available products. *But, chances are good that once a lapse, always a lapse.*

The only way you can discover—for sure—the quality of your lapse file is to test. Test new solicitation material for the products you wish to sell. Then, carefully analyze the results of those tests over a significant period of time! Within six months you will see lapse rates stabilize to a large extent. By this time, you will be able to tell whether your lapse file is a good one or is not worth the time, effort, and money to resolicit.

So far, these discussions have been concentrating on procedures associated with the data-processing system, fulfillment, and premium billing and collection. All of these have an enormous impact on the persistency of the business you produce.

Underwriting is one of the least understood areas of insurance direct marketing. What underwriters do is a mystery to most marketers, since most of the products offered are guaranteed issue.

Underwriters contribute—especially in the product-development phase of the marketing system. Underwriters help establish and define risks, help develop retention limits, and adhere to general underwriting rules. These things are important in attempting to keep the company out of lines of business that can hurt the bottom line. One of the critical areas underwriters are involved with is term life insurance.

Almost all term life insurance is underwritten. That simply means the applicant is asked a series of questions concerning his health and that of other family members applying at the same time. Based on the answers to those questions, underwriters are expected to pick out the good guys and dump the bad ones, in order to minimize anti-selection against the company. That's true for any underwritten product.

Oddly enough, underwriting tends to decline in most insurance direct marketing environments, not because of good or bad health of policy-holders, but because of lack of information about them. It's a problem marketers can attack.

SECRET No. 141

Underwritten applications need to be easy to read and understand—through the use of clear, precise instructions to the consumer about how to fill out the form.

Instructional copy is critical. Many underwritten applications remain unissued, because they are incompletely filled out or not signed. The former problem requires the applicant's telephone number; the latter, some inventiveness.

Under no circumstance should you attempt to get incomplete information for your underwriters by sending the applicant a form letter! Start with a phone call. Assign a telemarketing representative—a registered nurse is ideal—to call the applicant in order to fill in the blanks on his application.

A registered nurse is suggested, because, for the most part, he or she can interpret what the applicant is trying to say regarding a former illness or hospitalization. If the applicant was unable to explain a medical condition adequately on his application, it is doubtful that he can do any better in response to a form letter. A nurse, on the other hand, can help the applicant describe in his own words, whatever the condition might have been. Then, the nurse can turn the information into useful data, understandable to an underwriter.

Refrain from the use of letters, which always need to be personalized (never form), until the time when it is impossible to engage the applicant in a telemarketing conversation.

By following these suggestions, issues will increase. Now, what about unsigned applications?

It has been generally accepted that you simply cannot issue unsigned applications, especially for life insurance. Yet, it is all too common that many applications, both underwritten and guaranteed issue, are returned unsigned. Normally, a company tries to obtain the signature through the mail. Most have been remarkably *unsuccessful* in their efforts.

In life insurance, a basic tenet recognized as early as 1774 by the English Parliament is that no person can have a policy issued on his life without his consent. The concept was generated because in those days it was considered "sport" to take out life insurance on public figures to see if a profit might be made on their early demise.

It is now law, as well as strong public policy, that an *insurable interest* must exist before any life insurance policy is issued. Hence, the requirement for an insured to sign an application.

The procedure for issuing a policy without a signature is relatively simple. You employ the services of an outbound telemarketing rep, who is also a licensed agent.

Signature omission is most often oversight. The telemarketing representative calls the applicant, identifies the program, and asks the applicant to confirm that he or she was indeed applying for the insurance.

For record purposes, the applicant is then asked to provide his mother's maiden name (or, if unwilling to do so, his city of birth) as verification.

The telemarketing rep then records the date and time of the conversation and mother's maiden name or applicant's place of birth on the calling document or card. After which the rep initials the card and provides his/her employee number.

The card is filed with the application. Then the policy or certificate is issued. In a sense, you have obtained a telephonic signature on the application, attested to by a licensed insurance agent.

Both these techniques will increase issue rates. Telemarketing can also be used to obtain an attending physician's statement—another way to increase issue rates.

The fact is that the major role played by underwriting in the direct marketing insurance system is the devising of procedures which increase issue rates.

Conservative underwriting rules are often pointed to as the culprit for low issue rates. Yet, as you have seen, incomplete information and unsigned applications are the most frequent reasons for policies not to be issued.

It is possible to increase issue rates by widening the type of risks your underwriters are willing to accept—in short, reducing your underwriting standards. Of course, since all insurance product pricing is a function of balances, you will end up with higher rates when you do so.

One alternative you might consider is the creation of a substandard issue program. This is the *rated* risk. All this does is offer an applicant a policy, even when the applicant does not meet your existing underwriting criteria.

In the case of life insurance, the prospect may be offered a reduced benefit, an increased premium, or some combination of both. The rationale here is that an applicant is likely to take a rated policy rather than face the reality that he cannot get the insurance for which he applied.

The principle is applicable to both life and health insurance. It is less applicable to property and casualty coverages, most specifically automobile coverages.

The relationship between *issue rates* and *persistency* is an obvious one. Without issues, there simply can be no persistency.

Without strong customer service, persistency will suffer in any case. *Of all the elements of the insurance direct marketing system, this is the one that most frequently suffers benign neglect.*

SECRET No. 142

Knowledgeable and courteous customer service representatives are the key to the success of your insurance direct marketing programs.

Your customer service department is at the front line of your company. These representatives may be the only human contact that your policyowners and prospective policyowners ever have with your company. It is essential that your representatives be well-trained folks. Because many of the problems they are asked to solve are the kind that might have given Solomon pause.

There are two sides to customer service—inbound 800 telemarketing and correspondence.

Inbound 800 operators take calls concerning current promotions, coverage questions, claims problems, policy and certificate changes, and more. These representatives can pull up on their CRTs the whole spectrum of customer files on a random-access basis.

The important thing here is that *every customer service contact requires an action* of some sort. Your customers have problems that need solving. The more adept your customer service people are at helping deliver policyowner satisfaction, the more credibility you establish and the greater the contribution this group makes to the persistency of your business.

Customer service correspondence functions are equally important. Here's where your service referral data file comes in handy, as well as the correspondence text file.

Utilizing both these datasets allows your customer service people to accurately handle tens of thousands of incoming calls and letters. And, what is most important, allows them to efficiently satisfy customer problems and complaints.

Moreover, every incoming call or letter represents an opportunity to sell—especially when the situation ends on a positive note. Most frequently, this happens in the telemarketing area of your customer service group.

You might choose to use the subtle J.C. Penney technique of "switch the pitch and pitch the switch." Here, the telemarketing rep requests permission from a satisfied customer to send further information on a crossload product—life insurance to health insurance policyowners, for example.

Or, you might choose the more aggressive "tel-comm" procedures, pioneered by National Liberty and Montgomery Ward Life, where the telemarketing representative determines the customer's eligibility to receive an offer—and then sells like crazy.

Both techniques were discussed in Chapter XI. The point is, customer service can be more than just a cost center. It can be a viable contributor to the corporate coffers.

But, no matter how you choose to use this group, training is critical. *Customer service is not a clerical function.* Representatives need to thoroughly know the products you are selling—all the products, inside out. They need to know what every department in your company does. There needs to be more than a passing familiarity with your claims procedures. In fact, product knowledge, programs in progress, and policy provisions are as much a part of the customer service representatives arsenal as they are the marketers.

Once again, communications is the key. If you expect to succeed as a marketer, don't keep secrets from the folks who are there to help you.

Now, what about claims?

SECRET No. 143

The surest way to lose a customer is to unfairly deny a claim!

The best way to ensure fair claims settlement is to adhere to a philosophy that demands it . . . and to put that philosophy in writing so that everybody understands the ground rules.

It is unfortunate that insurance frequently deals with personal disaster—specifically, the personal disasters of the policyowner. Claims are seldom filed in an emotional vacuum.

Typical are the anguished loss of a loved one, a terrifying automobile accident, the theft of valuable—frequently irreplaceable—personal property, and the turmoil of long hospitalization. These are the events that claims are made of. And, at the heart of every claim is a fellow human being.

Therefore, at the hub of the claims procedure are these elementary principles: courtesy, compassion, communication, and fairness.

Courtesy is an absolute requirement. A claimant must feel that he is not a number, but rather a human being, and that your company stands ready, willing, and able to help him in any way possible.

Compassion in correspondence and conversation is an equal requirement. Forget the cold impersonality of corporate correspondence. Deal with the claimant as you want to be dealt with.

Communication is critical. Keep the claimant informed during the course of the procedure. Anticipate questions. Answer them before they are asked, and answer them accurately.

Fairness is an acute need. If there is a disappointing settlement, don't walk away from the responsibility of explaining why the decision was reached; and do it clearly, reasonably, and politely. If a claim is rejected, try a telephone conversation to explain why. Then follow up with a letter.

But, above all, adhere to the basic philosophical tenet: Is there any way we can pay this claim? Not: How can we reject this claim? If there is any doubt about the validity of the claim, always give the benefit of the doubt to the claimant.

The fact is: Insurance companies are in the business of paying claims. Marketing companies specializing in insurance sales must make doubly sure that every valid claim is paid—and paid promptly and fairly.

To follow this type of philosophy is to garner the greatest intangible asset a company can possess—GOODWILL! This helps admirably in retaining customers.

Customers are your lifeblood. And, to the direct marketing insurance organization, there can be nothing more important than the customer base!

The final area of administration to touch on is the mail room. Sophisticated, mail-order insurance operations handle millions of pieces of incoming mail *every year*. One leader in this business handles more than thirty million pieces. That includes applications, premium payments, customer correspondence, claims, corporate business letters, and business-to-business direct mail...and probably several other forgotten categories.

Mail-room operations are people intensive and are subject to the upward pressures of the economy and technology. Yet, ask yourself where you might end up without an efficient mail-room system. The mail room *receives* millions of pieces of mail, and it *mails out* hundreds of thousands of pieces of mail every year. It is the window into your company, and the window out of it as well.

So, it makes sense to treat your mail-room operation well. Invest in technology to increase efficiency. Foster excellence, demand competence, and reward innovation. You won't be sorry.

Administration, as you have seen, is complicated. Administration and operations focus on cost control and containment. But there is ample room for creativity. That's been the whole point to this overview.

Such things as effective data processing, efficient premium billing and collection, accurate fulfillment, keen underwriting, automated claims procedures and fair claims handling, sensitive customer service, and innovative mail-room techniques yield startlingly good results.

One leading direct-response insurance company spent nine years innovating, creating, improving, and fine tuning its administrative operations. The result? Administrative expenses were cut from 14% of earned premium to 8%. Not too shabby!

Reducing administrative expenses is one of the key functions in creating long-range profitability. Nowhere in the direct marketing business is profit as important as it is in the field of insurance. This is because insurance is essentially a *numbers* game, the product is a numbers product. Marketing programs succeed or fail "by the numbers."

The next stop on this tour of insurance direct marketing is unraveling the secrets of insurance direct marketing mathematics.

The Secrets of
Insurance Direct Marketing
Mathematics

OK, insurance direct marketing is a "numbers" business. In fact, direct marketing is the most quantitative of all marketing methods.

If you are determined to prosper as an insurance direct marketer, it is critical that you understand the impact of response rates, cost per application, indexing, acquisition allowances, policyholder lifetime value, and a host of other calculations and terms.

This understanding allows you to cogently plan, execute, and evaluate your programs. Now, genius is not a specific requirement for understanding. If you are one among our marketing brethren intimidated by mathematics, *relax*!

Insurance direct marketing mathematics is really arithmetic in disguise. Addition, subtraction, multiplication, and division handle most of the iterations for which you are responsible.

And, keep in mind that it is not the marketers' place to put the actuaries out of business. It is, however, clearly the marketers' job to understand the elements of profitability, and to help the actuaries understand that traditional calculations are, frequently, inappropriate for the insurance direct marketing system.

Most non-insurance companies using the direct marketing system have developed a business formula that is simplicity itself:

Selling price - cost of sale = gross profit.

Gross profit - operating expenses = net pre-tax profit.

In the direct marketing system environment, this simple formula lets the entrepreneur know how much money he is making.

Ah...if you suspect that insurance direct marketing is somewhat more complicated, you win the gold ring. As you saw in Chapter VI, at the center of insurance-profit reality is the *profit-study* concept.

It does not matter whether your company is mutual or stock!

SECRET No. 144

If profit is not the motivation behind every marketing program you run, you're in the wrong business!

Consider this. A stock company's basic objective is to return profit to its shareholders in the form of *dividends*. A mutual company's basic objective is to return profit to its policyholders in the form of *dividends*.

Shareholder dividends can be delivered in a check—so much dividend per share. Policyholder dividends can be delivered in a check, a reduction of premium, or an expansion of benefits.

The point is: Dividends are the owners' share of the profit you create with your programs. So, if you agree that profit is your motive, the first critical formula you need to work out on any program is acquisition allowance.

Why? If you don't know how much you can afford to spend to acquire a policyholder, you're barking up a bare tree! Here's the point at which your company decides to pursue a *product-marketing orientation* or a *customer-marketing orientation*—the concept of relational marketing.

If you are a product marketer, your acquisition allowances will be calculated for each individual product you sell. It does not take into account the future income streams from your customer base.

As you have seen in Chapter VI, this is a relatively restricting financial strategy. And you market to an acquisition allowance created for one product at a time. If you look at Figures 6-2 through 6-7, the acquisition allowances calculated for each of the separate profit studies indicate what you can spend to acquire a policyowner for each individual product in the marketing stream.

Using the *iteration-method* formula:

AA = Acquisition Allowance

$$AA = \sum_{N=1}^{10} \left(\frac{\text{Annualized}}{\text{Premium}} \bullet \left[1 - \text{loss \%} - \text{expense \%} - \frac{\text{Premium}}{\text{Tax \%}}\right] + \frac{\text{Investment}}{\text{Income}}\right)\frac{1\text{-lapse \%}}{(1+I)^N}$$

The iteration is done for the number of years selected by the figure indicated (in this case, 10 years). It is calculated for each of the years you are examining. Then a present value of the sum of the acquisition allowances is calculated, and you end up with the product's acquisition allowance for your product program.

To discover this allowance manually is a cumbersome procedure. Therefore, using LOTUS 1-2-3, the program setup illustrated in Appendix C will help you arrive at the result faster. When you complete your programming, it will look like Figure 15-1.

Keep in mind that these formulas do not take into account a variety of factors that were demonstrated in Chapter VI, although the product is the same as displayed in Figures 6-2 through 6-8. The biggest difference between the acquisition allowance displayed in Figure 15-1, and the acquisition allowance displayed in Figure 6-8 is mere detail.

In the example above, the period (n) calculation was made on a simple 1-year basis. While in Figure 6-8 that one year was broken down into 12 months. This "parsing" effect allows interest, and correspondent cash flow, to accumulate faster, thereby making a difference of $44.77 in the indicated acquisition allowances.

SECRET No. 145

The more detailed your mathematical inputs, the
more accurate your results.

Setting up your acquisition allowance model allows you to view results in several ways.

First:

Net lead cost/response x conversion + fulfillment cost/conversion. This figure must be < or = acquisition cost.

This formula views a program in an inquiry-conversion environment. All it is stipulating is that what you spend to acquire a policyholder must be less than the acquisition allowance assigned to the program.

```
Acquisition Allowance Calculation
------------------------------------------------------------------
Value Screen                      CALCULATION SCREEN
PRODUCT    HIP
AARP     285.20 LAPSE-1  0.36 AAA-1      80.27 INT-1      3.31
CLAIM-1    0.60 LAPSE-2  0.23 AAA-2      50.75 INT-2      5.51
CLAIM-2    0.75 LAPSE-3  0.18 AAA-3     137.33 INT-3      6.61
CLAIM-3    0.45 LAPSE-4  0.18 AAA-4     152.38 INT-4      7.71
CLAIM-4    0.40 LAPSE-5  0.12 AAA-5     138.52
CLAIM-5    0.45 RESV-1   0.15 AAA-6     138.52
ADMIN-1    0.10 RESV-2   0.10 AAA-7     138.52
ADMIN-2    0.06 RESV-3   0.05 AAA-8     138.52
PREM TA   0.025 RESV-4   0.05 AAA-9     138.52
   M       4.00 P1      42.78 AAA-10    138.52
                P2      71.30 TOTAL    1251.86
   I       0.15 P3      85.56
   N       1.00 P4      99.82
   i       0.06              Acquisition Allowance    309.44
------------- --------------------------- --------------
```

Figure 15-1: Acquisition allowance model screen for a single product

Second:

Solicitation material cost/response. This figure must be < or = acquisition allowance.

This formula allows you to view a direct-mail or space solicitation in the same basic configuration. Now, what about more detail?

Chapter VI has walked you through the concept of lifetime value and has displayed the profit-study models and the formulas to help you derive an acquisition allowance, using the LTV method.

Keep in mind that the values displayed are assumed to be for an inquiry/conversion program generated by a hospital indemnity product through television. The model is flexible (Figures 6-2 through 6-8). You can substitute your own values for life, accident or health products. But, these model formats are not truly appropriate for casualty products.

Appendix D provides the LOTUS 1-2-3 programming to allow you to create these models on your own personal computer.

Once you complete this programming exercise, you will be able to input variable values into the appropriate cells and build your own lifetime value profit studies.

Eventually you need to become familiar with LOTUS, or some other spreadsheet program, to understand how to create your own formulas. The important thing is that you try. Nothing worthwhile is ever accomplished, if you don't try.

SECRET No. 146

Mathematics is a rational, logical body of knowledge that can help the insurance direct marketer arrive at precise results.

By developing axioms, essentially unproved mathematical statements, you have the ability to deduce consequences. That's what modeling is all about.

Here are the "what-ifs" of the direct marketing business:

Now, there are many formulas you use in calculating the various elements of the insurance direct marketing spectrum. Think of them as descriptive terms that help you achieve your objectives.

Understand this: One man's total annualized renewal premium is another's annualized premium, cost per application is as critical as cost per inquiry, a standard measure of performance is expressed as applications per thousand.

Here's a neat little trick. Express apps per thousand instead of response %. It makes comparisons easier. Remember in inquiry-conversion programs to slip a decimal in place of the comma in your circulation number and then divide into the number of apps and you end up with apps per thousand.

Through it all, do not be apprehensive about making a mistake. Mistakes, especially in mathematics, can be fixed quickly. But...

SECRET No. 147

Check, double check, and triple check your numbers before you present them. One glaring error can destroy your credibility and a good program before it ever gets off the ground.

Remember, too, the more you work with the math of direct marketing, the more comfortable you will grow with the mathematical manipulations.

Once you have an acquisition allowance using either the iteration method or the more precise LTV method, you can move on to calculating a breakeven for any program. In insurance direct marketing, *breakeven* is the point at which acquisition allowance equals marketing cost. *All breakeven means is that you have successfully marketed to a stipulated financial objective.* It is an objective that meets the return-on-investment and profit objectives of your company.

If you use the iteration method of calculating acquisition allowance and you follow a "product-marketing orientation," not meeting your acquisition-allowance objective means that your product will deliver a lower profitability and a lower return on investment *than desired.* Exceeding your financial objective (spending less than your acquisition allowance to obtain a policyholder) means that your product will deliver a higher profitability and higher return on investment than originally desired.

The same is true for an acquisition allowance that is calculated, using the LTV method. Except, in this case, exceeding your acquisition allowance increases the *risk factor* in your program. This assumes, of course, you have used the risk percentage method of designating your acquisition allowance. If, on the other hand, you spend more than 100% of your LTV acquisition allowance, you will have to manage your relational marketing program aggressively to make up the difference.

Figure 15-2 displays a breakeven analysis for a lead-generating program. This model allows you to view *unit* cost as the basic measure. Under cost-lead assumptions, you examine the individual unit costs for each component in your inquiry-conversion program. Recall that in this case you are using a three-effort conversion series—three direct-mail kits designed to generate an application. The point is to arrive at a unit fulfillment cost.

Next, you examine the number of leads on a per-lead total basis. This includes: how much you pay (net) for each lead [media]; commissions per lead you have to pay—if any; the cost per call for your answering service; the cost of the "free gift" you offer—if any; production of the solicitation material, including the TV commercial, co-op mailing piece, etc.; and finally the unit fulfillment cost.

The column under "calculation" indicates how you treat each of the values. If you anticipate 10% invalid leads—invalid state, garbled name, and such, your net lead cost increases by 10%. If you pay 17.65% commission (net 15%) per lead, you convert this number to a factored number. Obviously, you will not receive 100% inbound calls from any program. In a TV program, for example, you will receive 85% to 90% of your leads via telephone. In a print program, you will receive 15% to 30% of your leads through telephone. You factor that number. Next, you transfer your unit cost for production and fulfillment to the calculation column and then add it up.

What you now have is the unit total cost per lead for your program. In short, every lead you bring in will cost you X number of dollars.

Part three of the calculation is to determine what paid-policy conversion

```
COST/LEAD ASSUMPTIONS
KIT                    #1        #2        #3        #4        #5
COMPONENT
-------------------------------------------------------     -------------------
LABELS/OSE            0.010     0.010     0.010
OSE                   0.009     0.009     0.009
SLSLTR                0.020     0.020     0.020
APP                   0.020     0.020     0.020
BROCHURE              0.040     0.030     0.030
HOT SHEET             0.010     0.010     0.010
CARD                  0.063
BRE                   0.009     0.009     0.009
OTHER                 0.003     0.003     0.003
-------------------------------------------------------     -------------------
TOTAL                 0.184     0.111     0.111     0.00      0.00      $0.41
-------------------------------------------------------     -------------------
D.P.                  0.15      0.04      0.03
LTRSHOP               0.05      0.04      0.04
POSTAGE               0.45      0.167     0.167
SHIP                  0.01      0.01      0.01
REPORTS               0.00      0.00      0.00
-------------------------------------------------------     -------------------
TOTAL                 0.660     0.257     0.247     0.000     0.000     $1.16
-------------------------------------------------------     -------------------
UNIT FULFILLMENT COST            $1.57
-----------------------------     ----------------------     -------------------
LEADS (PER LEAD TOTAL)
                  DATA                   CALCULATION         CIRC(M)     25000
MEDIA             $6.69                   $7.36              CP/M        $3.00
COMMISSIONS       17.65%                  $1.30              TLT/COST    $75,000
ANS. SERV         $1.25                   $0.14              TLT/LEADS   50000
GIFT/ENDORSER     $1.00                   $1.00
PRODUCTION                                $1.50 (AD PRODUCTION)
FULFILLMENT       $1.57                   $1.57
-----------------------------     ----------------------     -------------------
TOTAL                                    12.87
-----------------------------     ----------------------     -------------------
UNIT TOTAL COST PER LEAD                 12.87
-------------------------------------------------------------------------------
PRO-FORMA DATA ENTRY SCREEN
                                         APPS%        8.58%
CIRCULATION          50.000              TLTAPPS      4290
TLT PAID POLICIES     4.20%              ISSUE%       98.00%
AARP                $285.20              APP/ISSU     4204
MC/LEAD             $12.87               PAID%        50.00%
ACQ ALLOW            107%                PDAPPS       2102
-----------------------------     -----------------------     -------------------
PRO-FORMA
                                         COLPRE(M)    $599.52
CIRCULATION          50.000 (m)          TMC(M)       $643.27
CONVERSION %          4.20%              T/MC         $1.90
RENEWALS             2102                COST/APP     $306.01
AARP                $285.20              ACQ. ALLO    $306.30
```

Figure 15-2: Lead management model used to calculate breakeven and profitability

rate you need in order to meet your financial objectives.

First, you enter the circulation—the number of leads you plan to receive. *"TLT PAID POLICIES" you leave blank. This value is what you are going to solve for.* You next enter your anticipated average annualized renewal premium. Then, you transfer your unit total cost per lead to MC/LEAD (marketing cost per lead). Then, you enter acquisition allowance—expressed as a percentage of average annualized premium.

Skip down to issue %. Enter the number of policies or certificates of insurance you expect to issue. Then, skip down to paid % and enter the percentage of policies you issue that you anticipate will pay the first premium amount.

Now, using inspection, you return to the APPs % cell. By entering the % of converted applications, you can determine the number of total paid policies you will need to break even. All the elements of the PRO-FORMA are automatically calculated. The idea is to make the COST/APP (cost per application) equal to the ACQ.ALLO (acquisition allowance) just below it.

The LOTUS 1-2-3 programming for this model is contained in Appendix E. You can modify or refine it to create your own breakeven model for the programs you run. With a little imagination, you can use this same model for a direct-mail campaign. Simply eliminate efforts #2 and #3 and modify the data you input under the "Leads" section.

You can also use your LTV model to determine breakeven. Figures 15-3 and 15-4 display what happens to the HIP TV inquiry program when you are looking for the apps per thousand that are necessary to produce a 10% profit on the *initial book of business* and a 15% return on investment.

It is assumed that nothing changes in the model except the ISSUES/M. The original model showed that 45.59 applications per thousand were issued. This resulted in a profit of 16.46% for the initial product marketed. So the question is: How many issues per thousand do you need to break even in order to achieve the 10% profit and 15% ROI?

By substituting for the variable ISSUES/M, you discover that you need to issue 36.07 policies per thousand to achieve that objective. Figure 15-4, the summary, now shows an overall profit on your relational marketing of 14.27%, down from the 19.81% on the original model.

Looking at the relationship between acquisition allowance and cost per application, you discover that you can safely market to a 60% LTV acquisition allowance—perhaps a little less. But you will not achieve breakeven, if you market to a 50% LTV acquisition allowance, because your cost per application exceeds your allowable acquisition allowance.

Extending this one more step, the model displayed in Figure 15-3 shows

```
Jackson/Insurance: LOTUS 1-2-3 PROFIT STUDY (Breakeven--15%ROI, 10% Profit)

MODEL PROFIT STUDY--DIRECT MARKETING HEALTH INSURANCE

SCREEN VALUES (INPUT DATA + AUTOMATIC CALCULATION)

PRODUCT   HIP/TV     LAPSE(1)   0.52  ULTCLAIM    0.36  RESERV(1)   0.15  INFORCE-1   1000  PRESVAL    28,583.34
AARP      $285.20    LAPSE(2)   0.23  CLAIM(1)    0.60  RESERV(2)   0.10  INFORCE-2   640
ISSUES/M  36.07      LAPSE(3)   0.18  CLAIM(2)    0.75  RESERV(3)   0.05  INFORCE-3   493
CICR(M)   27.72      LAPSE(4)   0.18  CLAIM(3)    0.40  RESERV(4)   0.05  INFORCE-4   404
MC/M      12864.19   LAPSE(5)   0.12  CLAIM(4)    0.40  RESERV(5)   0.03  INFORCE-5   331  LTV          $28.58
TMC       356645.13  PREMTAX    0.025 CLAIM(5)    0.45                    INFORCE-6   292  ALLOW        107.40%
T/MC      0.80       INT.RATE   0.06  CLAIM(6)    0.45  N     1.00        INFORCE-7   257  COLFACT      79.49%
COMMISFY  0          MODPAYFAC  0.10  CLAIM(7)    0.45                    INFORCE-8   226
COMMISREN 0          PAY/N      12.00 CLAIM(8)    0.45  POLCYFEE $10.00   INFORCE-9   199  ACQUSITION   $306.31
ADMIN(1)  0.10       YEARS      10.00 CLAIM(9)    0.45                    INFORCE-0   175  ALLOWANCE
ADMIN(RE) 0.06       ROI        15.00%CLAIM(10)   0.45
```

PROFIT STUDY (AUTOMATIC CALCULATION)

YEARS	COLPREM	CLAIMS	ADMIN	COMMISS	TMC	PREMTAX	RESERVES	TOT/RESERV	INT	INCOME	EXPENSE	P(L)	PROFIT%	ACQALLOW
1	226,714	135,575	22,671	0	356,645	5,668	34,007	34,007	2,628	229,342	554,566	(325,224)	-141.81%	80.46
2	174,569	130,718	10,474	0		4,364	17,457	51,464	3,977	178,547	163,013	15,534	8.70%	50.06
3	143,147	57,242	8,589	0		3,579	7,157	58,621	4,530	147,677	76,566	71,111	48.15%	150.14
4	117,381	46,938	7,043	0		2,935	5,869	64,490	4,984	122,365	62,784	59,580	48.69%	150.47
5	103,295	46,462	6,198	0		2,582	3,099	67,589	5,224	108,518	58,341	50,177	46.24%	136.67
6	90,899	40,887	5,454	0		2,272	(13,518)	54,071	4,179	95,078	35,095	59,983	63.09%	135.87
7	79,992	35,980	4,799	0		2,000	(13,518)	40,554	3,134	83,126	29,262	53,864	64.80%	135.07
8	70,393	31,663	4,224	0		1,760	(13,518)	27,036	2,089	72,482	24,128	48,354	66.71%	134.27
9	61,945	27,863	3,717	0		1,549	(13,518)	13,518	1,045	62,990	19,611	43,380	68.87%	133.47
10	54,512	24,519	3,271	0		1,363	(13,518)	0	0	54,512	15,635	38,877	71.32%	132.68
TOTALS	1,122,846	577,846	76,439	0	356,645	28,071	(0)		31,791	1,154,637	1,039,002	115,636	10.01%	1,239.18
%		51.46%	6.81%	0.00%	31.76%	2.50%								

Figure 15-3: Use the basic profit model to determine how many policies you need to issue to "breakeven."

SUMMARY: PROGRAM TOTAL LINES TO CALCULATE LIFETIME VALUE

	COLPREM	CLAIMS	ADMIN	COMMISS	TMC	PREMTAX	RESERVES	TOT/RESEV	INT	INCOME	EXPENSE	P(L)	PROFIT%	ACQALLOW
BASIC	1,122,846	577,846	76,439	0	356,645	28,071			31,791	1,154,637	1,039,002	115,636	10.01%	1,239.18
RIDER1	39,697	20,314	2,658	0	800	992			1,447	41,144	24,765	16,379	39.81%	68.00
RIDER2	48,248	24,540	3,173	0	800	1,206			1,633	49,882	29,719	20,163	40.42%	295.91
RIDER3	32,829	16,587	2,117	0	800	821			1,020	33,849	20,325	13,524	39.95%	260.51
RIDER4	36,867	18,495	2,327	0	800	922			1,035	37,902	22,543	15,359	40.52%	303.24
RIDER5	26,891	13,385	1,657	0	1,000	672			668	27,559	16,715	10,844	39.35%	367.39
CRSLOAD1														
CRSLOAD2														
CRSLOAD3														
TOTALS	1,307,379	671,167	88,372	0	360,845	32,684	0	0	37,593	1,344,973	1,153,068	191,904	14.27%	2,534.21

	COMMISS	TMC	PREMTAX
	80%	60%	50%
	37.95	28.46	23.72
	501.13	375.85	313.21
	356.65	356.65	356.65

PRESENT VALUE: 47435.77
LIFETIME VALUE: 47.44
ACQ.ALLOW: 626.42
Cost/App: 356.65

Figure 15-4: The summary shows the impact of a "breakeven" program on your overall profitability.

that your target T/MC ratio is now .80; that is, for every $1.00 of marketing cost, you need to produce $.80 of total annualized renewal premium.

The point to this demonstration is to show how flexible modeling really is. You can use these techniques to determine acquisition allowance, to generate lifetime value, to calculate breakeven, and to show you what happens when you have hard numbers from a program...actual results.

By inputting actual values into your model, you can discover the real results of your program. You can analyze the impact of actual apps-per-thousand issues, examine actual loss ratios, fluctuations in interest rates, different levels of ROI, and the impact of actual lapse rates.

These examples of mathematical modeling, considering acquisition allowance, lifetime value profit studies, and breakeven calculation, are important parts of your marketing background. But, keep in mind that each one represents a possible solution to the financial complexities of the insurance direct marketing system. Companies develop individual arithmetic methods to solve for the various values necessary for their own financial health.

The objective is to offer concepts that have achieved success in a variety of insurance direct marketing environments. You can find concepts that can lead you in new directions and ideas that can illuminate new possibilities.

One final point before leaving this area: Profitability is the goal insurance direct marketing programs seek to achieve, and the path to profitability is testing. It was pointed out earlier that test programs seldom, if ever, achieve profitability goals. Therefore:

SECRET No. 148

Create a "testing budget" for insurance direct marketing programs, and treat testing as a cost of doing business—an overhead expense!

Don't demand profit from a test! In this day and age, unless you're exceeedingly lucky, it isn't going to happen.

Finally, a good insurance direct marketer has an obligation to display a frequently overlooked quality. He or she must be a good risk taker. So:

SECRET No. 149

Treat every dollar you spend of your company's money as if it were coming out of your savings account.

If you don't think you'd risk your own money, don't risk the company's. It works every time. Keep in mind that the direct marketing system matured through the vision and aggressiveness of entrepreneurs. Be one, within—of course—the limits of your own corporate environment.

So far the ideas presented have been fairly fundamental. Next, consider the concept of *marketing cost as an investment.*

Up until now, marketing cost has been treated as an "expense." Since marketing cost is charged to the first year of your expense stream, it usually results in a loss when deducted in the profit column. There is no doubt that you've spent the money in the first year to acquire the business you've put on the books.

But, two questions are generated by your expenditure: In what year will you recover your marketing cost ["investment"]? And, was it a good idea to have invested the money in your program in the first place?

Frequently, insurance direct marketers are faced with a choice of what programs to promote. Decisions are often made on experience and instinct rather than on hard data. You can make better decisions on what programs to market if you use a comparison called "Net Present Value."

Net present value (NPV) measures cash flow against investment. It views marketing cost as an investment and measures what the return on that investment is, based on a constant discount rate that management uses as a standard at which funds can or should be invested. The rate is a long-term opportunity rate, and is a judgment of the earning power of the amount you are putting in your marketing investment. It provides you with a dollar basis for making decisions between marketing opportunities or product marketing opportunities.

Return now to Figures 6-2 through 6-8. The first step in calculating NPV is to extract the $286,371 of TMC (shown on Figure 6-8) from first-year expenses for each of the products offered.

This subtraction results in an expense figure of $197,921 for the primary HIP/TV product. Or a cash flow profit in the first year of business of $31,421. You calculate the same way for each of the five riders. Next, you sum the cash flow profit by years 1 through 10.

Now, use the following formula to calculate NPV:

$$NPV = \frac{P^N}{(1+r)^N} + \frac{A^N}{(1+r)^N}$$

Does it look complicated? It's not, really. Using substitution, it looks like this, where P = investment, A = cash flow by year, and r = rate of return.

Here, let the rate of return = 10%, as follows:

$$\frac{-286,371}{(1+0.10)^0} + \frac{33,411}{(1+0.10)^1} + \frac{21,537}{(1+0.10)^2} + \frac{83,737}{(1+0.10)^3} + \frac{70,578}{(1+0.10)^4} + \frac{59,608}{(1+0.10)^5}$$

$$\frac{70,483}{(1+0.10)^6} + \frac{63,246}{(1+0.10)^7} + \frac{56,731}{(1+0.10)^8} + \frac{50,852}{(1+0.10)^9} + \frac{45,531}{(1+0.10)^{10}}$$

When you are all done, the NPV = $49,158. Now, follow exactly the same technique for the marketing plan or program or the product you are thinking of marketing. Compare the two and choose the program with the higher NPV.

A second technique for determining the acceptability of investing in a given marketing program or product is the "payback" method. It focuses on how long it will take to recover your marketing investment.

The formula is: $r = A/P$.

The rate of return (r) is the average annual flow of funds (A) divided by the original investment (P).

An easy way to determine the average annual flow of funds is to add the TMC (total marketing cost) to the profit total for this program as reflected in Figure 15-4. The result is $552,749.

By substitution then:

$r = 552,749/360,845 = 1.531$

Now, use the formula $1/r$ to determine recovery. In this case, by substitution $1/1.531 = .65$. This means that it will take 7.9 months to recover the invested funds, since recovery of the invested funds comes out of the profit cash flow.

Both of these techniques allow you to view your programs objectively, using financial-based measurements in place of "seat-of-the-pants" comparisons.

Finally, the last part of the mathematics of direct marketing: reporting and projecting results.

First, reporting formats.

SECRET No. 150

The more detail you provide in your reports, the more credibility you will enjoy.

One of the more frustrating events which insurance direct marketing managers go through is trying to read reports that compare apples and oranges. For reports to be effective, it is necessary to give enough detail so that a stranger will understand what it is you're trying to say.

Regardless of what your program happens to be—third-party, broad-market, direct-mail, television, print inquiry, or telemarketing—each shares common characteristics which, when reported properly, illuminate results.

The most effective format for reports seems to be:

Circulation The circulation of a program, which can be: the number of names mailed, the circulation of a press advertisement, or the number of leads generated. Generically, this is the source from which applications are derived.

Applications In hard numbers...30, or 50, or 5,000.

Apps/M Simply divide applications by circulation to get applications per thousand of circulation.

Issues Even in guaranteed issue, not every application is issued. This number is the actual number of applications sent to policyowners or prospective policyowners.

Issues/M Again, divide application by circulation to get issued policies per thousand of circulation.

Renewals Renewals are the number of *paid* applications generated by the program. If it is a cash-with-application program, this number will match issues per thousand. If it is a send-no-money program, it will likely be considerably less.

Renewals/M Divide renewals by circulation.

AARP Average annualized renewal premium or average annualized premium.

TARP The number of applications multiplied by the AARP.

TMC Total marketing cost spent on the project to produce the applications. Remember, if it is a third-party program, this number includes commissions.

T/MC The TARP to market cost ratio. For every $1.00 of marketing cost, it shows how much premium is brought in.

CPA Cost per application. This is a useful measure when you know your acquisition allowance.

Figure 15-5 shows the reporting format for a hypothetical program which divides the year into quarters. In this case, less than all the quarters have been completed. It provides a comparison between what you planned to sell [Plan], what your current estimate of sales is [Est], and what your actual sales are [Actual].

Reporting results in this format for every program you execute makes it considerably easier to read the reports, and to compare your plan, pro-

PROGRAM: HIP TV LEAD PROGRAM

	1ST QTR PLAN	CUR-EST	ACTUAL	2ND QTR PLAN	CUR-EST	ACTUAL	3RD QTR PLAN	CUR-EST	ACTUAL	4TH QTR PLAN	CUR-EST	ACTUAL	TOTAL YEAR PLAN	CUR-EST	ACTUAL
CIRC(M)	500.0	500.0	0.0	0.0	0.0	0.0	100.0	100.0	0.0	0.0	0.0	0.0	600.0	600.0	0.0
APPS	26214	26214	ERR	0	0	ERR	5243	5243	ERR	0	0	ERR	31457	31457	0
APPS/M	52.43	52.43	0	ERR	ERR	ERR	52.43	52.43	0	ERR	ERR	ERR	52.43	52.43	ERR
ISSUES	22795	22795	0	0	0	0	4559	4559	0	0	0	0	27354	27354	0
ISSUE %	87%	87%	0%	0%	0%	0%	87%	87%	0%	0%	0%	0%	87%	87%	0%
ISSUES/M	45.59	45.59	ERR	ERR	ERR	ERR	45.59	45.59	ERR	ERR	ERR	ERR	45.59	45.59	ERR
RENEWALS	17096	17096	0	0	0	0	3419	3419	0	0	0	0	20515	20515	0
RENEWAL %	75%	75%	0%	0%	0%	0%	75%	75%	0%	75%	75%	0%	75%	75%	0%
RENEWAL/M	34.19	34.19	ERR	ERR	ERR	ERR	34.19	34.19	ERR	ERR	ERR	ERR	34.19	34.19	ERR
AARP	285.20	285.20	0.00	0.00	0.00	0.00	285.20	285.20	0.00	0.00	0.00	0.00	285.20	285.20	0.00
TARP	4875.78	4875.78	0.00	0.00	0.00	0.00	975.10	975.10	0.00	0.00	0.00	0.00	5850.88	5850.88	0.00
TMC	6432.00	6432.00	0.00	0.00	0.00	0.00	1286.40	1286.40	0.00	0.00	0.00	0.00	7718.40	7718.40	0.00
T:MC	0.76	0.76	ERR	ERR	ERR	ERR	0.76	0.76	ERR	ERR	ERR	ERR	0.76	0.76	ERR
COST/APP	376.23	376.23	ERR	ERR	ERR	ERR	376.25	376.25	ERR	ERR	ERR	ERR	376.23	376.23	ERR

Figure 15-5: Report format displays—at a glance—how your program is performing.

jection and actual performance, one against another, among marketing efforts.

For testing, display your results two ways: First, the actual results, and, second, projected results for a rollout. Figure 15-6 displays an example of reporting test results. Test reporting should contain a narrative analyzing what happened and evaluating what should happen next as the result of the testing.

One great advantage of these reporting formats is their consistency. You always end up comparing apples with apples.

As well, there are two other ideas you will find useful in insurance direct marketing measurement and projection.

SECRET No. 151

Program results, adjusted for seasonality and sample size, give a clearer view of what you can expect in the future.

Insurance direct marketers are constantly asked to project results—sometimes years ahead—of programs they are running or they are thinking about running. In the reporting formats above, the "Plan" numbers, as well as the "Current Estimate" numbers, are forms of projection. The quandary faced by most marketers is how to project results with confidence.

First, consider seasonal variation. If you test (or run a program) in either May or June or August or September and you plan to roll out your testing (or continue your program) in January, February, and/or March, you need to adjust your results for seasonal variation.

Even though insurance is a twelve-months-a-year business, the fact remains that January results are always better than June results. The trick is to be able to index response in such a way as to account for the difference.

Obviously, you must keep very detailed internal records over a reasonable period of time in order to measure these differences. If January—with consistency—delivers a 25% boost in response over June for three to five years running, it is reasonable to predict that response will be higher by that percentage every year.

To index numbers, you adjust them according to some experienced or assumed relationship. Multiplying the response received in June by, in this example, 1.25% will yield a relatively conservative estimate of the increase in response you can expect in January over June. For example, if you received 153 responses to your testing in June and you can expect to re-

CREATIVE TESTING REPORT FORMAT

PROGRAM:		Group Trust DIRECT MAIL
TARGET DATE:		12/26/87
PERSUASION DATE:		2/15/88
PRODUCT:		HIP
PROJECT NO.:		00000000
CREATIVE:	Control:	Good News Kit
	Vs.	
	Test:	Good/Better/Best Kit
STATES:		Standard
OBJECTIVE:		To achieve a 25% increase in T/MC efficiency
T/MC GOAL:		2.00

FINANCIALS:

	CONTROL		TEST	
	Estimated	Actual	Estimated	Actual
Circ(M)	100.0	100.0	25.0	25.0
Apps	450	460	140	135
Apps/M	4.5	4.6	5.6	5.4
Issues	400	391	123	115
Issue%	88%	85%	88%	85%
Issues/M	4.0	3.91	4.93	4.6
Renewals	300	283	92	97
Renewal %	75%	75%	75%	84.3%
Renewals/M	3.0	2.83	3.7	3.88
AARP	285	291	285	280
TARP(M)	85.5	82.35	26.3	27.16
Test MC	----	----	13.75	13.9
Test MC/M	----	----	550	555
Roll MC	33.0	33.0	7.9	7.9
Roll MC/M	330	330	315	315
T/MC TEST	----	----	1.91	1.95
T/MC Roll	2.59	2.49	3.33	3.44
Cost/App	110.00	116.60	85.86	81.44

ANALYSIS: In this example both the control and the test kit exceeded the required T/MC. However the test kit T/MC efficiency increased by 27.7%. The testing objective was met.

ACTION: The action indicated by the test result is to retest the Test package Vs. Control in much larger quatity to verify the result. If the results are verified (at least a 25% increase in efficiency) the test package becomes the new control. This format is easy to read and gives a clear look at test performance. With some modification it is appropriate for any type of testing program--Direct Mail, Lead Generation, Telemarketing, Space, Free Falls and so on.

Figure 15-6: Test report format

ceive 25% more response in January...multiplying 153 by 1.25 equals 191.25 responses. There is your projection.

Developing your own unique seasonal variation chart allows you to adjust for response patterns and deviations for the types of products you sell to the various markets you service. While it is true for broad-marketing programs, it is uniquely true for endorsed-marketing programs. In third-party marketing, seasonal variation plays a less important role. It is the endorser and the quality of the list that plays the most important role.

While your seasonal variation may be different, the following table provides a very general rule of thumb:

Month	Index	
	Broad Market	Endorsed Market
January	1.25	1.15
February	1.10	1.05
March	1.00	1.00
April	.90	.95
May	.85	.90
June	.80	.85
July	1.00	.90
August	1.08	.80
September	1.05	.95
October	.95	1.00
November	.80	.90
December	.50	.50

To adjust expected results for seasonality, all you do is establish the percentage relationship of index numbers between months: The index number for May is .85, while that for August is 1.08. You know that you received 140 apps from a product in May. The question: How many apps should you expect from the project if carried out in August? First, establish the relationship between months: 1.08 for August/.85 for May. This means that August should do 1.27 as many apps as for May. Taking 1.27% of 140 = 178 apps, giving an increase of 38 apps.

Seasonal variation adjustments are most often used in a testing environment. However, when creating a plan, it is useful to adjust anticipated response rates according to the impact of these monthly response variations.

The second adjustment to response made by smart marketers, who are projecting future patterns, is dependent on the sample size of circulation.

You should consult Robert C. Blattberg's "Decision Rule and Sample Size Selection for Direct-mail Testing," found in *The Direct Marketing Manual*, Release No. 601.1, published by The Direct Marketing Association.

Statistically, the response you receive on a test needs to be modified by the degree of confidence you have in the test results. If you have structured your testing to deliver a 90% confidence level (in a sense, mailed enough names so that 90 out of 100 times your results will be the same), you will still have a modest swing in rollout response.

This is especially true for insurance, since response rates are relatively low, perhaps only 1 to 5 apps per thousand. The key to this whole procedure is your circulation.

For example, if you are willing to accept a .05% difference in response (decision parameter) for a product you anticipate will respond at .5% (read 5 apps per thousand), then your circulation has to be 65,400. If you get your 5 apps per thousand, on a rollout you will have a 90% chance of pulling 4.75 to 5.25 apps per thousand.

On the other hand, if you are willing to accept a .01% deviation, you need a circulation of 1,635,306. In such case—on a rollout—you have a 90% chance to pull 4.95 to 5.05 apps per thousand. But remember the other ten chances.

You may want to view your results with a higher confidence level. At a 95% confidence level, a .05% deviation requires a circulation of 1,077,000. And a deviation of .01% requires a circulation of 2,692,494.

There are two issues involved here: *First*, rollouts are subject to a range of response. If you hope to achieve 5 apps per thousand and are projecting results, you should stay at the low end of the range—4.75 apps per thousand, instead of 5.

In fact, it's a good idea to widen the app swing by increasing the acceptable deviation. If you accept a .10% deviation, your circulation needs to be 16,353 at a 90% confidence level. Then you project response at 4.5 apps per thousand.

For the most part, a 5-apps-per-thousand result is most likely to come from a direct-mail campaign. A television campaign producing 40-apps-per-thousand circulation requires a circulation of 5,049 leads to produce a 90% confidence level with a .50 decision parameter. The app swing is from 20 to 60 apps. If your program can be successful at 20 apps per thousand, go with it. But, if your breakeven is 32 apps per thousand, you'll need to produce 31,556 leads at 40 apps per thousand and a .20 decision parameter to be 90% sure your results will hold up.

The same general statistical reference points exist for all forms of insurance direct marketing. The smart marketer will look up in the published tables the desired confidence level—85%, 90%, 95%—and identify the acceptable percent of deviation (decision parameter) from test results. He will then determine what the circulation has to be to ensure the results.

Second, determining sample size (circulation) and making decisions based on the adjusted results is especially important to the small insurance direct marketer. In the long run, setting values for confidence level and the decision parameter is dependent on the economic importance of the decision you are trying to make.

The more important the decision, the more confidence you want to have in your results. But there is an enormous amount of difference in the cost of testing a circulation of 16,000 and a circulation of 64,000 or more. It's important to know the difference. And, to use it to your advantage.

OK, it's over. This tour of insurance direct marketing mathematics has suggested the importance of modeling, determining breakevens, reporting results, and the tricks of decision making and projection based on financial principles. These were included to help you get your programs approved and working. It is essential that you learn to manipulate and report your numbers effectively. If you do, it will help you, your company, and the business for which *you are responsible.*

As fascinating as the mathematics of insurance direct marketing is, so too is the intellectual exercise of trying, today, to discover the trends that will affect the business tomorrow. Not the day after today—but rather in the years, and even decades, that face us.

The question is: Does insurance direct marketing have a future?

XVI

Vexing Issues and Tomorrow's Trends

If you are like most insurance direct marketers, you keep your "pet" frustrations locked away in a mental vault, ventilated infrequently, and—even then—only to your most trusted companions or associates.

But the truth is that I know of one "pet" frustration we probably share in common—compliance.

Compliance is one of the nasty "four-letter" words that takes ten letters to spell. Of the *vexing issues* that face the insurance direct marketing community, it is No. 1.

In all fairness, the tussle between marketers and compliance specialists did not have its origin in the office. It started years before—in the late 19th century. And, through 1950, insurers were licensed to operate under the authority of their home state, but were able to mail solicitations into any other state, issue policies, and conduct business. Some companies abused the privilege.

During the 1960s, states began to adopt "unauthorized-insurers" legislation, making it illegal for insurance companies to sell insurance in any state in which they were not licensed. By 1970, the problem of un-authorized insurers disappeared.

Not content with that control (and the added revenues from premium taxes), the insurance commissioners singled out the direct-response insurance industry for special consideration.

The adoption of the NAIC (National Association of Insurance Commissioners) model rules in 1972, amended in 1974 and several times since, is the culprit in the schism between marketer and compliance specialist. Back in 1974, the state insurance commissioners discovered that "an ever-increasing volume of insurance is being marketed solely through direct-response advertising..." So, they decided to develop a body of rules that applied to direct-response insurance.

They did so because they claimed that insurance was unique...and so, too, were insurance buyers. In their convoluted reasoning: "By the time an insured discovers that a particular insurance product is unsuitable for his needs, it *may be* too late for him to return to the marketplace to find a more satisfactory product." Please note the italicized "may be."

"Hence," the Commissioners believe, "the insurance-buying public should be afforded a means by which it can determine, in advance of purchase, the desirability of the competing insurance products proposed to be sold. This can be accomplished by advertising which accurately describes the advantages and *disadvantages* of the insurance product without either exaggerating the benefits or minimizing the limitations. *Proper advertising can provide such description and disclosure without sacrificing the sales appeal* which is essential to its usefulness to the insurance-buying public and the insurance business."

Imagine how ignorant and misinformed these people must have been to assemble such a mixture of idiotic incantation, pompous presumption, and phony reasoning!

Think about the words in the first quotation..."may be." Presumably, "may be" means a consumer discovers—after the fact—that he or she is not covered, or not covered adequately, for a particular claim concerning an injury or accident.

Certainly that can never happen in an agent sale. Rather, it is solely the result of the insurance direct marketer misleading the consumer.

Oh, it may be true that the consumer has received the *actual policy* before paying for it (SNM offers). Or, if the consumer has paid for the policy in advance (CWA offers), it is true that a return privilege is extended for ten, fifteen, or even thirty days. But, according to the insurance commissioners, that is not enough time for the consumer to determine what is covered and what is not.

In the second quotation, the insurance commissioners believe that insurance companies using the direct marketing system have an obligation to *report the disadvantages of their products!*

Why, that is like requiring Ford to include a warning in its advertising that riding in this car can kill you. But, that doesn't matter—according to the commissioners—because, if you say riding in this car can kill you, *it will not have any impact on sales!*

Consider this: Some years ago a major national insurance direct marketer ran an advertising copy test, split three ways.

Copy A *Strictly adhered* to the NAIC Guidelines.

Copy B *Adhered* to the *spirit* of the Guidelines.

Copy C *Adhered* to a *creative interpretation* of the Guidelines.

The result? The Copy C approach was the clear winner, beating Copy A and B by a wide margin. Copy B did slightly better than Copy A.

It seems clear to me that adherence in the strict sense to the advertising guidelines promulgated by state insurance commissioners severely restricts the sale of insurance products through the direct marketing system. And, that's what the NAIC had in mind to start with.

If the insurance direct marketing system is to survive, it is time to challenge insurance commissioners in every state.

I say this because two things have happened: First, state insurance statutes are seriously vague. And, they deliver broad discretionary powers to insurance commissioners. Thus, insurance commissions are very powerful.

Second, using their power, the commissions politically maneuver legislatures into passing detailed and specific additional statutes similar to the NAIC Model Regulations, under the guise of reform.

The result of these procedures is that insurance commissioners rule by fiat and intimidation. Many of their regulatory rules are not supported by statute. Or, if they are so supported, it is by statutes that the commissioners have "created." So companies are blackmailed into adhering to ill-conceived regulations at the expense of their license to do business in the state.

Take this case, for example, from a mid-1980 decision by the insurance commissioner of Washington State. The Washington Insurance Department proposed a rule (WAC 284-30-600) stating that it shall be an unfair business practice to effect life or disability coverage under a group policy delivered outside the state unless four requirements are met:

1. Compliance with advertising requirements
2. Compliance with claims-settlement practice requirements
3. Compliance with certain loss-ratio requirements

4. Compliance with both standard-provision requirements and policy-benefit requirements.

Moreover, the proposed rule did not apply to all out-of-state group coverages. In fact, it applied only to "discretionary groups"—groups formed for the purpose of marketing insurance to such groups as veterans, credit-card holders, credit unions, etc. It was, virtually, aimed at direct marketers.

The guts of the issue is a concept described as "extraterritoriality," which means that the state can regulate group certificates issued under the laws of *another state*. This is an idea that is totally antithetical to the accepted concept of *group insurance*.

What is most important, however, the Insurance Commissioner did not have the statutory authority to require that group policies delivered or issued for delivery in another state must meet the benefits or the coverage requirements of Washington law under the provision of RCW 48.39.010(2) as cited by the Commissioner.

Moreover RCW 48.02.060(3)(a) permits the commissioner to make only *reasonable rules and regulations* for effectuating any provision of the insurance code. Clearly, discrimination is not reasonable—at least in the United States.

At any rate, although the industry argued, the rule was passed, effective April 1 of the following year. The result was that Washington State consumers were denied access to lower-cost, out-of-state group coverages, and companies were forced to file individual policy forms—with their greater expense—if they decided to continue to do business in the state at all.

In all fairness, Washington State is not the only one wishing to destroy out-of-state groups with onerous "discretionary" group regulation. Oregon, New York, Tennessee, and others thirst for extraterritorial control over products offered to their residents.

To agree with the enormous regulatory authority exercised by the states, you have to buy into the fact that insurance and insurance buyers are unique. And, that is not a fact.

Of course, the problem is that, up until now, the insurance industry has *accepted* the authority of the state commissioners. In regard to out-of-state companies, there is—through these various regulations—a presumption of guilt...not the presumption of innocence.

Think about the issue of pre-approval of advertising. In law or logic, by what possible standard is *censorship* allowed in the United States?

The Insurance Department of New York State prevents the sale of cancer insurance to its residents, because—in its infinite wisdom—it doesn't think such coverage is a very good product. *Even if the residents of the state want the product, they cannot purchase it.* Naturally, the state held hearings to determine the needs and wants of its citizens. If you believe that, then cows can fly.

The California and Tennessee Departments have decided that banks can no longer endorse insurance products. What can be the possible basis for an insurance commissioner's interference in state banking?

The Florida Department arbitrarily decided that television-inquiry advertising run by four national insurance direct marketing companies was misleading. They issued a cease and desist order and fined the companies. Of course, precisely the same advertising is run in forty other jurisdictions. But to Florida that doesn't make any difference. Pay up or lose your license. Two of the four paid. The other two are going to court to— finally—*challenge the right of the Department to make such a decision.*

Perhaps insurance companies will start to take notice of the need to challenge. And, perhaps they will begin to build around a recent U.S. Supreme Court decision in which the justices *established the principle* that "targeted mailings don't represent any of the dangers of in-person solicitations, such as invasion of privacy or exertion of undue influence."

It was just such "undue influence" that led, in the late seventies, to the congressional hearings that resulted in the Bacchus amendment, which governs the sale of Medicare supplement insurance. The culprits were insurance agents, not *direct-response marketing advertisers*!

Perhaps it is time to recognize that the insurance regulators of the states are *stifling competition*—not fostering it—by imposing ridiculous restrictions and reaching unreasonable interpretations of words and phrases.

Perhaps it is time to recognize that political appointees and professional politicians are the wrong people to be regulating an industry.

Perhaps it is time to recognize that consumer complaints do not focus on advertising, but focus on claims payments.

Perhaps it is time to recognize that the American consumer is not dumb! And as soon as the people realize that regulators (not legislators) are telling them what they can and cannot buy, what they can and cannot read, what they can and cannot hear...there are going to be some pretty angry folks out there. Among marketers, we're pretty angry already.

Because of insurance regulation, two things have happened—and will continue to happen in the future. First, all creative work is beginning to look, sound, and read alike. Direct mail, telemarketing scripts, TV commercials, print advertising...there is a dull sameness to it all. Consumer-desired products that have the capacity to generate excitement in presentation are crushed in the advertising pre-approval mill of Arizona and Maryland.

The difficult states in which to do business—Arizona, North Carolina, Minnesota, New York, Florida, Michigan, Maryland, Washington, California, and a host of others—need to be brought up short. Because they are basically denying their citizens the right to purchase supplemental insurance products in a free, open, competitive market.

But, what may be sadder than all regulation—internal guidelines have split companies right up the middle! Insurance direct marketers have become the "shysters and hucksters" of their companies, *according to the insurance companies' compliance departments.*

Compliance specialists, who ought to be spending their time building business, are too busy tearing it down in an effort (futile at best) to interpret the *interpretive* guidelines. All that is accomplished is animosity and frustration. In a sense, it's a corporate civil war...with the "Direct Marketer-South" fighting a holding action against the "Compliance-North."

Now, just because a problem has been defined, I don't expect things to change. And, I don't believe all regulation is bad. Since insurance is a financial product, it makes sense to have some authority watch over the industry. But perhaps the industry needs to get involved, too. Why single out direct-response advertising for special regulation? Before trying to stifle the direct marketing system, why not learn more about it—and the good it has brought to millions of consumers?

To that end, it seems to me, a commission needs to be established with its members drawn from state insurance departments, insurance companies using the direct marketing system, and the direct marketing industry. Its purpose would be to educate regulators, and to draft advertising regulations that make sense, if any regulations are needed at all. And, to ensure that those regulations are accepted uniformly by every state.

It all comes down to some pretty simple ideas, it seems to me: *If you're not part of the solution, you're part of the problem.*

And, this problem of regulation is a dandy. Each year regulators are eroding our ability to do business. Not just the ability of insurance direct marketers, but that of agents, brokers, direct-selling companies—actually, the entire insurance industry. According to the Ernst & Whinney study, among insurance company CEOs, regulation and legislation is the number one enemy of expansion.

I repeat the two choices: To be part of the solution, or to be part of the problem. To accept the status quo is definitely to be part of the problem. I hope the alarm clock rings soon to wake us all up. If we sleep much longer, it will be too late.

Fortunately, it's not too late to do something about *vexing issue No. 2*—people.

In 1980, there were 89 mail-order and agency/brokerage insurance company members of DMA. In 1988, there were 108—only a 21% increase in eight years. Of the 89 in 1980, 44 disappeared by the time of the 1988 roster. That means 63 new companies were added during those eight years. Excluding the companies who disappeared, the increase is 140%.

And that's significant. Because every one of those companies—and many have expanded enormously in eight years—need good people. Companies just getting into the business especially need good people. Companies deciding to re-enter the business also need good people. The problem is: *Good people are just not around.*

If we are going to populate insurance direct marketing with good people, we have to *find them*, we have to *train them*, and we have to *keep them*.

From 1984 through 1987, one moderate-sized national insurance direct marketing company followed a strategy of serious expansion. Sales skyrocketed from about $10 million in new business in 1984 to $46.9 million in 1987. In the process, the company filled its various marketing divisions with experienced people, novices in training, and internal staff people—all talented, all dedicated.

And today, all are gone. Of the original group that began with the company, only 2 remain. The marketing department, from a high of almost 40 employees, has only five or six people left. And that team will produce less than $5 million in new business. Of all those people who left, *less than half remained in insurance direct marketing*. Think of it—more than 50% of those talented people are working in other industries. That is dramatic.

Now, why did it all happen? Remember Secret No. 1? That's why. The company dabbled. It grew—without the commitment necessary to make it grow. Its management, enchanted with short-term numbers, never examined what was actually happening.

There was no leadership. I don't mean *management*, I mean *leadership*. And the result? A feeling of disenfranchisement among a very talented group of marketers, half of whom found jobs in other industries!

Just hiring people is not the answer. Nor is "just" training people. Insurance direct marketing must become a people-persistent industry. We must start attacking the people-pool problem by, first, keeping the people we have.

Insurance direct marketing people are not "insurance" people under the definition most companies use. The good people are entrepreneurial, intelligent, talented, dedicated, and hardworking. They are not nine-to-fivers. They thrive on challenge, and demand opportunity. And, I think, they seek leadership—not management.

Insurance direct marketers don't need a policeman or a devil's advocate. They blossom under the sure hand of enthusiasm. Force them to work under a cheerleader, a coach, a nurturer, a facilitator...and they will deliver.

To keep good folks, we have to pay them well. But, a big portion of their compensation comes more from the doing. In one company I've worked with, a marketing director was making $30,000 a year when the going rate was twice that much. But prying him loose was out of the question. It wasn't the money; it was the challenge and opportunity of the job.

Once we learn how to keep the good people, we have to concentrate on recruiting others to, someday, fill their shoes. Here, we have to concentrate on training. USAA, CNA, and other insurance direct marketing organizations have in-house training programs. DMA runs important seminars, and DMIC holds an annual conference in April of each year. Send your people.

The key here is investment. Newcomers to insurance direct marketing have to learn two disciplines: Insurance and direct marketing. That means we have to ensure that we're making a proper investment in our new people.

An argument often heard is: Why make much of an investment at all? Just as soon as the new marketer becomes productive, he or she will fly the coop and join another company. It doesn't have to happen. Think about that. It doesn't have to happen—if expectations are realistic and progress brings reward.

Perhaps *it is time* for the industry to bite the bullet. Or there will not be any good people in fewer years than any of us want to think about.

The impact of and fragmentation caused by regulation and, additionally, the *talent-pond problem* are two of the most serious issues facing insurance direct marketers in the next several decades. But, there is another.

Vexing issue No. 3 Product and customer-service qualtiy are two particular problems for the insurance direct marketer. It seems to me a process currently at work that will shape our destiny in the years ahead is the growing bifurcation of markets. This relates to the increasing distance between high-priced, up-market insurance products and low-priced, down-market insurance products.

At the low end of the insurance direct marketing spectrum, price is a dominant factor in purchasing decisions. It is part of the persistency problem, which—it is generally agreed—plagues the direct marketing system. Because of the nature of products offered to this segment, product switching, based on price decision, is prevalent.

The impulse purchase—especially in health-insurance indemnification products—has fallen victim to this market characteristic.

At the high end of the insurance direct marketing spectrum, the upscale markets, price is less a barrier. This segment will seek products which express and reflect a sense of individualism. Appeals to status, style, and reliable service will be more persuasive than price.

So, there are two opportunities brewing. And there is a large hole between the two segments. Companies offering insurance products that are not competitively priced or particularly individualistic will fail.

The strategies to follow during the next two decades in order to deliver the best potential for future profits are *high volume* or *high price*.

Pursuing either strategy is not going to be easy. Telemarketing makes up-market penetration manageable and effective. Television and direct mail focus on down-market penetration.

But, to make either strategy work, companies must provide imaginative direct marketing insurance products, and deliver high-quality coverage—at the right price to both market segments.

Then, customer service on two levels will be absolutely critical—contact and claims. It is absolutely necessary for companies engaged in insurance direct marketing to *provide insureds with toll-free telephone access to the company.*

Claims-handling procedures must be sharpened. Claims will have to be settled faster than they are today. There can be no long-term claims settlement procedure. To a large degree, claims-payment automation, using computer algorithms, is in the future.

By coupling claims handling and payment with strong, policyowner marketing programs, it is likely that persistency problems in the low end of the market will be alleviated.

At the high end of the market, assignment of a personal services representative, in periodic telephone contact with the policyowner and available by name during business hours, will have an enormous impact on a unique policyowner marketing level.

This technique is available on a national level to direct marketing insurance companies. Or, on a local level, to aggressive agents and brokers.

In short, product and service quality is not the key to direct marketing success. It is the necessary prerequisite for success!

Vexing problems have been discussed, each of which offers opportunity and challenge to a new generation of insurance direct marketers. Now, for the trends that will shape insurance direct marketing in the years ahead. Far and away, the most important is the Graying of American—*Trend No. 1.* The 50+ market has been the primary insurance target for some of the largest insurance companies in America for the last three decades.

Old American Insurance Company, Colonial Penn Group, Prudential, and The Hartford have led in the insurance marketing efforts to this age segment. This market is not frail. It reflects the vitality of the people who populate it—currently one out of every three Americans. And in just a few years—when the "baby boom" generation turns fifty—it will account for 40% of the American population!

The psychographics of the market are dramatic. The "seniors" consider themselves mature and in the prime of life. Perceptively, they see themselves—compared to younger people—as more calm, more cost conscious, more careful, more logical, more confident, more practical, and more likely to plan ahead.

They demand to be treated as useful, competent, confident, coping individuals—with a zest for life and a desire to be self-sufficient and active.

In fact, the senior market is divided into two distinct subsegments. Subsegments that, taken together, account for 50% of current discretionary income available today—and 70% of the nation's net worth.

The "prime-life generation" (ages 50 to 64) is the larger of the two. Numbering 33 million—47% male, 53% female. Of the total, 80% are homeowners, 75% are employed, and 75% are married. They enjoy a median income of $25,557. Seven out of 10 are vets.

Seven out of 10 are at least high-school graduates, and 15% are college graduates. They are widely dispersed: 34% live in the Southern region; 18%, out West; 26%, in the North Central region; and 23%, in the Northwest.

This segment is characterized by an intense sense of optimism. The two greatest fears shared by its members are dependence on others and unexpected health and related financial catastrophe.

Interestingly, 40% of those in the 50-to-54 age band have no confidence in the Social Security System. Only 19% in the 55-to-64 age band have no confidence in the system.

The retired generation (ages 65+) numbers 28.6 million members—40% male, 60% female. Of the total, 70% are homeowners, 15% are employed (54% full time, 46% part time), and 65% are married. They have a median income of $13,254 (average income is $19,918). The mean financial asset base of this subsegment is $68,000.

Thirty-eight percent are vets, 4.7 out of 10 are at least high-school graduates, and 9.2% are college graduates. Sad to say, 10.5% of the market live at or below the poverty level, with women dominating this group.

In general, this subsegment shares the optimism of the younger (50-64) group. It, too, has fears of dependency and health and financial catastrophe.

Overall, neither subsegment has a clear understanding of Medicare—especially as to provisions relating to nursing home care.

It is estimated that within two years the national nursing home bill will grow to $52 billion annually. Of this, 48% will be covered by Medicare/Medicaid. The other 52% will be covered by consumers themselves. Few understand that Medicare covers only short-term nursing care (under 100 days).

Not many know that the average cost of nursing home care, for example, runs approximately $1,900 a month. While the price of the typical plan offered to provide protection against lengthy stays in nursing homes runs between $50 and $140 a month, consumers estimate that such protection costs between $10 and $40 per month. While the market represents a prime opportunity for insurance direct marketers, a considerable amount of time has to be spent on "education." And, a considerable amount of energy needs to be expended to convince these consumers that the benefit is worth the cost.

Finally, this trend toward a growing fifty-plus market will stay with us through the end of the 1990s. And, based on a proprietary study conducted to determine the buying habits of this market segment, you have—in general—a 14.7% better chance of selling insurance to folks over fifty than under fifty. And a whopping 75.8% better chance of selling insurance to the "affluent" over-fifty market.

There is one more element of this trend worth commenting on. It is the idea of older Americans as the new wave of entrepreneurs. Large and growing numbers of older employees want to continue working past normal retirement age. This group has the motivation to go into business for themselves. They have the resources to do so. And, thanks to advances in medicine and health care—which not only increase life span, but improve physical fitness—they have the energy to run their own businesses.

This may well have a large impact on business-to-business insurance direct marketers.

Trend No. 2 for the astute insurance direct marketer to watch is the New American Family.

The demise of the American family has been vastly overrated. As a point of identification, the *new American family* is defined as a married couple with children under 18 at home. They account for about 25% of all households today. Nine out of ten have heads of households between 25 and 54 years of age. The Congressional Budget Office takes the view that, as they go, so goes the middle class.

In general, this group is enjoying prosperity. But it is distinctly different from the "traditional" family. A growing conservatism among its members has brought back the concept of "joining" the family. It is, increasingly, composed of two wage earners...both parents working. It is smaller than the former *traditional* family. A growing concern is the care of elderly relatives—the grandparents.

In general, this group faces a growing challenge of balancing competing demands of work and home. Time is at a premium; convenience is important, but not at the expense of price.

One important impact of this group on the insurance industry as a whole, is the changing face of work: demand for day care, flexible working hours, job sharing, maternity/paternity leave with full job protection, and continuation of health benefits. These are all issues that may be somewhat embryonic today, but will grow in importance tomorrow.

Cafeteria-type employee-benefit plans—to avoid duplication of benefits in the two-wage earner family—will be part of the growing requirements of this group. And, historical ways of looking at group insurance will be forced to change.

The key word here is *flexibility*. To the insurance direct marketer, this offers the opportunity to view product development in a *completely different* way. That new way calls for shaping the new products to meet the needs and demands of flexibility. It's certainly worth considering.

Trend No. 3 is the New Reality in Consumer Marketing. There was significant reaction to the upheaval of the late sixties and all of the seventies...Watergate, Vietnam, and OPEC. Such things as Iran, high inflation, soaring interest rates...and a multitude of other problems worked against any tendency toward euphoria.

The Reagan era, marked by public enthusiasm and a general "grand" feeling about being an American, fostered a remarkable feeling of well-being among consumers in the eighties.

In the later stages of the cheerful Reagan optimism, the public mood became divorced from economic reality. October 19, 1987 marked the bubble-burst for the country. The stock market plummet—*decline* is too soft a word—somewhat belied the trends in the general economy, as to reduced inflation, a growing GNP, and the relatively low interest rates.

Americans learned that security, "feeling good" about their country, and real economic well-being carried a stiff price.

Main street and wall street are now going through a period of "reality therapy." The stock market crash changed the American consumer's perception of the economy. Today—and I expect for at least the next five to ten years—there will be an economic sobriety in consumer markets.

The psychological "highs" of the Reagan era have given way to the sobering reality we face every day. Yet, Americans are determined to "make things work." There is a national determination—a "grit," if you prefer—engendered in all consumers today.

Perhaps the reality is not quite as cheerful, or as lighthearted, as it was at the peak of the Reagan years. However, consumers are not scared, but they are cautious.

After euphoria, comes *austerity*. It is the national manic-depression. For insurance direct marketers, the new national mood and the new marketing reality are likely to restrain confidence in institutions, advertising claims and, in general, they make it more difficult for companies without national recognition to penetrate desirable market segments.

That is, of course, the downside. The upside is that the insurance direct marketing *offer* becomes even more critical. *Make your offers believable to the right list or target market, for the right product, at the right price, and chances are good that you will succeed.*

Chances are good, as well, that third-party marketing will begin to experience a resurgence. This will depend on the credibility of the endorser in breaking down the initial sales-resistance barrier thrown up by the consumer.

There is also a terrific opportunity for the broad marketer. Especially if devices can be developed to lend credibility to their offers.

All in all, Trend No. 3 doesn't appear to be all that bad—in either the short or long term.

Trend No. 4 is Geographic Relocation. Americans are an enormously mobile people. The latest available figures indicate that 46 million people in the U.S. moved from one place to another within one year...

more than ever before.

For the most part, people move short distances. But, approximately 10% move from one region to another. In recent years, the Northeast and Midwest have been losers in the regional population shifts. The South is staying about even. The West has been the big winner.

These migratory patterns are important to the insurance direct marketer. First, they identify the geographic areas where "markets" are available.

To the regional insurer, loss of market—through the migration of people composing a chosen regional market—ultimately will mean a decline in sales. There are simply not as many people available to purchase products. On the other side, a gain in market means opportunity for expanded sales.

Second, to the national marketer, migratory patterns indicate future business opportunities. The loss of population in the Northeast and Midwest, for instance, may shift the focus from the harsh regulatory environments represented by New York State and Michigan to more acceptable environments.

Another example: If there is movement of the 50+ market segment to restrictive regulatory states like Florida, California, and Arizona, the company may want to alter marketing strategies so as to follow their market. It becomes incumbent to find particular ways to deal with the regulators in those states.

Third, the action of a family's moving is a "life" event. Taking up residence in a new area—especially when the move is a regional one— means the consumer needs to find new anchors in his new community: a new bank, homeowners insurance, automobile insurance, and new retail credit cards. Perhaps additional life, health, or accident insurance.

Movers represent insurance sales opportunities. Perhaps not in the way such opportunity was defined by the marketer described in the introduction to this book. But, nonetheless, definite possibilities exist. Since "moving" is in our population's blood, and since regional migration to the sun belt is an important trend, it will pay you to watch it and to make the best use of it you can.

Trend No. 5 is of particular concern to insurance direct marketing creative people. It is the Video/Visual revolution. The impact of VCRs, the growing illiteracy rate among our young people, the number of hours consumers spend in front of television sets, and—to some extent— intellectual laziness...all these taken together mean that there are going to be some dramatic changes in the decades ahead in the way we communicate our messages to the public.

Chances are good that, more than ever before, visual identification will be the key to sales. Strong, bold, arresting, eye-catching graphics will play a greater role than ever before in direct marketing creative material.

Copy will have to be better written than it is today. It will have to be more incisive, more interesting, and more compelling.

New opportunities will develop in the VCR markets for including advertising messages on rental cassettes. Twenty-four-hour television will take on new meaning. Late-night and early-morning time slots—once the preserve of direct-response advertisers—will be more competitive, because of the VCR recording habits of consumers.

To attract consumers, striking new formats will have to be developed for direct mail, press advertising, and television.

What may be most important in this area is media fragmentation. The diversity of choices available to consumers today is staggering. Just as we identify specific market segments in list selection, so can we do among a startling number of magazines.

Both the growth of cable television—with its diversity of programming—and the growth of direct satellite transmission have expanded consumers' choices. Evidence exists that consumers, increasingly, know what they want to watch and when they want to watch it. *Just as the old radio networks were replaced by hundreds of local and specialty stations... so will network television be fragmented.*

This trend indicates an increasing specialization, diversity, and localization in the media markets. Couple this with the need for arresting graphics and compelling copy. It offers insurance direct marketers both an extraordinary challenge and opportunity to effectively communicate with their markets.

Finally, *Trend No 6* is the New American Lifestyle: *individualism.* Perhaps the most powerful trend during the next decade will be the shift from societal segment identification to a new individualism among American consumers.

Increasingly, Americans seek to control their *time.* They are segmenting it, allocating it better, using it more efficiently in seeking ways to increase the benefits of their leisure hours.

The new lifestyle is not merely a quest for convenience. It is a growing necessity, and it mirrors consumer desire to tailor their daily schedules to their needs, as opposed to having schedules imposed upon them.

Consider ATMs. Bank customers are no longer limited by "banking hours." Both the boom in home shopping through outlets like HSN and QVC and the growth of VCRs speak directly to the issue of the growing trend for consumers to manage their own time.

The trend is the result of two developments: the growth of two-income households and the revolution in electronic technology. The microchip revolution makes it possible for individuals to exercise greater control over their own lifestyles. And, the relative scarcity of free time, particularly for working couples, makes greater control necessary.

Because of the greater control consumers can exercise over their own time, as well as the almost limitless choices available to them, former patterns of consumer demographics and psychographics are rapidly and increasingly becoming meaningless.

Consumer behavior is also becoming more individualistic, and less defined by easy reference to identifiable social groups. Perhaps most noticeable today among affluent Americans is this movement toward self-expression. It is being seen, as well, in the less affluent.

Clearly, the trend is away from social conformity and toward the new individualism. The result of all this is that new combinations of consumer interests, spending habits, and buying patterns will emerge.

Insurance direct marketers will be forced to pay more attention to actual, and less to presumed, behavior. It means that research—in particular, the qualitative kind—will be more important than ever before.

New products will be developed that support this need for individual identification. Successful insurance direct marketers will emphasize consumer desire to save time and to enjoy a high degree of purchasing convenience.

In fact, it is likely that occasion-specific selling will become second nature to insurance direct marketers in this emerging consumer environment.

So, as I see it, there are three vexing problems facing the insurance direct marketing industry: regulation and its fragmentation, the shortage of talent, and product and customer-service quality.

And there are six major trends: the graying of America, the new American family, the new American reality, geographic relocation, the video/visual revolution, and the emerging American lifestyle—individualism.

Each problem and each trend will have some impact on the way you do business—right into the twenty-first century. You might look at them in this way: *Each problem represents opportunity. Each trend represents possibilities.*

That's what we've been discussing throughout this book—opportunities and possibilities. The insurance direct marketing system offers, I believe, exceptional opportunities and limitless possibilities for underwriting companies, agents, and brokers to serve the best interests of policyowners and prospects, using multi-channel distribution.

In reality, direct marketing is a *concept*. It most certainly is *not* a fancy term for mail order. And, for those smart insurance marketing companies adopting the concept, the decades ahead will be bright indeed. The seeds have been sown, already.

Consider Old American Insurance Company. Under the leadership of Martin Baier, the company built a marketing database for the sale of insurance to the 50+ market segment through the mail-order distribution channel. Now they are using the same dynamic database to generate new leads and tips for a variety of products sold through the agency distribution channel. In fact, one half of their $50 million annual sales are agent generated. With the acquisition of Old American by CenTrust of Florida, insurance will be sold at the counter in savings and loan banks—opening a third distribution channel—direct selling. Direct mail and television synchronize the multi-channel, relational database marketing.

Or consider Forethought Insurance. A sensitive TV commercial— created by Olgivy & Mather Direct, Chicago—develops phone leads for an insurance policy which funds final burial plans that are agent-sold through some of America's 15,000 funeral homes. Leads are generated far below the $50 allowable lead cost. Their hi-tech system ties manufacturing, insurance, and retailing together, in a coordinated marketing effort.

Finally, on the business-to-business side, a unique direct-mail effort presented by Safeco Insurance to its independent agents resulted in more than $6 million in sales, surpassing its goal by more than 150 percent among agents who had not previously contributed.

All of these stories are available on videotape from HCI Video (Hoke Communications, Inc.). Each story identifies for you one of the astounding possibilities offered by the direct marketing concept.

In the years ahead, the *possibilities* will increase in importance. Multi-channel distribution and integrated, relational, database marketing, I believe, will become the norm. Single-channel distribution, effectively, will not survive into the next century.

Expanding consumer and business-to-business demand will dictate new, aggressive ways of viewing insurance and allied financial services— regardless of product. In fact, we are seeing elements of this today— everywhere we look.

Dedicated mail-order insurance marketing companies are disappearing. They are swallowed up by larger financial service organizations, in an acquisition frenzy, to add special and unique talent and expertise to the overall success of their parents.

So, to answer the question posed at the end of Chapter XV: Is there a future for insurance direct marketing? YOU BET!

You are limited only by your imagination. For more than two decades I have been an attentive student of insurance direct marketing, seeking—and sometimes finding—the success offered by this system and concept. What is the final secret?

All it really takes to succeed in insurance direct marketing is commitment, enthusiasm, thought, attention to detail, courage, curiosity, teamwork, experience, judgment, and finally...passion!

Good Luck.

GLOSSARY

800 Service :   An inbound long-distance service which is free to the caller, paid for by the recipient.

A.I.D.A. :   A popular formula for the preparation of direct-mail copy. The letters stand for attention, interest, desire, and action.

AAP (Average Annual Premium) :   Annualized premium of all policies in group divided by total number of policies in group.

AARP (Average Annualized Renewal Premium) :   The average amount of annualized premium per policy associated with a designated group of policies.

Accident :   An unforeseen, unintended, and unexpected event, mishap, or casualty.

Accident policy :   A policy which provides benefits only as the result of an accidental injury, never as the result of illness.

Accidental death and dismemberment :   A form of insurance affording benefits in the event of accidental death, accidental loss of a member(s), e.g., an arm or a leg, or the accidental loss of sight.

Accidental death benefit :   1) A benefit in addition to the face amount of a life insurance policy, payable if the insured dies as the result of accidental means. Such policy is sometimes referred to as "double indemnity." 2) A lump sum payment for loss of life due to an accident which was the direct cause of death.

Accounting-G.A.A.P. (Generally accepted accounting principles) :   Accounting method in which a company reports its financial condition and operations based on income and expense items adjusted to reflect income actually earned and expenses benefiting mostly that accounting period.

Accounting - statutory :   Accounting method in which a company reports its financial condition and operations as required by state statute. Statutory earnings or losses are those as shown on the NAIC Convention Blank (essentially a cash basis), in contrast to earnings or losses that would be shown if a generally-accepted accounting procedures statement were used.

Acquisition allowance :   The sum of money allocated to be spent to acquire a new policyowner.

Action devices :   Items and techniques used in a mailing to stimulate the

311

response desired.

Active buyer : A buyer whose latest purchase was made within the last twelve months.

Active customer : A term used interchangeably with "active buyer."

Actives : Customers on a list who have made purchases within a prescribed time period, usually not more than one year; premium-paying policyholders.

Actuary : A person who calculates policy rates, reserves, and dividends; and prepares various other applicable statistical studies and reports.

Add-on : An increment of insurance coverage added to an existing policy wherein the additional coverage is of the same type as that of the base; policy "riders," for example, are considered add-ons.

Add-on service : Service of Direct Marketing Assn., which gives consumers an opportunity to request that their names be added to mailing lists.

Additions : New names, either of individuals or companies, added to a mailing list.

Address-coding guide : Contains the actual or potential beginning and ending house numbers, block group and/or enumeration district numbers, ZIP Codes, and other geographic codes for all city delivery service streets served by 3,154 post offices located within 6,601 ZIP Codes.

Address correction requested : An endorsement which, when printed in the upper left-hand corner of the return address portion of the mailing piece (below the return adress), authorizes the U.S. Postal Service, for a fee, to provide the known new address on the mailing piece.

Adverse selection : The tendency of more poor risks than good ones to buy insurance or maintain existing insurance in force, i.e., selection against the company.

Agent : An insurance company representative, licensed by the state, who solicits insurance for the company or companies with which he is licensed.

Alphanumeric : A contraction of "alphabetic" and "numeric." Applies to any coding system that provides for letters, numbers (digits), and special symbols such as punctuation marks. Synonymous with alphameric. Also means that a file is maintained on an alphabetic (first) and numeric (second) basis.

Alternate offer : An insurance solicitation made to "house" names including lapses and non-buying inquiries presenting an alternative offer for another type of insurance.

Annuitant : The person during whose life an annuity is payable, usually the one who receives the annuity payments.

Annuity . A contract providing for specified payments to be made at regular intervals for a specified period of time or for life.

312

Glossary

Annuity certain : A contract guaranteeing payments at regular intervals for a specific period of time, even if the annuitant has died.

Antiselection : See adverse selection.

APL (Automatic premium loan) : A provision in a life insurance policy authorizing the insurer to automatically pay any premium not paid by the end of the grace period through a policy loan, providing the policy has sufficient cash value to cover the amount due.

APO (Automatic premium option) : An offer made in the fulfillment package for a new insured to automatically increase his insurance coverage by one unit.

Applicant (Insurance) : The individual requesting insurance coverage.

Application : A statement signed by the prospective insured giving information on the basis of which the insurer determines the acceptability of the risk, the contract to be drawn, and the premium.

Application form (Insurance) : A legal document filed with and approved by the various state insurance commissions, containing blank spaces to be filled with particulars regarding the prospective policyowner. The particulars to be filled in are designed to give the insurance company two general kinds of information: One is general contractual information providing identifying data concerning the applicant and describing the insurance coverage applied for. The other is risk-appraisal information needed to decide whether the person meets the company's standards of insurability.

Assignment : The legal transfer of ownership rights under a life insurance policy from one person to another.

Assignment of benefits : A statement by the policyowner which instructs the insurance company to pay claim benefits directly to a third party, usually a doctor or hospital. If an assignment has been properly made, the assignee acquires legally enforceable rights under the insurance policy.

Attained age : The current age of the insured.

Audience : The total number of individuals reached by a promotion or advertisement.

Audit : Printed report of the counts involved in a particular list or file. Also used in reference to the verification of facts, figures, or claims made by an insurance company.

Automatic answering machine : Plays and records short messages.

Automatic call distributor (ACD) : Equipment that automatically manages and controls incoming calls evenly and sends calls to the telephone rep who has been idle the longest, answers and queues calls during busy periods.

Automatic call sequencer (ACS) : Distributes incoming calls by allowing operators to make the decision on longest idle phones.

Automatic dialing recorded message player : A machine that dials preprogrammed telephone numbers, automatically plays a pre-recorded message (normally a sales pitch), then records responses.

Automatic number identification (ANI) :   Part of a PBX management report which allows the phone company to generate a bill broken down by telephone number extension for individual accountability.

Automatic premium loan :   A policy loan effected by a life insurance company, by previous authorization of the policyowner, to pay a premium which remains unpaid at the end of the grace period.

Automatic route selection (ARS) :   A switching system that chooses the least costly path from available owned or leased circuits. (See least-cost routing.)

Back end :   The activities necessary to complete a mail-order transaction once an order has been received and/or the measurement of a buyer's performance after he has ordered the first item in a series offering.

Band :   With WATS, the geographic areas from which the customer can call, or to which you may call.

Bangtail :   Promotional envelope with a second flap, which is perforated and designed for use as an order blank.

Barge-out device :   A machine that announces the same outgoing message to all callers.

Batch processing :   Technique of executing a set of computer programs/selections in batches as opposed to executing each order/selection as it is received. Batches can be created by computer programming or a manual collection of data into groups.

Batched job :   A job that is grouped with other related jobs as input to a computer system, as opposed to a transaction job entry, where the job is done singly to completion.

Behavior modeling :   A training technique that ignores attitudes and shows participants exactly how to implement desirable skills in typical on-the-job situations.

Beneficiary :   The person to whom the proceeds of a life insurance policy are payable at the death of the insured.

Benefits :   The financial reimbursement and other services provided to insureds by the insurer. Also the specifics of how a product benefits the prospect, i.e., saves money, saves time, eliminates worry.

Bill enclosure :   Any promotional piece or notice enclosed with a bill, an invoice or a statement not directed toward the collection of all or part of the bill, invoice, or statement.

Billing kit :   The collection of components sent to a policyowner in a given mailing, which includes a notice that a premium payment is due or past due. Elements usually include letters encouraging premium payments, premium notices, reinstatement forms, and payment option promotions—like credit card or automatic checking account

314

deduction.

Binary : Involves a selection, choice, or condition in which there are two possibilities, such as the use of the symbols "0" and "1" in a numbering system.

Binder, binding receipt : See conditional binding receipt.

Bingo card : A reply card inserted in a publication and used by readers to request literature and samples from companies whose products and services are either advertised or mentioned in editorial columns.

Birthday life - marketing approach : A marketing technique designed to sell life insurance wherein a solicitation is made just prior to the individual's next birthday, therefore, qualifying him for the lower premium rate associated with his then current age.

Blocked calls : Calls that receive busy signals.

Boiler room : Refers to telephone selling lacking appropriate professionalism, controls, positive atmosphere, telecommunications equipment, etc.

Book billing : Method of premium billing by which monthly payers receive in advance sufficient premium notice cards to last them for an entire year. If an address or any other detail should change, the policyowner takes advantage of the address-change card in the packet in order that records can be updated.

Bounce back : An element in a fulfillment kit which allows the prospect to apply for additional coverage, a different coverage, or additional infomation.

Broadcast media : A direct-response source that includes radio, television, and cable TV.

Broadside : A single sheet of paper, printed on one side or two, folded for mailing or direct distribution, and opening into a single large advertisement.

Brochure : That element of a direct-mail kit which explains all the features and benefits of an insurance program.

Broker : An insurance solicitor, licensed by the state, who represents various insureds, and who is permitted to place insurance coverages with any insurance company authorized to transact business in the state in which he holds a license.

Bulk mail : A category of third-class mail involving a large quantity of identical pieces but addressed to different names, which are specially processed for mailing before delivery to the post office.

Bump-up : A term used to indicate, normally, a telemarketing intervention in a direct marketing program that proposes, to a prospective insured, an increased benefit amount at an appropriate increase in premium prior to issuing a policy.

Burnout : A phenomenon of exhaustion and lack of motivation often experienced by TSRs working long shifts without proper breaks and assignment changes.

Burst : To separate continuous form paper into discrete sheets.

Business-to-business telemarketing : Telemarketing of insurance services to individuals at their places of business. Frequently used by agents and brokers to generate new business and to service existing customers.

Buyer : One who applies for, and is issued, an insurance policy or certificate. Unless another modifying word or two is used, it is assumed a buyer has paid for all premium due to date. Synonymous with policyholder, policyowner under the same circumstances.

Byte : A single character or element in a binary number (digit). The smallest element of binary machine language represented by a magnetized spot on a recording surface or a magnetized element of a storage device.

CPI (Cost per inquiry) : A simple arithmetical formula derived by dividing the total cost of a mailing or an advertisement by the number of inquiries received.

CPM (Cost per thousand) : Refers to total cost per thousand pieces of direct mail "in the mail."

CPO (Cost per order) : Similar to cost per inquiry except based on actual orders rather than inquiries. Synonymous with CPA—cost per application.

Call accounting : Refers to equipment that provides a record of calls placed by extension, time, date, number dialed, and length of call.

Call detail recording (CDR) : A PBX and electronic key system feature that generates a chronological listing of every call leaving the system, including extension that made the call, duration of call, etc.

Call forcing : A call-distribution feature which automatically directs a waiting call onto an available TSR as soon as that person has completed a previous call.

Call guide : An informal roster of points to be covered during a telephone sales presentation which allows for personalization. May also refer to formal presentation script.

Call parking : By "placing" a call on hold or an imaginary extension ("parking it"), the call can be retrieved from any other phone within the system.

Call queuing : Places incoming calls in a waiting line for access to an operator station.

Camp-on : Allows incoming call to wait on a line until it is available, at which time the call goes through automatically.

Cancellation request : This is a request from the policyowner, the main insured only, to discontinue the policy.

Cash buyer : A buyer who encloses payment with order.

Cash on delivery (COD) : Sometimes used as synonymous with SNM (send no money).

Cash surrender value :   The cash value of a whole life or endowment insurance policy upon surrender to the company prior to its maturity as a claim or an endowment. Some term policies may have small cash surrender values.

CC (Credit card) :   DC, AMEX, VISA, MASTERCARD, used to pay premium.

Census tract :   Small geographical area established by local committees, and approved by the Census Bureau, which contains a population segment with relatively uniform economic and social characteristics, with clearly identifiable boundaries averaging approximately 1,200 households.

Certificate holder :   An individual who has been issued a group certificate stating the coverage and general provisions of the group master contract under which the individual is insured. This status is generally identical to that of an individual policyholder except that the continuance of coverage is dependent upon the continuance in force of the master group policy and continuance as a member of the group for which the master policy was issued.

Circulation :   The number of pieces of direct mail or the number of leads for a specific program to which a promotion is directed. A quantitative term.

Claim :   The demand upon an insurance company for payment of benefits under the terms of an insurance contract.

Claim philosophy :   The operating guidelines of the claim service division used and interpreted by the claims service representatives as their basis for making decisions regarding claim settlements.

Cleaning :   The process of correcting and/or removing a name and address from a mailing list because it is no longer correct or because the listing is to be shifted from one category to another.

Closed-ended questions :   Used to elicit a specific ordered choice answer of "a, b, or c," or an unordered choice where the customer can choose more than one specific answer. Applies to telemarketing.

Cluster selection :   A selection routine based upon taking a group of names in series, skipping a group, taking another group, etc. E.g., a cluster selection on an nth name basis might be the first 10 out of every 100 or the first 125 out of 175, etc.; a cluster selection using limited Zip Codes might be the first 200 names in each of the specified Zip Codes, etc.

Clustering :   Grouping names on a list according to geographic, demographic, or psychographic characteristics.

Coding :   1) Identifying devices used on reply devices to identify the mailing list or other source from which the address was obtained. 2) A structure of letters and numbers used to classify characteristics of an address on a list.

Cold calls :   Unsolicited sales calls to an audience not familiar to the caller.

Collected premium : Premiums which the policyholder has remitted in cash or check to the insurance company and which have been applied to the specific policy, but not necessarily earned. (See earned premium.)

Commission : 1) That part of the collected premium paid to an agent, broker, or third party to compensate for this person's sales efforts or endorsement. 2) A percentage of sale, by prior agreement, paid to the list broker, list manager, or other service arm for their part in the list usage.

Communicator call report (CCR) : Identifies, for each telephone sales representative, what calls were handled, the date, the contact name, and all information pertaining to the details of each call made during a shift.

Compile : The process by which a computer translates a series of instructions written in a programming language into actual machine language.

Compiled list : Names and addresses derived from directories, newspapers, public records, retail sales slips, trade show registrations, etc., to identify groups of people with something in common.

Compiler : See list compiler.

Compliance : A term used to mean acting in accordance with the various state statutes, regulations, and guidelines dealing with insurance policies, applications, insurance product development, advertising, and all forms of policyholder solicitation.

Component : A letter, flyer, brochure, card, outside envelope, return envelope, premium notice, policy jacket, or advertising materials, which will be used by the company, generally in combinations, to form a kit for soliciting new business, communicating the notice of premium payments due, transmitting a new policy, and the like.

Component number : A control number assigned to components of direct mail and fulfillment kits which identifies and distinguishes one from another.

Comprehensive : Complete and detailed layout for a printed piece. Also: "comp" or "compre." Also a term describing coverage under auto and homeowners policies.

Compromise settlement : An offer by the company on a basis other than for the full amount for which a claim was submitted. This may be a result of the fact that part of the diagnosis has already been excluded because of a pre-existing clause. If a lawsuit against the company is being considered and if the company—though knowing the correctness of its decision—feels that the suit may not be in its favor, an agreed settlement may be favored. In some cases, the policyowner is requested to surrender his policy before a specified payment is made.

Computer : Data processor that can perform substantial computation, without intervention by a human.

Computer compatibility : Ability to interchange the data or programs of one computer system with one or more other computers.

Computer letter : Computer-printed message providing personalized, fill-in information from a source file in pre-designated positions. May also be fully printed letter with personalized insertions.

Computer personalization : Printing of letters or other promotional pieces by a computer using names, addresses, special phrases, or other information based on data appearing in one or more computer records. The objective is to use the information in the computer record to tailor the promotional message to a specific individual.

Computer program : Series of instructions or statements prepared to achieve a certain result.

Computer record : All of the information about an individual, company, or transaction stored on a specific magnetic tape or disc.

Conditional binding receipt : A receipt given to the applicant who pays all or a specified portion of the initial premium with his application for insurance. This receipt declares that if the proposed insured is found to be insurable, insurance under any policy issued as the result of the application shall be effective as of the date of the conditional receipt or, in some cases, the date of the application approval.

Consumer list : A list of names (usually at home address) compiled, or resulting, from a common inquiry or buying activity indicating a general or specific buying interest.

Contestable clause : A provision in an insurance contract setting forth the conditions under which, or the period of time during which, the insurer may contest or void the policy. (See time limit on certain defenses.)

Continuity program : Products or services bought as a series of small purchases, rather than all at one time—insurance, for example.

Continuous form : Paper forms designed for computer printing that are folded, and sometimes perforated, at predetermined vertical measurements. These may be letters, vouchers, invoices, cards, etc.

Conversion : 1) Privilege - The exchange of an insurance policy of one kind for a policy of a different kind, usually without evidence of insurability. Examples are: a) the exchange of a term life insurance contract for a whole life or endowment contract in accordance with the terms of a specific policy provision, or b) the right of a certificateholder under a group insurance contract to purchase individual insurance without evidence of insurability at the termination of his group coverage. 2) To secure specific action, such as the purchase of insurance from a name on a mailing list or as a result of an inquiry. 3) Process of changing from one method of data processing to another, or from one data processing system to another. Synonymous with reformatting.

Convertible term insurance policy : A specific-period life insurance policy that, by its terms, may be exchanged for a whole-life or endowment plan of insurance without evidence of insurability.

Cost per hour (CPH) : The hourly cost of running a telemarketing program, including salaries, telephone communication charges, list cost, and a portion of monthly overhead.

Cost per inquiry (CPI) : Average cost for each response (or inquiry) received.

Cost per thousand (CPM) : Common rate for list rentals where fee is based on every 1,000 names rented to telemarketer. Also a unit of measure applied to the cost of mailing kits, fulfillment material, etc.

Countersignature : The requirement by some states that a policy be personally signed by a licensed resident agent prior to delivery to the policyowner. (A favorite of Florida.)

Coupon : Part of an advertising promotion piece intended to be filled in by the inquirer or customer and returned to the advertiser.

CPA (Cost per application) : The average marketing cost of securing an insurance application.

Cross selling : Selling an additional insurance product to a current policyholder that is different from the coverage owned. Also applies to the sale of products to inquirers that are different from the original product inquired about.

Customer cycling : Planned, regular contact with customers and cancelled or lapsed policyholders.

Customer profile : Pertinent information about a customer, including purchase history, address and phone number, demographic and psychographic information, etc.

Customer service representative (CSR) : One who handles client concerns, complaints, and inquiries.

CWA : Acronym for cash with application.

Cycle : As related to computer processing, a processing routine which is repetitive in nature and generally at timed intervals.

Database : A collection of data to support the requirements and requests for information of a specific group of users. The difference between data and information can best be illustrated by imagining all the names and telephone numbers from a phone book written on different pieces of paper and thrown into a barrel. The barrel contains a huge amount of data, but unless it is organized (as in the phone book) its value as information is questionable.

Decoy : A unique name especially inserted in a mailing list to verify list usage.

Deductible : The portion of an insured loss to be born by the insured before he is entitled to recovery from the insurer.

Glossary

Deductible period : Used interchangeably with the term "elimination period" to describe the specified number of days of hospital confinement due to illness which are to be excluded from benefit coverages or number of days excluded on a loss of time policy.

Deferred annuity : An annuity under which income payments are not to begin until some future date, such as in a specified number of years or at a certain age.

Deferred policy acquisition costs : Marketing costs which are incurred but not recognized as a cost of the current accounting period. However, they are recognized proportionately in the periods in which the associated premium revenues are earned. A foundation concept of GAAP accounting.

Deferred premium : The unpaid and as yet undue mode premiums on insurance policies which are required to provide the policyholder with coverage to the next policy anniversary date. Deferred premiums are an asset and may be considered the same as accounts receivable. The deferred premium amount is reduced as the policyowner makes periodic mode payments.

Demographics : Socio-economic characteristics pertaining to a geographic unit (county, city, sectional center, ZIP Code, group of households, education, ethnicity, income level, etc.). As well, specific information on individuals such as age, income, marital status, family members.

Dependent : Person(s) listed on application of main insured for whom premiums are paid by the main insured.

Detailed station message accounting (DSMA) : Record of calls made through each telephone.

Deviated premium : A term used to describe the marketing technique of charging less than the normal premium for insurance protection for a given period of time as an incentive to buy. Used as a "trial" offer.

Dials per hour (DPH) : Number of telephone calls placed, not necessarily completed, by a TSR or group during a one-hour period.

Direct distance dialing (DDD) : Calls made without operator assistance.

Direct-mail advertising : Any promotional effort using the Postal Service, or other direct delivery service, for distribution of the advertising message.

Direct Marketing Association (DMA) : The direct-response industry's trade association, representing direct-mail, direct-response advertising, mail-order and telemarketing agencies, and companies which sell goods or services to industry participants.

Direct-response advertising : Advertising, through any medium, designed to generate a response by any means (such as mail, telephone, or personal visit) that is measurable.

Disability benefit : A benefit to which the insured is entitled if he becomes totally and permanently disabled as defined in his policy. It may provide only a waiver of premium, or both waiver and payment of a monthly income.

Dividend : An amount allocated from surplus and payable to the policyowners of participating insurance contracts, if the company has operated with sufficiently favorable mortality, morbidity, interest, and expense experience.

Double indemnity : See accidental death benefit.

Doubling day : A point in time established by previous experience when 50% of all returns to a direct-response solicitation will normally be received.

Downgrading : A term used to describe the process by which an insured is offered an alternative coverage, less than the coverage applied for, to induce the insured to maintain his policy, or to pay his premium.

Due date : Date on which a policy is due for renewal, and to which coverage is provided. Includes month, day, and year. Also refers to date on which premium payment is due.

Dummy : 1) A mock-up giving a preview of a printed piece, showing placement and nature of the material to be printed. 2) A fictitious name with a mailable address inserted into a mailing list to check on usage of that list.

Dupe (Duplication) : Appearance of identical or nearly identical records more than once.

Duplication elimination : A specific kind of controlled duplication which provides that no matter how many times a name and address appear on a list, and how many lists contain that name and address, it will be accepted for mailing only once by that mailer. Also referred to as "dupe elimination."

Earned premium : That amount of premium income applicable to the expired or elapsed part of the period for which the premium has been charged and insurance coverage has been provided.

Effective date : 1) Date on which coverage under a policy begins. This is sometimes known as the "policy date." On a "send-no-money" policy, no effective date is shown, even though a policy form is sent. As soon as the initial premium has been received, the policy goes into effect on the date of receipt. The policyowner is sent a rider giving the effective date. 2) The date from which insurance coverage begins under a policy or rider and from which time the company is liable for any benefit claims due under the terms of the contract.

Endorsement : A written or printed form attached to the policy to alter provisions of the contract relating to such facts as the name of the insured, the property covered, the perils insured, and the locations covered. Sometimes loosely used to refer to any change in the printed policy or any rider.

Endowment insurance : A contract that pays an amount of insurance, if the insured should die during a specified term of years, or a stated amount as an endowment if the insured survives to the end of that term.

Enrollment deadline :   The end of a specified period of time (as short as 2 or 3 days) during which application for insurance coverage under a given solicitation must be made. To be accepted, the application is to be postmarked by midnight of the deadline date. The purpose served by an enrollment deadline can be two-fold: 1) to serve as a stimulus for immediate response from the prospective insureds. 2) to prevent people from waiting until they have reason to believe they are, or will become, sick and then apply for coverage. The disadvantage in employing an enrollment deadline in a solicitation is that the state insurance commissions who allow its use do not allow the using company to run another solicitation in that state for the same product for a specified period of time following, which can be as short as one month or as long as six months.

Enrollment form :   A "group" application form against which a certificate of insurance is issued, as opposed to an individual policy.

Envelope stuffer :   Any advertising or promotional material enclosed in an envelope with business letters, statements, or invoices.

EP (Elimination period) :   In health insurance contracts, a specified number of days of hospital confinement due to ILLNESS which are to be excluded from the benefit coverage. For example, an elimination period of 3 days means that benefit coverage begins on the 4th day of hospitalization. A zero-day elimination means that benefit coverage begins the very first day of hospitalization.

Exclusion clause :   A policy provision stated within the insurance contract that denies coverage and thereby any benefit or loss payments for certain specific perils or conditions. Such a provision might read: "Your policy does not cover conditions caused by: war or any act of war, any mental disease or disorder, or the use of intoxicants or narcotics."

Exclusions :   Specified hazards for which a policy will not provide benefit payments.

Extended term insurance :   Term life insurance granted under the nonforfeiture section of a life insurance contract if a policyowner ceases to pay premiums at any time after the contract has acquired a cash value. The cash value will be applied to purchase term insurance in the face amount of the policy, less indebtedness, for as long a period as it will provide or for the term of the policy, if shorter. Under endowment contracts, any excess is used to purchase a pure endowment payable on the date the contract matures.

Face amount :   The amount stated in the policy that is payable at the death of the insured or at the maturity of the contract, subject to adjustments for indebtedness, dividend additions, additional benefits, or grading. Grading means that a portion of the face amount (as a percentage of face or in fixed dollars) is payable in the first in-force year, a higher amount for the second in-force year, and

323

the full amount in the third in-force year and thereafter.

Facsimile transmitting machine/message (FAX) : A method of information transfer of text and illustrations. Image is scanned by the FAX equipment, transmitted over telephone lines and reconstructed and duplicated at a receiving FAX.

Family life policy : A policy that provides insurance on the lives of all members of a family. The typical form provides permanent insurance on the life of the father and a lesser amount of term insurance on the lives of the wife and children. Children born or legally adopted after the policy is issued are automatically insured under the policy with no increase in premium.

Family member : Dependent, adult or child, who is covered by a policy written as a family plan.

Federal Communications Commission (FCC) : A federal agency whose duty is to regulate communication by wire and radio—including licensing of communications providers.

Field : Reserved area in a computer which services a similar function in all records of the file. Also, location on magnetic tape or disc drive which has definable limitations and meaning. E.g., Positions 1-30 is the Name Field.

File maintenance : The activity of keeping a file up to date by adding, changing, or deleting data (all or part). In most instances synonymous with list maintenance. (See "update.").

Fill-in : A name, address, or other words added to a preprinted letter.

Fixed field : A way of laying out, or formatting, list information in a computer file that puts every piece of data in a specific position relative to every other piece of data, and limits the amount of space assigned to that data. If a piece of data is missing from an individual record, or if its assigned space is not completely used, that space is not filled (every record has the same space and the same length). Any data exceeding its assigned space limitation must be abbreviated or contracted.

Follow-up system : An automated or manual telemarketing system that keeps track of calls that should be recycled into the outgoing program and rescheduled at a later time. Its purpose is to trap information and release it back to communicators at the appropriate time.

Franchise insurance : In life and health, a plan for covering groups of persons with individual policies uniform in provisions (although they may differ in benefits). Individual contracts are issued to each and with individual underwriting. The solicitation usually takes place among an employer's work force with his consent. Franchise Insurance is usually applied to groups too small to qualify for true group coverage. Also, in life insurance, sometimes called "wholesale insurance."

Glossary

Free-standing insert : A promotional piece loosely inserted or nested in a newspaper or magazine.

Frequency : The number of times an individual has ordered a product or service within a specific period of time. (See monetary value and recency.)

Friend-of-a-friend (Friend recommendation) : The result of one party sending in the name of someone considered to be interested in a specific advertiser's product or service; a third-party inquiry.

Front end (Marketing) : 1) Solicitation of business from individuals who are not already policyowners—as distinguished from internal marketing, wherein additional business is solicited from those who are or have been policyowners. 2) Activities necessary for the measurement of direct marketing activities, leading to an order or a contribution.

Fulfillment (General) : The process of completing an agreement. Fulfillment for requested insurance coverage - The issuing of the policy, sending a fulfillment package, and sending the first billing notice. Fulfillment for inquiries - The sending of information and application to the person who inquired about insurance coverage.

Fulfillment package : 1) The collection of pieces sent to the individual who has applied and been accepted for insurance coverage, which includes an identification card and welcoming letter from the company, the actual policy, first billing notice, and an insurance add-on offer. 2) The collection of pieces mailed to an individual who has requested information about a particular coverage, designed to persuade the individual to apply for the coverage.

Full premium : The full premium under a particular policy for a given coverage and period of time—as opposed to reduced or deviated premium.

Geodemographics : Any method of subdivision, based on geographic or political subdivisions—ZIP Codes, sectional centers, cities, counties, states, regions, ADIs (areas of dominant influence), or DMAs (designated marketing areas), and combined with quantified data such as age, sex, marital status, etc.

Gimmick : Attention-getting or participation device, usually dimensional, attached to a direct-mail printed piece.

Grace period : The period of 30 or 31 days, granted under the terms of an insurance contract, following the day a premium becomes due and during which the payment may be made without loss of any rights. The policy remains in force during this period, but lapses if the premium is not paid at the end of the grace period. If the insured dies during the grace period, the death benefit is payable, but the premium is deducted from the proceeds. Usually applicable to life and health insurance. Property and casualty coverages normally have no such device.

Graded death benefit (GDB) : Type of life insurance protection for which

325

full face-amount benefits are not paid for a specific period of time, can apply to whole life coverages or guaranteed-issue term coverages. It is an underwriting technique to reduce the impact of antiselection.

Grading periods : The specific period of time during which the full face amount of a GDB (or guaranteed-issue term policy) is not paid—usually two or three years.

Group certificate : The document provided to each participant or member of a group insurance plan, which states the coverage and general provisions of the group master contract and which serves as evidence of their insurance. The holder of this document is referred to as a certificate holder rather than a policyholder.

Group insurance contract : The master policy or contract of insurance issued to an employer (or other entity authorized by state law) under a group insurance plan. The contract covers a group of persons eligible for coverage due to their relationship to the entity.

Group insurance trust : A marketing device through which products are marketed to a broad affinity group (e.g., Veterans, credit-card holders) and which requires a bank to act as trustee for the group.

Group life insurance : Insurance on the lives of several persons as a group—written under one policy, called a master contract—and evidenced by individual certificates issued to the persons whose lives are insured. Also applicable to health insurance, accident insurance, and all forms of property & casualty consumer insurance.

Guarantee : A pledge of satisfaction made by the seller to the buyer and specifying the terms by which the seller will make good his pledge.

Guaranteed renewable : The option of renewal to a specified age, or for a lifetime, vested solely in the insured. However, the insurance company has the right to increase premiums applicable to an entire class of policyholders.

Guaranteed renewable policy : A policy that the insured has the right to continue in force by the timely payment of premiums for a specified period of time as set forth in the contract. During this period the insurer has no right unilaterally to make any in-force changes, other than a change in the premium rate for classes of insureds. Premiums may not be changed for an individual, but can be for classes of insureds, objectively determined. (See non-cancellable policy.)

Guiding scripting : The use of key words or prompters, rather than fully worded scripts, to guide a TSR through the sales process.

Hardware : Physical equipment, excluding functional software properties, e.g., switchboards, telephone instruments, etc.

Health insurance : A broad term covering the various forms of insurance relating to the health of people. It includes coverages such as accident, sickness, disability, hospital and medical expense.

Glossary

Hot-line list : The most recent names available on a specific list, but no older than three months. In any event, use of the term *hot-line* should be further modified by "weekly," "monthly," etc.

House list : Any list of names owned by a company as a result of compilation, inquiry or buyer action, or acquisition that is used to promote that company's products or services.

In-force business : Insurance for which premiums are being paid or for which premiums have been fully paid. The term usually refers to the face amount of a life insurer's portfolio of business, whereas in health insurance it refers to the premium volume of an insurer on policies which are either in a premium-paying status or have not extended beyond the grace period. In property and casualty, it most frequently refers to "written" premium.

In-house telemarketing : Telemarketing done within a company as a supplementary or primary method of marketing when selling that company's own products.

Inbound : Calls that are received by a telemarketing center. (See outbound.)

Incontestable clause : (Time Limit on Certain Defenses) A policy clause making a contract indisputable by a company regarding an insured person's application statements after a specified period of time has elapsed. In life insurance, the period of time is normally two years.

Incurred losses : Loss occurring within a fixed period, whether or not adjusted and paid during the same period.

Indemnity : The payment of a benefit for a loss insured under a policy. The insured is indemnified for a specific loss, or part thereof.

Industrial life insurance : Life insurance under which premiums payable are collected more frequently than under ordinary life insurance, typically weekly. Collection of premiums and servicing of the policy normally take place at the home of the insured by agents, called debit agents.

Initial premium : The first premium paid on a policy.

Injury : Usually defined as bodily injury, caused solely by an accident occurring while policy is in force.

Inpatient : One who is confined within a hospital at his or her expense and is charged for room and board by the hospital for each day of confinement.

Inquiry : A request for information about an insurance product by a prospective buyer. Inquiry, unsolicited - A request by a prospective buyer for information about insurance products which cannot be directly attributed to an advertising campaign.

Insufficient funds : Lack of funds in a checking account to cover a given check. Such a check is therefore returned as non-negotiable.

Insurability : Those qualifications of age, health, occupation, etc., which enable the proposed insured to meet the requirements of an insurance company for the issuance of insurance.

Insurable interest : Relationship between an insured and a beneficiary; i.e., one of blood, marriage, or economic dependence.

Insurance : Protection by written contract against financial hazards (in whole or in part) of the happening of specified fortuitous events.

Insurance direct marketing : An interactive system of marketing that ascertains, creates, and satisfies the insurance wants and needs of people by performing organized tasks affecting the transfer of services between seller and buyer; using one or more media for the purpose of soliciting a response by phone, mail, or personal visit from a prospect or customer; maintaining complete information on each transaction in a database; and doing so at a profit.

Insurer : The insurance company which makes insurance available.

Invitation to contract : A form of new-business solicitation which invites the prospect to complete an application, requiring a signature, on the basis of which an insurance contract is issued.

Invitation to inquire : A solicitation inviting the prospect to obtain free information about an insurance offer.

Issue age : The age of an insured at the time the policy is issued.

Issue slip : A form used by underwriters which is attached to applications being processed. The form provides spaces to record the progress being made in the processing, as well as other data on the policy form and, when approved, gives the effective date.

K : Used in reference to computer storage capacity, generally accepted as 1,000. Analogous to M in the direct marketing industry.

Key : One or more characters within a data group that can be used to identify it or control its use. Synonymous with key code in mailing business.

Key code : A group of letters and/or numbers, colors, or other markings used to measure specific effectiveness of media, lists, advertisements, offers, etc., or any parts thereof.

Kit : That specific combination of components which, when assembled, comprises a unit designated for a specific purpose by the company. Examples of such kits include: inquiry, direct mail, fulfillment, and billing kits.

Lapse (Insurance general) : Termination of an insurance contract because of nonpayment of premium. A policy is generally said to lapse if a premium remains unpaid at the end of the grace period. (The grace period is the 30 or 31 days granted under the terms of the insurance contract following the day a premium comes due and during which the payment may be made without loss of any benefit rights.) In P&C, a lapse occurs the day after a due date on which premium has not been paid. Life insurance (LOMA) - Termination of an insurance contract because of nonpayment of premium past the grace period. If a lapse occurs and there are nonforfeiture values, the policy lapses but may remain effective as extended term or reduced paid-up insurance. Lapse, Promotional (Trial) - A lapse which occurs before the policyowner has made one full modal premium payment.

Lapse rate : The rate at which a designated group of insurance policies terminate because of nonpayment of premium past the grace period (including cancellations). The lapse rate is the rate of "nonpersistence," the opposite or complement of the persistency rate.

Layout : 1) Artist's sketch showing relative positioning of illustrations, headlines, and copy. 2) Positioning subject matter on a press sheet for most efficient production. (Also called imposition.)

Lead qualification : Determination of a customer's qualification, level of interest, willingness and ability to buy a product or service.

Least-cost routing (LCR) : Equipment that automatically makes a decision for the user as to the most economical method of calling telephone numbers, routing outgoing calls via the most cost-effective lines available to the system.

Letterhead : The printing at the top of a sheet of paper that identifies the sender.

Lettershop : A business organization that handles the mechanical details of mailings—such things as addressing, imprinting, collating. Most lettershops offer some printing facilities, and many offer some degree of creative direct-mail services.

Level premium : A premium which remains unchanged throughout the life of a policy.

Life annuity : A contract providing for specified payments at regular intervals for the lifetime of the annuitant.

Life expectancy : The average number of years a group of persons of a stated age may be expected to live.

Lifetime value : The present value of a future stream of net contributions to overhead and profit expected from the policyowner.

Lift note : A second letter enclosed in a mailing package to stress a specific selling point. In third-party marketing it frequently carries the endorsement.

Limited-payment life policy : A policy of whole life insurance on which the premium payments will terminate at the end of a specified term of years or at the death of the insured, if it occurs before that date. Once the policy has been paid for the specified term, it remains in force with no further premium due.

Line capacity : The total number of in-house telephones that a switch can accommodate.

List (Mailing list) : Names and addresses of individuals and/or companies having in common a specific interest, characteristic, or activity.

List broker : A specialist who makes all necessary arrangements for one company to use the list(s) of another company. A broker's services may include most, or all, of the following: research, selection, recommendation, and subsequent evaluation.

List buyer : Technically, this term should apply only to one who actually buys mailing lists. In practice, however, it is generally used to identify one who orders mailing lists for one-time use; a list user or mailer.

List cleaning : The process of correcting and/or removing a name and/or address from a mailing list because it is no longer correct. Term is also used in the identification and elimination of house-list duplication.

List compiler : One who develops lists of names and addresses from directories, newspapers, public records, sales slips, trade show registrations, and other sources for identifying groups of people or companies with something in common.

List maintenance : Any manual, mechanical, or electronic system for keeping name and address records (with or without other data) up to date at any specific point in time.

List management system : A database system that manages customer and prospect lists. Its major function is to merge and purge duplicates between in-house lists and those obtained from outside sources. It is also utilized to select names for both direct-mail promotions and outgoing telemarketing programs.

List selection : Characteristics used to define smaller groups within a list (essentially, lists within a list). Although very small, select groups may be very desirable, may substantially improve response and decrease cost; however, the smallness often renders them impractical.

List sequence : The order in which names and addresses appear in a list. While most lists today are in ZIP-Code sequence, some are alphabetical by name within the ZIP Code; others are in carrier sequence (postal delivery); and still others may (or may not) use some other order within the ZIP Code. Some lists are still arranged alphabetically—by name or chronologically, and in many other variations, or combinations.

List sort : Process of putting a list in a specific sequence, or from another sequence or no sequence.

List test : Part of a list selected to try to determine the effectiveness of the entire list.

Local access transport area (LATA) : Geographic area in which the local telephone company provides local and long-distance service, plus access to telephone network.

Local area network (LAN) : A privately owned network which integrates voice, and/or data and video technologies, and supports this communication.

Glossary

Local exchange carriers (LEC) : Regional Bell operating companies (BOCs) and approximately 1,500 other telephone operating companies that provide local services and connections to long-distance carriers.

Look-up service : A service organization that adds telephone numbers to lists.

Loss adjustment expense : That sum expended to determine the actual loss against a property and casualty insurance policy.

Loss ratio : The percentage of benefits paid to the policyowners in relation to the premium written or collected during a specified period of time.

Losses : A term used in property & casualty insurance indicating the losses (claims) paid or anticipated to be paid against a particular policy form.

Mail order buyers (MOBs) : Individuals who have purchased goods or services through the mail—the most desirable insurance direct marketing target.

Mailgram : A combination telegram-letter, with the telegram transmitted to a postal facility close to the addressee and then delivered as first-class mail. Popular form of first-effort, inquiry-conversion direct mail.

Main insured : Person who signed the original application for the policy. All billings are sent to the main insured who is held responsible for all payments on the policy. If reinstatement should ever be necessary, the main insured would sign the reinstatement form for himself and all dependents, if any, on the policy. *Main insured* and *principal insured* are identical terms.

Management information systems (MIS) : Systems, automated or manual, that provide sales support information for both the sales representative to enhance sales activity and for management to evaluate sales performance. Now being used in place of EDP (electronic data processing).

Market : The total of all individuals or organizations that are potential buyers.

Marketing costs : (See MC - Marketing costs.)

Marketing mix : The various marketing elements and strategies that must be used *together* to achieve maximum effectiveness.

Master contract/master policy : See group insurance contract.

Master file : File of a permanent nature that is regarded in a particular job as authoritative, or one that contains all subfiles.

Match code : A code determined either by the creator or the user of a file for matching records contained in another file.

Maturity date : Date on which a life insurance policy reaches its full value.

MC (Marketing costs) : MC, as included in the calculation of TARP/MC, are all marketing costs incurred to solicit the first, full-modal premium remittance (including fulfillment costs). This total does not include any allocatable and applicable overhead or interest charged on any funds borrowed to provide for marketing costs.

Mental and nervous disorders :   Any disorder of the mind or nerves. Mental ailments pertain to the mind. Nervous ailments pertain to excitability states and instability of nerve action—both without apparent organic cause. Mental disease is manifest by behavior. Senile disorders would be considered a disorder of the mind and would, therefore, fall under the exclusion in the policy contract of mental and nervous disorders. Nervous disorders and bodily disorders induced by mental or emotional disturbances, include such disorders as nervous breakdown, anxiety, psychoneurosis, neurasthenia, psychosomatic disorders—those having bodily symptoms of a psychic, emotional, or mental origin.

Merge-purge :   Combining two or more lists for list enhancement, suppression, or duplication-elimination, by a computerized matching process.

Mode of payment :   The frequency with which the policyowner has elected to pay premiums. The four modes generally available are monthly, quarterly, semiannually, and annually. However, payments may be made in any other mode acceptable to the insurer, including the payment of a single premium.

Modem :   A device which converts computer-generated digital signals into analog (voice) signals, or vice versa, to allow transmission over telephone lines.

Monetary value :   Total expenditures by a customer during a specific period of time, generally twelve months.

Monitoring :   The ability to listen in on telephone conversations from other extensions, usually for TSR training. Also known as "service observing."

Morbidity table :   Shows the incidence and extent of disability (illness) which may be expected from a given large group of persons. Used to calculate rates.

Mortality table :   A statistical table showing the number of persons living, the number dying, and the rate of mortality per thousand at each age from 0 through 99. Calculated on the basis of large groups. Currently using 1984 CSO.

Multiple buyer :   One who has bought two or more times (not one who has bought two or more items, one time only); also a multi-buyer or repeat buyer.

Multiple regression :   Statistical technique used to measure the relationship between responses to a mailing with census demographics and list characteristics of one or more selected mailing lists. Used to determine the best types of people/areas to mail to. This technique can also be used to analyze customers, subscribers, etc.

Multi-policy trailer : Record of all other existing policy numbers for a policyowner, which follows the basic record of a policyowner on a magnetic tape in data processing.

Mutual insurance company : A life insurance company owned and controlled by its policyowners. Profits are usually distributed to policyholders in the form of dividends.

Negative option : A buying plan in which a customer or club member agrees to accept and pay for products or services announced in advance at regular intervals unless the individual notifies the company, within a reasonable time after announcement, not to ship the merchandise. Rarely used in insurance sales in the United States.

Nesting : Placing one enclosure within another before inserting a mailing envelope.

Net collected premium : The expected premium to be collected from a program. Most frequently used to calculate third-party endorser compensation or commissions.

Nixie : A mailing piece returned to a mailer (under proper authorization) by the Postal Service because of an incorrect, or undeliverable, name and address.

Noise cancelling : A feature of some telephone headsets which drastically reduces or eliminates background noise.

Noncancellable policy : A contract of insurance that the insured has a right to continue in force by the timely payment of premiums for a substantial period of time.That is, the insurance company has no right to cancel the coverage. Normally the term is applicable to accident, life, and health coverages. In property & casualty coverages, policies can be issued for a specified term—usually not exceeding one year—and are noncancellable for the issued term. However, in most P&C coverages, insurance is provided subject to the validation of information provided to the company. If information is incorrect, the company has a right to terminate during the first sixty days.

Nonforfeiture provisions : Provisions required to be included (in the United States but not in Canada) in any long-term, whole life, or endowment life insurance contract, guaranteeing at least minimum values at various ages to the policyowner who has paid premiums long enough to establish an equity in the policy.

Nonmedical form : Form on which an applicant provides, for the underwriters, additional background data of a medical nature. It is termed "nonmedical" because the applicant, rather than a medical person (including physician), provides the desired information.

Nonparticipating policy : A policy under which no policy dividends are payable; that is, one that does not participate in any division of the surplus or profit of the company.

Novelty format : An attention-getting direct-mail format.

Nth name selection : A fractional unit that is repeated in sampling a mailing list. For example, in an *every tenth* sample, you would select the 1st, 11th, 21st, 31st, etc., records—or the 2nd, 12th, 22nd, 32nd, etc., records, and so forth.

OCR (Optical character recognition) : Machine identification of printed characters through use of light-sensitive devices.

Offer (Direct marketing) : The deal you are offering the prospect.

Offer (Legal) : A proposal which requires only acceptance to create a contract. Insurance offer — A life or health insurance contract is completed in the same way as any other formal contract—that is, through an offer made by one party and accepted by the other. In some instances, the company is making the offer, and in others the applicant is making the offer, in the legal sense.
Company Makes Offer — The company is in the position of making an offer to a prospective insured when an application submitted without money is approved and a policy is issued. The applicant shows acceptance by making an initial premium payment and thus forming a valid contract.
Applicant Makes Offer — The applicant is in the position of making an offer to buy insurance from the company when his completed application is accompanied by a premium payment. The company shows acceptance by issuing a policy and thus forming a valid contract.

Open-ended question : Sales technique designed to elicit respondents' replies in their own words—as opposed to giving a "yes" or "no" response.

Optical scanner : An input device that optically reads a line of printed characters and converts each character into its electronic equivalent for processing.

Option : As it applies to processing applications for A&H insurance coverage: *Benefit Option*— Identifies the base policy benefit level classification. Examples include $1,000 a month with a 5-day elimination period vs. $600 a month with a 3-day elimination period, etc. *Front-end Rider Option* — Identifies the riders which the applicant may select as coverage in addition to the base policy coverage. This selection is made at the time the application is initially submitted to the company. Most life insurance policies provide options with respect to settlement arrangements, dividends, and nonforfeiture values. This is equally true with regard to automobile and homeowners coverages. Auto policies offer collision deductible options, for example.

Order card : A reply card used to initiate an order by mail.

Ordinary life insurance : One of the broad classes of life insurance. The others are group and industrial. The term *ordinary* is also used to refer to continuous premium, whole life contracts.

Other common carrier (OCC) : Refers to geographic areas not accommodated by a long-distance service company.

Glossary

Outbound : Calls that are placed by the telemarketing center. (See inbound.)

Package : A term used to describe all of the assembled enclosures (parts or elements) of a mailing effort. (See kit.)

Package insert : Any promotional piece included in a product shipment. It may be for different products (or refills and replacements) from the same company or for products and services of other companies.

Package test : A test of part or all of the elements of one mailing piece against another.

Paid-up policy : A life insurance policy under which no further premiums are payable, but that will pay the full amount if the insured dies within the term stated in the original policy.

Para sales force : A sales team that works alongside another sales team—either on the telephone or in the field—as a supplement to the other.

Participating policy : A policy under which dividends are payable—that entitles its owner to participate in any allocations of surplus.

Payer benefits : Coverages, available in connection with juvenile insurance policies, that provide waiver of premiums under such policies in the event the premium payer, usually a parent of the insured, becomes totally and permanently disabled or dies within the term specified (usually during the minority of the child insured).

Payment mode : A billing-related term used to describe payment intervals. Premiums generally may be paid at annual, semiannual, quarterly, or monthly intervals at the company's designated premium rate applicable for each.

Peel-off label : A self-adhesive label attached to a backing sheet, which is attached to a mailing piece. The label is intended to be removed from the mailing piece and attached to an order blank or card.

Peg count : A tally of the number of calls made or received over a set period of time.

Pending claims : Claims currently being processed. Frequently, claims remain in the pending category because hospitals or physicians are slow in completing and returning forms sent to them.

Penetration : Relationship of the number of individuals or families on a particular list (by state, ZIP Code, S.I.C., etc.), compared to the total number possible. Also used in third-party programs to indicate the overall number of respondents (or insureds) relative to the total number of members of the third party.

Persistency (General) : The continuance of an insurance contract by the insured as the result of continued payment of premium. (This is the reciprocal of "lapse.") *Persistency Rate* — The rate at which a designated group of insurance policies remain in force through continued premium payments. The persistency rate may be based on, and expressed in, numbers of policies, premium rates, or face amounts of policies for life insurance.

335

Glossary

Personalizing : Individualizing of direct-mail pieces by adding the name or other personal information about the recipient.

Phone list : Mailing list compiled from names listed in telephone directories.

Piggy-back : An offer that hitches a free ride with another offer.

Pilot : Trial program designed to test feasibility of a potential telemarketing program.

Policies issued : A policy is counted as having been issued when the policy forms are completed and the recording of such is on the master file.

Policies issued and delivered (Legal - LOMA) : If the initial premium has been paid and the application approved for the plan of insurance applied for, the act of mailing is construed to be delivery of the policy to the owner, since the insurance company has parted with possession with the intention of completing the contract.

Policy : 1) The written instrument issued to the applicant, which expresses the insurance contract between the company and the applicant. 2) The written statement of the contract effecting insurance and including all clauses, riders, endorsements, and papers attached thereto and make a part thereof.

Policy-activation deadline : A time limit imposed upon the recipient of a policy issued under a send-no-money/full-premium marketing approach to respond with an initial premium payment in order to put the received policy in force or in an active status. This time limit is usually, but may not always be, imposed by states. Current allotted intervals include 10-, 21-, or 30-day periods.

Policy anniversary : Date on which renewal of a policy is necessary to continue in force—expressed by month, day, and year. Usually corresponds to modal payment chosen by insured.

Policy change : A transaction, manual or generated internally by computer, which affects a change to the contents of the computerized master-policy record.

Policy face : The part of the policy which provides relevant data as to the type of policy and its coverages and may include a policy schedule and endorsements.

Policy form : Printed contract which stipulates the obligations of both the insurer (the company) and the insured (the policyowner).

Policy issue : 1) *Process* — The process of preparing the written document to be delivered to the policyowner, which expresses the insurance contract between the company and the policyowner. 2) *Computer System* — The name given to the computer system which prepares the computerized portion of the policy to be delivered to the policyowner, which expresses the insurance contract between the company and the policyowner. 3) *Insurance Company Department* — A department in the insurance company which participates in the processing and preparing of the insurance policy which will be delivered to the policyowner.

Policy loan :   An advance made by a life insurance company to a policyowner at the latter's request, and secured by the cash value of the policy.

Policy maintenance :   Standard, recurring activities which take place on policy records; i.e., changes to address, coverage, dependents, and premium rates; recording of claims and premium payments; and producing the first two billing notices. Fulfillment and conservation activities are not included in the policy maintenance function with respect to cost allocation.

Policy schedule :   Policy data which is printed and included with the policy form. The information includes such items as policy benefit statements, listing of main insured and individuals covered under the policy, the policy type, policy number, policy effective date, which of the four modal premium rates applies to that policy, initial term, first premium, and issue state code.

Policyholder :   The individual in actual possession of an insurance policy.

Policyowner :   The person who has ownership rights in an insurance policy and who may or may not be either the policyholder or the insured. Often used loosely to refer to the policyholder and/or the insured. Also the person responsible for paying premium.

Pop-up :   A printed piece containing paper construction pasted inside a fold and which, when the fold is opened, "pops up" to form a three-dimensional illustration.

Positive option :   A method of distributing products and services incorporating the same advance notice technique as *Negative Option* but requiring a specific order each time from the member or subscriber. Generally, it is more costly and less predictable than negative option. Almost all insurance is positive option.

Post card :   Single sheet self-mailer on card stock.

Pre-call planning :   Preparation before a sales call to promote maximum effectiveness.

Pre-existing conditions :   A health or physical condition which was manifested or symptomatic during a specified time period prior to the time an insurance policy goes into effect and for which benefit coverage is generally not provided until the policy has been in force for a specified period of time. The period of time during which the pre-existing condition is not covered depends on the policy and state requirements.

Pre-recorded message :   Taped message, often recorded by celebrities or authority figures, which are played to inbound callers or interjected within an outbound call.

Premium :   1) The payment required to keep an insurance policy in force. 2) An item offered to a buyer, usually free or at a nominal price, as an inducement to purchase or obtain for trial a product or service offered via mail order. In insurance, usually called "gift" or "free gift" to avoid confusion.

Premium (Step-rated) : A premium charged to individuals, normally in five-year bands, which increases as the individual passes from one age band to another.

Premium (Level) : A premium which remains unchanged throughout the life of the policy.

Premium (Step-rated) : A premium charged to individuals, normally in five year bands, which increases as the individual passes from one age band to another.

Preprint : An advertising insert printed in advance and supplied to a newspaper or magazine for insertion.

Principal sum : 1) Lump-sum payment made under a policy upon the insured's accidental death, dismemberment, or loss of sight, according to the terms of the specific policy. 2) A term used in accident insurance and certain property and casualty coverages to indicate the maximum amount payable under the terms of the policy.

Proactive telemarketing : Seller-initiated or outbound calling.

Program : A sequence of steps to be executed by the computer to solve a given problem or achieve a certain result. Also refers to those steps required to execute an insurance solicitation.

Programming : Designing, writing, and testing of a program.

Project (General) : A planned undertaking. *Marketing Project* — Denotes a plan to make a specific offer or solicitation, generally over a specified period of time.

Prospect : A name on a mailing list considered to be a potential buyer for a given product or service but who has not previously made such a purchase.

Prospecting : Mailing to get leads for further sales contact rather than to make direct sales.

Protocol : 1) The established format for sending and receiving messages. 2) Rules and procedures under which research is conducted.

Psychographics : Any characteristics or qualities used to denote the lifestyle(s) or attitude(s) of customers and prospective customers.

Pure endowment : A sum of money payable at the end of a stated period, provided a designated person is living at that time. If the person specified dies before the end of the period, nothing is payable.

Purge : The process of eliminating duplicates and/or unwanted names and addresses from one or more lists.

Pyramiding : A method of testing mailing lists, in which one starts with a small quantity and, based on positive indications, mails increasingly larger quantities of the list balance to verify initial results, until the entire list has been mailed.

Glossary

Qualified leads : Potential customers that have been determined to need, want, and be able to purchase a specific product or service.

Queue : A function of an ACD which holds all inbound calls in the order in which they arrive until the next available TSR takes the first in line, moving the next call into the front position, etc.

Random access : An access mode in which records are obtained from, or placed into, a mass storage file in a non-sequential manner so that any record can be rapidly accessed. Synonymous with direct access.

Rate increase : Increase in a premium rate. Rates cannot be raised for guaranteed-renewable policies because a person gets older or because he has too many claims.

Re-application form (See reinstatement.) : New application required of previous policyowner because of lapsing of the previously held policy.

Reactive telemarketing : Customer-initiated buying by telephone (inbound calling).

Rebating : Paying, offering to pay or allow, the giving of any valuable consideration not specified in the policy to any person as an inducement to apply for and secure a policy of insurance. Absolutely illegal in every state.

Recency : The latest purchase or other activity recorded for an individual or company on a specific customer list.

Recurrent disability : A period of disability resulting from the same, or related, cause as a prior disability.

Recurring clause : A provision found in health insurance policies which sets the time period that must elapse between a disability or claim from a given cause and the recurrence of the disability from the same or related cause for the second disability to be considered the start of a new benefit period. If the recurrent disability falls short of the stated time period, benefits are paid as though the second disability were a continuation of the prior disability, subject to benefit maximums for a single disability.

Reduced paid-up life insurance : One of the nonforfeiture benefits, under which the cash value of the policy is used as a single premium to purchase paid-up insurance of the same kind as the policy itself (whole life under a whole-life policy, endowment under an endowment policy, term insurance under a long-term contract for the term of the policy) in such an amount as the cash value will provide.

Reduction of benefits : Automatic reduction in coverage under certain specific conditions—e.g., the insured reaching age 65.

Referral : The name of a prospective customer submitted to an insurance company by a third party.

Reformatting : Changing a magnetic tape format from one arrangement to a more usable format. Synonymous with conversion (list or tape).

Refund : Return to the insured or his estate all or part of the premium(s) paid by the insured.

Refund - initial premium : Return of a full initial premium to a new policyowner upon his request, providing he returns the policy within the guaranteed time allowed.

Refund - overpayment : Return to a policyowner the amount of excess premium paid.

Refund - unearned premium : Return to a policyowner the amount of premiums paid but not used (unearned). This may be the result of either the death of an insured or a cancellation of a paid-in-advance policy.

Reinstatement (Insurance general) : Restoration of a lapsed policy to premium-paying status on compliance with the conditions set forth in the policy. Such conditions could include resubmitting evidence of insurability, including good health of the insured satisfactory to the company. *Insurance — Life* (LOMA) — Reinstatement privilege is a specifically granted right under a life insurance contract subject to stated conditions. Such conditions would generally include payment of all premiums in default with a specified rate of interest and evidence of insurability, including good health of the insured satisfactory to the company. *Insurance — Accident & Health* (LOMA) — The right of the policyowner to reinstate his policy is assumed. The reinstatement provision of the policy merely clarifies the circumstances under which a reinstatement becomes effective, limits the amount of past-due premium that may be collected by the insurer, and specifies the losses that will be covered by the reinstated policy.

Reinstatement - automatic : Resumption of a policy which has been in a state of lapse without evidence of insurability requested. When P&C premium payments are a few days late, reinstatement upon payment of the premium is almost always automatic.

Reinstatement form : Reinstatement application form used by policyowner whose policy has lapsed, in order to request reinstatement. Space is provided for the furnishing of pertinent data.

Relational marketing : Marketing conducted as the result of a relationship having been established with a policyholder or a prospective policyholder.

Release : Signed statement by an insured that all liability of the company has been met.

Renewable term insurance : Term insurance that may be renewed for another term of the same length, usually subject to an upper-age limit, beyond which renewal will not be permitted. Frequently, premiums increase from one term to another.

Renewal : Premium payment after the first payment on a policy in order to continue a policy in force. Continuation of an insurance contract beyond the first-year anniversary date as a result of a premium payment, regardless of payment mode—monthly, quarterly, semiannually, or annually.

Reply-o-letter : One of a number of patented direct mail formats for facilitating replies from prospects. It features a die-cut opening on the face of the letter and a pocket on the reverse. An addressed reply card is inserted in the pocket and the name and address thereon show through the die-cut opening.

Request for quotation (RFQ) : A form completed by a potential buyer to provide information which enables the insurance company to prepare a price quotation. Most often used for homeowners and auto insurance.

Rescission : Consideration of an insurance policy as null and void from its effective date because of fraudulent misstatement of fact. Although guaranteed-renewable policies cannot be cancelled, the company can, when fraud is evident, rescind the policy by returning all premiums paid to the person who was listed as the main insured. During the contestable period a policy might be rescinded due to non-disclosure of information material to the risk.

Reserves : The amount required to be carried as a liability in the financial statements of an insurer to provide for future commitments under policies outstanding.

Response rate : The rate at which applications or inquiries are generated in relation to the total number of pieces circulated or to the total exposures of the material—e.g., television. Expressed as a percentage, or as applications per thousand, or as leads (inquiries) per thousand.

Response per thousand (RPM) : Referring to the number of orders or inquiries received per thousand calls as a result of a telemarketing or direct mail campaign.

Return envelopes : Addressed reply envelopes, either stamped or unstamped - as distinguished from business-reply envelopes which carry a postage payment guarantee - included with a mailing.

Return of premium rider (A&H) : A rider or provision in an insurance policy agreeing to pay a benefit equal to the sum of all premiums paid, minus claims paid, if claims over a stated period of time do not exceed a fixed percentage of the premiums paid. Benefit periods and percentages returned vary with policies and riders.

Return postage guaranteed : A legend imprinted on the address face of envelopes or other mailing pieces when the mailer wishes the Postal Service to return undeliverable third-class bulk mail. A charge equivalent to the single-piece third-class rate is made for each piece returned.

Returns : Responses to a direct-mail program.

RFMR : Acronym for recency-frequency-monetary value ratio, a formula used to evaluate the sales potential of names on a mailing list.

Glossary

Rider (Endorsement) General :   An amendment in writing (including printed, stamped, or separated form) added to and made part of the insurance policy in order to expand, limit, or change the benefits otherwise payable. An offer to policyowners of a new type of coverage or an increase in existing coverage which can be added to their base policy. This coverage is conveyed on a separate rider form and does *not* have the same effective date as the base policy.

Riders :   Term generally used to designate any of many additional benefits or coverages which may be added to an insured's basic policy. These additional benefit plans are primarily offered to existing policyholders by internal marketing, or policyowner marketing.

Rollout :   To mail the remaining portion of a mailing list after successfully testing a portion of that list.

Running charge :   The price a list owner charges for names run or passed, but not used by a specific mailer. When such a charge is made, it is usually to cover extra processing costs. However, some list owners set the price without regard to actual cost.

Sales conversion rate :   Number of sales in relation to number of responses received.

Salting :   Deliberate placing of decoy or dummy names in a list to trace list usage and delivery. Specifically used in house lists to determine unauthorized usage of the list. (Similar to "decoy.")

Sample package (Mailing piece) :   An example of the package to be mailed by the list user to a particular list. Such a mailing piece is submitted to the list owner for approval prior to commitment for one-time use of that list. Although a sample package may, due to time pressure, differ slightly from the actual package used, the list-user agreement usually requires the user to reveal any material differences when submitting the sample package.

Schedule page :   A separate page of policy data attached to each issued policy, containing such information as policy benefit statements, listing of main insured and individuals covered under the policy, the policy type, policy number, policy effective date, the four modal premium rates for that policy, initial term, first premium, and issue-state code.

Script :   A prepared text presentation that is closely followed by sales personnel or TSRs as a tool to convey a sales message in its entirety.

Sectional center (SCF or SCF center) :   A Postal Service distribution unit comprising different Post Offices whose ZIP Codes start with the same first three digits.

Seeding :   Dummy names "planted" in a mailing list to check usage, delivery, or unauthorized re-use. (Same as "salting.")

Segmentation :   The process of separating characteristic groups within a list for target marketing.

Selection criteria :   Definition of characteristics that identify segments or

342

sub-groups within a list. Also used to indicate specific audience characteristics for use in selecting lists or policyowners for mailings.

Self-mailer :   A direct-mail piece mailed without an envelope.

Send no money (SNM) :   Term used to describe a front-end marketing approach with the following characteristics: 1. The applicant does not send in any money with his application. 2. The company sends out a policy containing a date which will become the effective (or policy activation) date providing the company receives the first full modal premium due within a stated time period. 3. The receipt and application of the first premium within the specified time limit will activate the policy. 4. The time period allowed for the premium remittance is generally based on state requirements when such exist. The period is usually 10, 21, or 30 days from the indicated policy effective date.

Sequence :   An arrangement of items according to a specified set of rules or instructions. Refers generally to ZIP Codes or customer number sequence.

Settlement option :   A choice, other than lump sum, given the sums payable under a life insurance contract. Usually any substantial sum, whether payable as an endowment, death, or cash surrender benefit, may be settled under one of several alternative methods.

Software :   A set of programs, procedures, and associated documentation concerned with operation of a data processing system.

Solicitation :   Urging an individual to either make an offer to buy insurance or to invite the company to make an offer to sell insurance to him through the means of personal or telephone contact or advertising material. (See *offer*.)

Solo mailing :   A single mailing promoting a single product.

Source code :   Unique alphabetical and/or numeric identification for distinguishing one list or media source from another.

Source count :   The number of names and addresses, in any given list, for the media (or list sources) from which the names and addresses were derived.

Specified term :   *Specified term*, as indicated in the policy schedule, is the period of coverage provided by the first premium payment. The term remains the same as long as the policyowner continues to pay in the same manner. Since payments usually may be made monthly, quarterly, semiannually, or annually, the term may vary among policyowners. In any event, it is not necessary to have a new policy form with each premium payment.

Specimen policy :   Sample policy which is sent on request. Such a policy form is stamped "Specimen" and cannot become valid.

Speculator :   An individual or group of individuals who purchase insurance policies with the sole intention of profit through the filing of suspicious claims for benefits.

Speculator ZIP : A geographic area wherein a company does not solicit business or accept applications due to past misrepresentation on applications or applications received from speculators.

Split test : Two or more samples from the same list - each considered to be representative of the entire list - used for creative tests, offer tests, etc.

State count : The number of names and addresses, in a given list, for each state.

Statement stuffer : A small, printed piece designed to be inserted in an envelope, carrying a customer's statement of account.

Status : A computer-generated report containing the most current as well as historical information regarding a policy.

Stuffer : Advertising enclosures placed in other media - merchandise packages, mailings for other products, etc.

Substandard insurance : A rated policy is issued at higher than standard premium rate to cover the extra risk involved in certain cases where the insured has impaired health, a hazardous occupation, a poor driving record, etc.

Success model : A set of logical steps followed by successful sales people to sell a product or service and used as a training example for new sales people.

Supplementary contract : A contract issued by a life insurance company when a benefit is settled under one of the optional modes of settlement. It specifies the amounts and times of the payments to be made, the payee or payees, and all other pertinent factors in connection with such settlement.

Surgical schedule : Schedule of maximum payments made for specific surgical procedures.

Suspense : The status of a transaction or document which cannot be fully processed due to errors, misstatements, missing information, or missing money.

Syndicated mailing : Mailing prepared for distribution to multiple-endorser lists, where the size of the endorser's list is too small to make a solo mailing practical.

Tape density : The number of bits of information (bytes) that can be included in a specific magnetic tape—e.g., 556 BPI, 800 BPI, 1,600 BPI, etc.

Tape dump : A printout of data on a magnetic tape to be edited and checked for correctness, readability, consistency, etc.

Tape layout : A simple "map" of the data included in each record and its relative, or specific, location.

Tape record : All the information about an individual or company contained on a specific magnetic tape.

Target date : *Direct Mail* — The date on which a mailing is to go into the postal system. *Space* — The date on which a space piece (free-fall insert or run of press) is to appear in a newspaper, magazine, or other related media.

Target market : The most likely group—based on any number of criteria—determined to have the highest potential to buy a product or service.

TARP (Total annualized renewal premium) : The aggregate amount of annualized renewal premium of all policies associated with a specific insurance marketing project or any other designated group. TARP serves as input in the overall evaluation of the results of a marketing project aimed at selling insurance. TARP = total annualized renewal premium of all policies in designated group. Annualized renewal premium is the value of one year's premium based on the initial payment mode of the policy times the rate of premium due for that mode. For monthly payment mode, 12 x monthly premium rate = annualized premium. For quarterly payment mode, 4 x quarterly premium rate = annualized premium. For annual payment mode, 1 x annual premium rate = annualized premium.

Teaser : A copy device used on outside envelopes in direct mail to excite the recipient's curiosity, and to get the envelope opened.

Telemarketing : The discipline that puts advanced telecommunications technology to work as part of a well-organized and well-managed marketing program. It uses management information systems and emphasizes the use of personal selling skills to help companies keep in close contact with their customers, increase sales, and enhance business productivity, while reducing costs.

Telemarketing service vendor : One who sells the service of conducting telemarketing calls. Also called telemarketing service bureau.

Telephone list appending : The adding of telephone numbers to mailing lists.

Telephone preference service (TPS) : A program of the DMA which allows consumers who do not want telemarketing calls to have their names removed from a majority of rental lists offered to telemarketers.

Telephone sales supervisor (TSS) : Those who oversee the performance of TSRs.

Telephone sales/service representative (TSR) : The individual who makes outbound calls or receives inbound calls in a telemarketing program.

Term insurance : Life insurance issued for a term of years under which the benefit is payable only if the insured dies during that time, after which the insurance expires without value.

Test market : Trial market for a new product, service, or offer—usually selected in a manner that is representative of the total market.

Test panel : A term used to identify each of the parts or samples in a split test.

Test tape : A selection of representative records within a mailing list that enables a list user or service bureau to prepare for reformatting or

Glossary

converting the list to a form more efficient for the user.

Third party : An organization which permits an insurance company to solicit its members, clients, customers, subscribers and/or employees for insurance; and which typically lends its endorsement to the solicitation in return for some consideration or fee.

Third-party endorsed : A method of solicitation to the members, clients, customers, subscribers, or employees of an organization that supports (endorses) the company and its respective insurance product.

Time limit on certain defenses : One of the uniform individual accident and sickness provisions required by state law to be included in every individual health policy issued in a state, setting a limit on the number of years after the policy has been in force that a physical condition not excluded at the time of issue can be used as a defense against a claim (sometimes called incontestable clause).

Time-zone sequencing : Preparation of national telemarketing lists according to time zones—so calls can be made at the most productive time.

Tip-on : An item glued to a printed piece.

Title : A designation before (prefix) or after (suffix) a name to more accurately identify an individual. (Prefixes — Mr., Mrs., Dr., Sister, etc.; Suffixes — M.D., Jr., President, Sales Manager, etc.)

Token : An involvement device, often consisting of a perforated portion of an order card designed to be removed from its original position and placed in another designated area on the order card to signify a desire to purchase the product or service offered.

Traffic builder : A direct-mail piece intended primarily to attract recipients to the mailer's place of business.

Twisting : Inducing an insured to cancel his present insurance and replace it with insurance in the same or another insurance company by misrepresenting the facts or by presenting an incomplete comparison.

Underwriter : 1) An insurer; 2) One who selects and evaluates risks for insurance.

Underwriting : The process of selecting those applicants for insurance who meet the insurability requirements of the company and classifying them according to degrees of insurability so that appropriate premium rates may be assigned.

Universe : Total number of individuals fitting a single set of specifications, to whom a product is offered.

Update : Recent transactions and current information added to the master (main) list to reflect the current status of each record on the list.

Upgrading : A term used to describe the process by which an insured is offered increased benefits at an increased premium, by mail or some other method.

Variable field : A way of laying out for formatting list information that assigns a specific sequence to the data, but does not assign it specific positions. While this method conserves space on magnetic tape, it is generally more difficult to work with.

Waiver : An agreement by endorsement to the contract waiving some provision thereof.

Waiver of premium : A provision or rider agreeing to waive or forego premium payment during a period of disability on the part of the insured or (sometimes) premium payer, if other than the insured, as in insurance on children. During this time the policy continues to be in force.

WATS : Acronym for wide area telephone service. A service providing a special line allowing calls within a certain zone, on a direct-dialing basis, for a flat monthly charge.

White mail : Incoming mail that is not on a form sent out by the advertiser. All mail other than orders and payments.

Whole life : A life insurance policy, the coverage of which continues for the entire life of the insured or to age 100, whichever is longer. It includes ordinary (straight) life on which premiums are paid until death; or limited-payment life, on which premiums are payable for a specified number of years.

Workstations : The area where TSRs perform their jobs.

Written premiums : The total amount of premium on all policies issued by an insurance company.

ZIP Code : A group of five to nine digits used by the U.S. Postal Service to designate specific distribution centers, post offices, stations, branches, or carrier routes.

ZIP Code count : The number of names and addresses in a list, within each ZIP Code.

ZIP Code sequence : Names and addresses arranged in a list according to the numeric progression of the ZIP Code in each record. This form of list formatting is mandatory for mailing at bulk third-class mail rates, based on the sorting requirements of Postal Service regulations.

Appendix A

Listing of Secrets

movement, serious illness, graduation, starting school, beginning a new job, etc.—almost always outpull lists that do not offer such data.

analysis, execution of marketing efforts, and precise
measurements.

usually monthly!

Appendix B

Listing of Figures

Listing of Figures

Appendix C
Lotus Programming: Acquisition Allowance

```
A1:  'Acquisition Allowance Calculation
A2:  '---------
B2:  '---------
C2:  '---------
D2:  '---------
E2:  '---------
F2:  '---------
G2:  '---------
H2:  '---------
A3:  'Value Screen
E3:  'CALCULATION SCREEN
A4:  'PRODUCT
B4:  ^HIP
A5:  'AARP
B5:  (F2) 285.2
C5:  'LAPSE-1
D5:  (F2) 0.36
E5:  'AAA-1
F5:  (F2) +B5*(1-(B6+B11+B13))+H5*((1-D5)/(1+B16)^B17)
G5:  'INT-1
H5:  (F2) +D14*(1+B18/B14)^B14*(1+B18/B14)-D14
A6:  'CLAIM-1
B6:  (F2) 0.6
C6:  'LAPSE-2
D6:  (F2) 0.23
E6:  'AAA-2
F6:  (F2) +B5*(1-(B7+B12+B13))+H6*((1-D6)/(1+B16)^B17)
G6:  'INT-2
H6:  (F2) +D15*(1+B18/B14)^B14*(1+B18/B14)-D15
A7:  'CLAIM-2
B7:  (F2) 0.75
C7:  'LAPSE-3
D7:  (F2) 0.18
E7:  'AAA-3
F7:  (F2) +B5*(1-(B8+B12+B13))+H7*((1-D7)/(1+B16)^B17)
G7:  'INT-3
H7:  (F2) +D16*(1+B18/B14)^B14*(1+B18/B14)-D16
A8:  'CLAIM-3
B8:  (F2) 0.45
C8:  'LAPSE-4
D8:  (F2) 0.18
E8:  'AAA-4
F8:  (F2) +B5*(1-(B9+B12+B13))+H8*((1-D8)/(1+B16)^B17)
G8:  'INT-4
H8:  (F2) +D17*(1+B18/B14)^B14*(1+B18/B14)-D17
A9:  'CLAIM-4
B9:  (F2) 0.4
C9:  'LAPSE-5
D9:  (F2) 0.12
E9:  'AAA-5
F9:  (F2) +B5*(1-(B10+B12+B13))+H8*((1-D9)/(1+B16)^B17)
A10: 'CLAIM-5
B10: (F2) 0.45
```

```
C10: 'RESV-1
D10: (F2) 0.15
E10: 'AAA-6
F10: (F2) +B5*(1-(B10+B12+B13))+H8*((1-D9)/(1+B16)^B17)
A11: 'ADMIN-1
B11: (F2) 0.1
C11: 'RESV-2
D11: (F2) 0.1
E11: 'AAA-7
F11: (F2) +B5*(1-(B10+B12+B13))+H8*((1-D9)/(1+B16)^B17)
A12: 'ADMIN-2
B12: (F2) 0.06
C12: 'RESV-3
D12: (F2) 0.05
E12: 'AAA-8
F12: (F2) +B5*(1-(B10+B12+B13))+H8*((1-D9)/(1+B16)^B17)
A13: 'PREM TAX
B13: 0.025
C13: 'RESV-4
D13: (F2) 0.05
E13: 'AAA-9
F13: (F2) +B5*(1-(B10+B12+B13))+H8*((1-D9)/(1+B16)^B17)
A14: ^M
B14: (F2) 4
C14: ^P1
D14: (F2) +B5*D10
E14: 'AAA-10
F14: (F2) +B5*(1-(B10+B12+B13))+H8*((1-D9)/(1+B16)^B17)
C15: ^P2
D15: (F2) +B5*D11+D14
E15: 'TOTAL
F15: (F2) @SUM(F5..F14)
A16: ^I
B16: (F2) 0.15
C16: ^P3
D16: (F2) +B5*D12+D15
A17: ^N
B17: (F2) 1
C17: ^P4
D17: (F2) +B5*D13+D16
A18: ^i
B18: (F2) 0.06
E18: 'Acquisition Allowance
H18: (F2) +F15/(1+B16)^10
A19: '-------
B19: '-------
C19: '-------
D19: '-------
E19: '-------
F19: '-------
G19: '-------
H19: '-------
```

Appendix D
Lotus Programming: Model Profit Study—LTV

```
A1:  'MODEL PROFIT STUDY--DIRECT MARKETING HEALTH INSURANCE
A3:  'SCREEN VALUES (INPUT DATA + AUTOMATIC CALCULATION)
A5:  'PRODUCT
B5:  'HIP/TV
C5:  'LAPSE(1)
D5:  0.36
E5:  'ULTCLAIM
F5:  (F2) 0.52
G5:  'RESERV(1)
H5:  (F2) 0.15
I5:  'INFORCE-1
J5:  1000
K5:  'PRESVAL
L5:  (,2) +M32/(1+D15)^D14
A6:  'AARP
B6:  (C2) 285.2
C6:  'LAPSE(2)
D6:  0.23
E6:  'CLAIM(1)
F6:  (F2) 1.15*F5
G6:  'RESERV(2)
H6:  (F2) 0.1
I6:  'INFORCE-2
J6:  (1-D5)*J5
A7:  'ISSUES/M
B7:  45.59
C7:  'LAPSE(3)
D7:  0.18
E7:  'CLAIM(2)
F7:  (F2) 1.44*F5
G7:  'RESERV(3)
H7:  (F2) 0.05
I7:  'INFORCE-3
J7:  (F0) (1-D6)*J6
A8:  'CICR(M)
B8:  (F2) 1000/B7
C8:  'LAPSE(4)
D8:  0.18
E8:  'CLAIM(3)
F8:  (F2) 0.769*F5
G8:  'RESERV(4)
H8:  (F2) 0.05
I8:  'INFORCE-4
J8:  (F0) (1-D7)*J7
A9:  'MC/M
B9:  12864.19
C9:  'LAPSE(5)
D9:  0.12
E9:  'CLAIM(4)
F9:  (F2) 0.769*F5
G9:  'RESERV(5)
```

```
H9:  (F2) 0.03
I9:  'INFORCE-5
J9:  (F0) (1-D8)*J8
K9:  'LTV
L9:  (C2) +L5/1000
A10: 'TMC
B10: +B9*B8
C10: 'PREMTAX
D10: 0.025
E10: 'CLAIM(5)
F10: (F2) 0.865*F5
I10: 'INFORCE-6
J10: (F0) (1-D9)*J9
K10: 'ALLOW
L10: (P2) +L13/B6
A11: 'T/MC
B11: (F2) 1000*B6/B10
C11: 'INT.RATE
D11: 0.06
E11: 'CLAIM(6)
F11: (F2) 0.865*F5
G11: ^N
H11: (F2) 1
I11: 'INFORCE-7
J11: (F0) (1-D9)*J10
K11: 'COLFACT
L11: (P2) (B21/1000)/B6
A12: 'COMMISFY
B12: 0
C12: 'MODPAYFAC
D12: (F2) 0.1
E12: 'CLAIM(7)
F12: (F2) 0.865*F5
I12: 'INFORCE-8
J12: (F0) (1-D9)*J11
A13: 'COMMISREN
B13: 0
C13: 'PAY/N
D13: (F2) 12
E13: 'CLAIM(8)
F13: (F2) 0.865*F5
G13: 'POLCYFEE
H13: (C2) 10
I13: 'INFORCE-9
J13: (F0) (1-D9)*J12
K13: 'ACQUSITION
L13: (C2) +O32/(1+D15)^D14
A14: 'ADMIN(1)
B14: (F2) 0.1
C14: 'YEARS
D14: (F2) 10
```

```
E14:  'CLAIM(9)
F14:  (F2) 0.865*F5
I14:  'INFORCE-0
J14:  (F0) (1-D9)*J13
K14:  'ALLOWANCE
A15:  'ADMIN(RE)
B15:  0.06
C15:  'ROI
D15:  (P2) 0.15
E15:  'CLAIM(10)
F15:  (F2) 0.865*F5
A16:  '---------
B16:  '---------
C16:  '---------
D16:  '---------
E16:  '---------
F16:  '---------
G16:  '---------
H16:  '---------
I16:  '---------
J16:  '---------
K16:  '---------
L16:  '---------
M16:  '---------
N16:  '---------
C17:  'PROFIT STUDY (AUTOMATIC CALCULATION)
A19:  ^YEARS
B19:  ^COLPREM
C19:  ^CLAIMS
D19:  ^ADMIN
E19:  ^COMMISS
F19:  ^TMC
G19:  ^PREMTAX
H19:  ^RESERVES
I19:  'TOT/RESEV
J19:  ^INT
K19:  ^INCOME
L19:  ^EXPENSE
M19:  ^P(L)
N19:  ^PROFIT%
O19:  'ACQALLOW
A21:  ^1
B21:  (,0) (1-D5)*D13*((B6*D12)+(H13*D12))*J5
C21:  (,0) +F6*B21
D21:  (,0) +B14*B21
E21:  (,0) +B12*B21
F21:  (,0) +B10
G21:  (,0) +D10*B21
H21:  (,0) +H5*B21
I21:  (,0) +H21
J21:  (,0) +I21*(1+D11/4)^4*(1+D11/4)-I21
```

367

```
K21:  (,0)  +B21+J21
L21:  (,0)  @SUM(C21..H21)
M21:  (,0)  +K21-L21
N21:  (P2)  +M21/K21
O21:  (F2)  +B6*(1-(F6+B14+D10))+J21/1000*((1-D5)/(1+D15)^H11)
A22:  ^2
B22:  (,0)  (1-D6)*D13*((B6*D12)+(H13*D12))*J6
C22:  (,0)  +B22*F7
D22:  (,0)  +B15*B22
E22:  (,0)  +$B$13*B22
G22:  (,0)  +D10*B22
H22:  (,0)  +H6*B22
I22:  (,0)  +I21+H22
J22:  (,0)  +I22*(1+D11/4)^4*(1+D11/4)-I22
K22:  (,0)  +B22+J22
L22:  (,0)  @SUM(C22..H22)
M22:  (,0)  +K22-L22
N22:  (P2)  +M22/K22
O22:  (F2)  +B6*(1-(F7+B15+D10))+J22/1000*((1-D6)/(1+D15)^H11)
A23:  ^3
B23:  (,0)  (1-D7)*D13*((B6*D12)+(H13*D12))*J7
C23:  (,0)  +B23*F8
D23:  (,0)  +B15*B23
E23:  (,0)  +$B$13*B23
G23:  (,0)  +D10*B23
H23:  (,0)  +H7*B23
I23:  (,0)  +I22+H23
J23:  (,0)  +I23*(1+D11/4)^4*(1+D11/4)-I23
K23:  (,0)  +B23+J23
L23:  (,0)  @SUM(C23..H23)
M23:  (,0)  +K23-L23
N23:  (P2)  +M23/K23
O23:  (F2)  +B6*(1-(F8+B15+D10))+J23/1000*((1-D7)/(1+D15)^H11)
A24:  ^4
B24:  (,0)  (1-D8)*D13*((B6*D12)+(H13*D12))*J8
C24:  (,0)  +B24*F9
D24:  (,0)  +B15*B24
E24:  (,0)  +$B$13*B24
G24:  (,0)  +D10*B24
H24:  (,0)  +H8*B24
I24:  (,0)  +I23+H24
J24:  (,0)  +I24*(1+D11/4)^4*(1+D11/4)-I24
K24:  (,0)  +B24+J24
L24:  (,0)  @SUM(C24..H24)
M24:  (,0)  +K24-L24
N24:  (P2)  +M24/K24
O24:  (F2)  +B6*(1-(F9+B15+D10))+J24/1000*((1-D8)/(1+D15)^H11)
A25:  ^5
B25:  (,0)  (1-D9)*D13*((B6*D12)+(H13*D12))*J9
C25:  (,0)  +B25*F10
D25:  (,0)  +B15*B25
```

```
E25: (,0) +$B$13*B25
G25: (,0) +D10*B25
H25: (,0) +H9*B25
I25: (,0) +I24+H25
J25: (,0) +I25*(1+D11/4)^4*(1+D11/4)-I25
K25: (,0) +B25+J25
L25: (,0) @SUM(C25..H25)
M25: (,0) +K25-L25
N25: (P2) +M25/K25
O25: (F2) +B6*(1-(F10+B15+D10))+J25/1000*((1-D9)/(1+D15)^H11)
A26: ^6
B26: (,0) (1-D9)*D13*((B6*D12)+(H13*D12))*J10
C26: (,0) +B26*F11
D26: (,0) +B15*B26
E26: (,0) +$B$13*B26
G26: (,0) +D10*B26
H26: (,0) -I25/5
I26: (,0) +I25+H26
J26: (,0) +I26*(1+D11/4)^4*(1+D11/4)-I26
K26: (,0) +B26+J26
L26: (,0) @SUM(C26..H26)
M26: (,0) +K26-L26
N26: (P2) +M26/K26
O26: (F2) +B6*(1-(F11+B15+D10))+J26/1000*((1-D9)/(1+D15)^H11)
A27: ^7
B27: (,0) (1-D9)*D13*((B6*D12)+(H13*D12))*J11
C27: (,0) +B27*F12
D27: (,0) +B15*B27
E27: (,0) +$B$13*B27
G27: (,0) +D10*B27
H27: (,0) -I25/5
I27: (,0) +I26+H27
J27: (,0) +I27*(1+D11/4)^4*(1+D11/4)-I27
K27: (,0) +B27+J27
L27: (,0) @SUM(C27..H27)
M27: (,0) +K27-L27
N27: (P2) +M27/K27
O27: (F2) +B6*(1-(F12+B15+D10))+J27/1000*((1-D9)/(1+D15)^H11)
A28: ^8
B28: (,0) (1-D9)*D13*((B6*D12)+(H13*D12))*J12
C28: (,0) +B28*F13
D28: (,0) +B15*B28
E28: (,0) +$B$13*B28
G28: (,0) +D10*B28
H28: (,0) -I25/5
I28: (,0) +I27+H28
J28: (,0) +I28*(1+D11/4)^4*(1+D11/4)-I28
K28: (,0) +B28+J28
L28: (,0) @SUM(C28..H28)
M28: (,0) +K28-L28
N28: (P2) +M28/K28
```

```
O28:  (F2)  +B6*(1-(F13+B15+D10))+J28/1000*((1-D9)/(1+D15)^H11)
A29:  ^9
B29:  (,0)  (1-D9)*D13*((B6*D12)+(H13*D12))*J13
C29:  (,0)  +B29*F14
D29:  (,0)  +B15*B29
E29:  (,0)  +$B$13*B29
G29:  (,0)  +D10*B29
H29:  (,0)  -I25/5
I29:  (,0)  +I28+H29
J29:  (,0)  +I29*(1+D11/4)^4*(1+D11/4)-I29
K29:  (,0)  +B29+J29
L29:  (,0)  @SUM(C29..H29)
M29:  (,0)  +K29-L29
N29:  (P2)  +M29/K29
O29:  (F2)  +B6*(1-(F14+B15+D10))+J29/1000*((1-D9)/(1+D15)^H11)
A30:  ^10
B30:  (,0)  (1-D9)*D13*((B6*D12)+(H13*D12))*J14
C30:  (,0)  +B30*F15
D30:  (,0)  +B15*B30
E30:  (,0)  +$B$13*B30
G30:  (,0)  +D10*B30
H30:  (,0)  -I25/5
I30:  (,0)  +I29+H30
J30:  (,0)  +I30*(1+D11/4)^4*(1+D11/4)-I30
K30:  (,0)  +B30+J30
L30:  (,0)  @SUM(C30..H30)
M30:  (,0)  +K30-L30
N30:  (P2)  +M30/K30
O30:  (F2)  +B6*(1-(F15+B15+D10))+J30/1000*((1-D9)/(1+D15)^H11)
A32:  'TOTALS
B32:  (,0)  @SUM(B21..B30)
C32:  (,0)  @SUM(C21..C30)
D32:  (,0)  @SUM(D21..D30)
E32:  (,0)  @SUM(E21..E30)
F32:  (,0)  @SUM(F21..F30)
G32:  (,0)  @SUM(G21..G30)
H32:  (,0)  @SUM(H21..H30)
J32:  (,0)  @SUM(J21..J30)
K32:  (,0)  @SUM(K21..K30)
L32:  (,0)  @SUM(L21..L30)
M32:  (,0)  @SUM(M21..M30)
N32:  (P2)  +M32/K32
O32:  (,2)  @SUM(O21..O30)
A33:  ^%
C33:  (P2)  +C32/B32
D33:  (P2)  +D32/B32
E33:  (P2)  +E32/B32
F33:  (P2)  +F32/B32
G33:  (P2)  +G32/B32
```

Appendix E
Lotus Programming: Lead Program Breakeven Model

```
A1:  'COST/LEAD ASSUMPTIONS
A2:  'KIT
C2:  ^#1
D2:  ^#2
E2:  ^#3
F2:  ^#4
G2:  ^#5
A3:  'COMPONENT
A4:  '---------
B4:  '---------
C4:  '-----------
D4:  '---------
E4:  '---------
F4:  '---------
G4:  '---------
H4:  '---------
A5:  'LABELS/OSE
C5:  (F3)  0.01
D5:  (F3)  0.01
E5:  (F3)  0.01
A6:  'OSE
C6:  (F3)  0.009
D6:  (F3)  0.009
E6:  (F3)  0.009
A7:  'SLSLTR
C7:  (F3)  0.02
D7:  (F3)  0.02
E7:  (F3)  0.02
A8:  'APP
C8:  (F3)  0.02
D8:  (F3)  0.02
E8:  (F3)  0.02
A9:  'BROCHURE
C9:  (F3)  0.04
D9:  (F3)  0.03
E9:  (F3)  0.03
A10: 'HOT SHEET
C10: (F3)  0.01
D10: (F3)  0.01
E10: (F3)  0.01
A11: 'CARD
C11: (F3)  0.063
A12: 'BRE
C12: (F3)  0.009
D12: (F3)  0.009
E12: (F3)  0.009
A13: 'OTHER
C13: (F3)  0.003
D13: (F3)  0.003
E13: (F3)  0.003
A14: '---------
B14: '---------
C14: '-----------
D14: '---------
E14: '---------
F14: '---------
```

371

```
G14:  '---------
H14:  '---------
A15:  'TOTAL
C15:  (F3)  @SUM(C5..C13)
D15:  (F3)  @SUM(D5..D13)
E15:  (F3)  @SUM(E5..E13)
F15:  (F2)  @SUM(F5..F13)
G15:  (F2)  @SUM(G5..G13)
H15:  (C2)  @SUM(C15..G15)
A16:  '---------
B16:  '---------
C16:  '-----------
D16:  '---------
E16:  '---------
F16:  '---------
G16:  '---------
H16:  '---------
A17:  'D.P.
C17:  (F2)  0.15
D17:  (F2)  0.04
E17:  (F2)  0.03
A18:  'LTRSHOP
C18:  (F2)  0.05
D18:  (F2)  0.04
E18:  (F2)  0.04
A19:  'POSTAGE
C19:  (F2)  0.45
D19:  (F3)  0.167
E19:  (F3)  0.167
A20:  'SHIP
C20:  (F2)  0.01
D20:  (F2)  0.01
E20:  (F2)  0.01
A21:  'REPORTS
C21:  (F2)  0
D21:  (F2)  0
E21:  (F2)  0
A22:  '---------
B22:  '---------
C22:  '-----------
D22:  '---------
E22:  '---------
F22:  '---------
G22:  '---------
H22:  '---------
A23:  'TOTAL
C23:  (F3)  @SUM(C17..C21)
D23:  (F3)  @SUM(D17..D21)
E23:  (F3)  @SUM(E17..E21)
F23:  (F3)  @SUM(F17..F21)
G23:  (F3)  @SUM(G17..G21)
H23:  (C2)  @SUM(C23..G23)
A24:  '---------
B24:  '---------
C24:  '-----------
D24:  '---------
```

```
E24:  '---------
F24:  '---------
G24:  '---------
H24:  '---------
A25:  'UNIT FULFILLMENT COST
D25:  (C2) +H15+H23
A26:  '---------
B26:  '---------
C26:  '---------
D26:  '---------
E26:  '---------
F26:  '---------
G26:  '---------
H26:  '---------
A27:  'LEADS (PER LEAD TOTAL)
C28:  'DATA
E28:  'CALCULATION
G28:  'CIRC(M)
H28:  (F0) 25000
A29:  'MEDIA
C29:  (C2) 6.69
E29:  (C2) +C29*1.1
G29:  'CP/M
H29:  (C2) 3
A30:  'COMMISSIONS
C30:  (P2) 0.1765
E30:  (C2) +E29*C30
G30:  'TLT/COST
H30:  (C0) +H28*H29
A31:  'ANS. SERV
C31:  (C2) 1.25
E31:  (C2) +C31*0.11
G31:  'TLT/LEADS
H31:  (F0) 50000
A32:  'GIFT/ENDORSER
C32:  (C2) 1
E32:  (C2) +C32
A33:  'PRODUCTION
E33:  (C2) +H30/H31
F33:  '(AD PRODUCTION)
A34:  'FULFILLMENT
C34:  (C2) +D25
E34:  (C2) +C34
A35:  '---------
B35:  '---------
C35:  '---------
D35:  '---------
E35:  '---------
F35:  '---------
G35:  '---------
H35:  '---------
A36:  'TOTAL
E36:  (F2) @SUM(E29..E34)
A37:  '---------
B37:  '---------
C37:  '---------
```

```
D37:  '---------
E37:  '---------
F37:  '---------
G37:  '---------
H37:  '---------
A38:  'UNIT TOTAL COST PER LEAD
E38:  (F2) +E36
A39:  '-----------
B39:  '-----------
C39:  '-----------
D39:  '-----------
E39:  '-----------
F39:  '-----------
G39:  '-----------
H39:  '-----------
A40:  'PRO-FORMA DATA ENTRY SCREEN
E41:  'APPS%
F41:  (P2) 0.0858
A42:  'CIRCULATION
C42:  (F3) +H31/1000
E42:  'TLTAPPS
F42:  (F0) (C42*1000)*F41
A43:  'TLT PAID POLICIES
C43:  (P2) +F46/(C42*1000)
E43:  'ISSUE%
F43:  (P2) 0.98
A44:  'AARP
C44:  (C2) 285.2
E44:  'APP/ISSU
F44:  (F0) +F42*F43
A45:  'MC/LEAD
C45:  (C2) +E38
E45:  'PAID%
F45:  (P2) 0.5
A46:  'ACQ ALLOW
C46:  (P0) 1.074
E46:  'PDAPPS
F46:  (F0) +F44*F45
A47:  '-----------
B47:  '-----------
C47:  '-----------
D47:  '-----------
E47:  '-----------
F47:  '-----------
G47:  '-----------
H47:  '-----------
A48:  'PRO-FORMA
E49:  'COLPRE(M)
F49:  (C2) +C52*C53/1000
A50:  'CIRCULATION
C50:  (F3) +C42
D50:  '(m)
E50:  'TMC(M)
F50:  (C2) +C42*1000*C45/1000
A51:  'CONVERSION %
C51:  (P2) +C43
```

```
E51:  'T/MC
F51:  (C2)  ((F42*C44)/F50)/1000
A52:  'RENEWALS
C52:  (F0)  +C43*C42*1000
E52:  'COST/APP
F52:  (C2)  +F50/C52*1000
A53:  'AARP
C53:  (C2)  +C44
E53:  'ACQ. ALLO
F53:  (C2)  +C53*C46
```

INDEX

INDEX